Sustainable Development
Principles, Analysis
and Policies

Sustainable Development
Principles, Analysis
and Policies

I. Moffatt

Department of Environmental Science

University of Stirling

Stirling, UK

Cover illustration:

© 1995 M.C. Escher / Cordon Art - Baarn - Holland.

All rights reserved.

The Parthenon Publishing Group
International Publishers in Medicine, Science & Technology

NEW YORK   LONDON

Published in the UK and Europe by
The Parthenon Publishing Group Limited
Casterton Hall, Carnforth,
Lancs LA6 2LA, England

Published in the USA by
The Parthenon Publishing Group Inc.
One Blue Hill Plaza
PO Box 1564, Pearl River,
New York 10965, USA

British Library Cataloguing in Publication Data

Moffatt, Ian
Sustainable development: principles, analysis and policies
1. Sustainable development. 2. Economic development –
Environmental aspects
I. Title
333.7

ISBN 1-85070-731-6

Library of Congress Cataloging-in-Publication Data

Moffatt, Ian.
Sustainable development: principles, analysis, and policies /
by Ian Moffatt.
    p.   cm.
Includes bibliographical references and index.
ISBN 1-85070-731-6
1. Sustainable development.   I. Title
HC79.E5M627 1996
338.9--dc20
                                                    96-13441
                                                    CIP

First published 1996

Typeset by H&H Graphics, Blackburn, Lancs.
Printed and bound by Bookcraft (Bath) Ltd., Midsomer Norton

CONTENTS

LIST OF FIGURES

LIST OF TABLES

ACKNOWLEDGEMENTS

This book has been written whilst the author was engaged in research over the last six years in both Australia (1990–1993) and the United Kingdom (1993 to date). During this productive research period several people have been extremely helpful and have influenced my thoughts on sustainable development. In particular I would like to thank Professor David A. M. Lea, former Executive Director, and his staff at the North Australian Research Unit, Darwin for their support for my research whilst based there as a Senior Research Fellow at the Australian National University.

In Stirling, Scotland I would like to thank my colleagues for their support. Within the Department of Environmental Science Professor Donald Davidson, for maintaining a sense of humour and providing support when administrative matters kept endangering that rare species – the researcher. Bill Jamieson and David Aitcheson drew some of the figures and Tracey Grieve and John McArthur helped with the usual computing problems associated with file management on different computer systems which, if we believe the computing companies, their products should blend seamlessly! Dr Nick Hanley, Department of Economics, has contributed to the debate over the relevance of economics to environmental problems and we have worked together in a productive and friendly way over several years on joint research problems. I would like to acknowledge the contributions to the data anlaysis made by Nick Hanley and Paul Gill, our joint Research Assistant, in Chapter 5 and to Mike Wilson who collected much factually sound material for the index of sustainable economic welfare for Scotland in Chapter 6.

I would also like to thank the editors and publishers for permission to draw upon earlier versions of papers which appeared in the *Australian Geographical Studies* and *The International Journal of Sustainable Development and World Ecology*. In addition I would like to thank the following authors and publishers for their kind permission to use tables and figures from their work. Michael Common (McMillan Press); Robert Costanza (Columbia University Press); Paul Ekins (Routledge); Michael Jacobs (Pluto Press); Gareth Jones (Addison, Wesley, Longman); David Pearce (Earthscan); David Pearce and Giles Atkinson (Elsevier Science Publishers, Netherlands); Robert Repetto (World Resources Institute).

I am also grateful to Cordon Art for granting me permission to use Waterfall by M C Escher as a cover for this book. I would also like to thank my students, especially the M.Sc. Environmental Management students, for their questions as they helped me to clarify some of my thoughts in the research seminars. Andrew Cowling and Helen Lee made useful editorial comments on the text. To all of the above people I offer my thanks but they are not responsible for the views expressed in this book.

Finally, I would like again to thank Kath, Sean and Ewan for their encouragement and support whilst writing this text. Optimistically, the ideas contained in this book will contribute to make the world a better and sustainable place.

Dr I Moffatt
Stirling

PREFACE

Sustainable development is a grand ideal around which a vast literature has grown rapidly. The purpose of this book is to clarify the concept; to describe some ways of measuring sustainable development and to suggest ways in which the ideals can be translated into policy to make development sustainable.

The book is organised around six questions. First, how did the concept of sustainable development evolve? Next, what definitions underpin the concept of sustainable development? Third, what ethical principles can be used to judge whether or not actual or proposed development is sustainable? Fourth, what measures can be used to determine whether or not development is sustainable? Fifth, what methods can be used to explore different scenarios of sustainable development? Finally, what policy and associated instruments can be implemented to bring about sustainable development in the early decades of the twenty-first century?

The first chapter in Part One offers an overview of the arguments developed in the text. Chapter 2 then offers an interpretation of the evolution of the sustainable development debate. This chapter is an extension of a paper first published in Australia. Chapter 3 is concerned with definitions and ethical principles underlying sustainable development and draws upon the work of Rawls and Taylor. In particular it is argued that the twenty-seven principles produced at the United Nations' Rio de Janeiro *Earth Summit* in 1992 are more concerned with appearing to have reached some major international agreements than with the ethics underpinning sustainable development. It is suggested that if we are to move essentially unsustainable activity onto a potentially sustainable basis then closely argued and clearly stated ethical principles must help to guide our practices.

Much of the material in Part Two is concerned with the analysis of data to produce indicators of sustainable development. Chapter 4 examines some of the issues which surround the search for indicators of sustainable development. Chapters 5 and 6 present empirical research on ecological–economic and socio-political measures of sustainable development. These chapters draw upon the author's recent research into sustainable development in both Australia and Scotland. In particular, the Scottish case study was undertaken as part of a study funded by the Scottish Office Department of Agriculture and Fisheries and the Scottish Natural Heritage, although the views expressed are not those of the Department or of the Scottish Office or Scottish Natural Heritage. The seventh Chapter then summarises the results of the detailed case studies and discusses some of the problems inherent in developing indicators of sustainable development.

In Part Three attention is turned from measures of sustainable development to the attempts to put the principles into practice and then measure their impact. An attempt to develop a dynamic simulation model of sustainable development is described, based in part on work completed in both Australia and the United Kingdom. The early ideas were developed by Malcolm Slessor, at the University of Edinburgh, and several other researchers have undertaken the development of ecological–economic models. Rarely have these models been developed for addressing the issues involved in promoting sustainable development. The latter requires a translation of the ethical principles underpinning sustainable development so that alternative future patterns of sustainable development can be judged. An early version of the model has been developed and used in Australia and Scotland and currently detailed research has commenced in Scotland. Unlike many economic–ecological models the one descibed in Chapter 8 explicitly incorporates the ethical principles, discussed in Chapter 3, as a basis to guide political choices over the way in which we can collectively move our unsustainable activities onto a sustainable trajectory. This then leads on to a discussion, in Chapter 9, of a vision of a sustainable future, as influenced by writers from the Green movement. After briefly describing the various ideological positions within the Green movement some eco-liberal policy prescriptions to make development sustainable are described. Some of the problems involved in this demanding challenge faced by individuals, local communities, nations and the international community are discussed in the final chapter.

Dr Ian Moffatt
Stirling.

PART ONE

Principles of Sustainable Development

CHAPTER 1

FOREWORD

The term sustainable development became fashionable in the 1980s in both the *World Conservation Strategy* (IUCN, 1980) and the book entitled *Our Common Future*, known as the *Brundtland Report*, published in 1987 (WCED, 1987). These two publications have led to detailed discussions over the implications of sustainable development for academic enquiry, policy-making and action. For the academic community, there has been an explosion of interest in the definitions of the term sustainable development as well as numerous studies which have attempted to measure or model sustainable, as opposed to unsustainable, development. From the perspective of policy-makers, in both the private and public sectors of the economy, a growing number of agencies have seen that sustainable development appears to be an important paradigm for the twenty-first century. Unfortunately, the details of this new paradigm are unclear and hence the ways in which sustainable development can be implemented are more problematic.

One of the problems confronting policy-makers is the way in which sustainable development challenges much of orthodox policy thinking. For the orthodox policy-maker the major problem for implementing sustainable development resides in making the new ideas operational so that these can help to shape policies to move current economic and unsustainable development onto a sustainable track. These solutions are difficult to put into practice when many institutions are designed to support the unsustainable *status quo* rather than to change it onto a sustainable footing. Transport and energy industries and ministries, for example, are concerned with efficient use of resources and only slowly are they beginning to examine alternative forms of efficient, environmentally-friendly and socially-acceptable transport and renewable sources of energy. Paradoxically, if we are to translate the ideals of sustainable development into practice, the concept has to be integrated into the warp and woof of contemporary institutions. The solution to transforming unsustainable development to sustainable forms of development remains elusive although some ideas on the ways in which this can be resolved are suggested in this book.

In the following chapter we begin by offering a brief history of the concept of sustainable development. It will be argued that sustainable development has

3

taken a long time to mature from the ideas of early environmentalists and economists interested in contributing to participatory and ecologically sustainable economic development. The seeds of these ideas were first sown in the writings of early environmentalists such as Aldo Leopold's land ethic (Leopold, 1949), in Rachel Carson's *Silent Spring* (Carsons, 1965) in Commoner's *Closing Circle* (Commoner, 1972) and Fraser Darling's early ecological work on the Scottish Western Isles (Darling, 1955). These writings contained the idea that sustainable development must examine ecological, economic, social and ethical aspects of reality. These early ideas were slowly absorbed into the practices of some of the practitioners of eco-development in several so-called Third World nations. By the 1970s the idea of sustainable development had influenced decision-makers; under the influence of Maurice Strong, then Secretary General-designate to the United Nations, and the biologist Dubois and the economist Ward. The Stockholm Conference witnessed the first attempt to put the environment and development onto the international political agenda (Ward and Dubois, 1972). Later meetings resulting in the publication of the 1980s *World Conservation Strategy* (IUCN, 1980), the publication of the *Brundtland Report* entitled *Our Common Future* (WCED, 1987) and the 1992 *Earth Summit* at Rio have helped to maintain the high profile of environmental groups and political decision-makers as they agreed to support the concept of sustainable development. The second chapter, then, charts the development of the concept and offers a personal interpretation of the development of sustainable development up to and including the *Earth Summit* held at Rio de Janeiro in 1992.

The 1992 *Earth Summit* achieved several important agreements such as the Climatic and Biodiversity conventions as well as Forest protection statements. It also suggested some twenty-seven principles to guide sustainable development in practice. These twenty-seven principles were not brought together without heated debate and sometimes disagreements between the various national decision-makers taking part at the *Earth Summit*. Inevitably, such meetings result in compromises agreed over negotiations between different pressure groups and other vested interests. More disturbing, however, is the fact that the principles written as the Rio Declaration, which were announced at the end of the summit, are derived from different paradigms concerning the role of humanity and the natural world. Furthermore, without subjecting these principles to a careful critique they run the risk of offering little real guidance to individuals and groups who wish to make the concept of sustainable development operational and put it into practice in their everyday lives. The third chapter provides one way of making some sense of the principles which ought to be used to guide sustainable development.

Chapters 4 to 7 examine the different ways in which academics and policy-makers have been concerned with measuring some aspects of the concept of sustainable development. In the UK Sustainable Development Strategy (Anon., 1994), for example, it was noted that indicators of sustainable development need to be developed to help both researchers, policy-makers and practitioners to implement sustainable development strategies in their substantive work. Hence, these chapters are concerned with the problems of developing a set of indicators to help in substantive real world studies. Chapter 4 examines some of the desirable characteristics of, and problems associated with, indicators of sustainable development. In particular the work of Repetto *et al.* is used to show why many people believe that the orthodox paradigm of economic development needs to be enlarged (if not replaced) to try and account for the real cost of the wealth of nations, and not just the financial aspects of this activity (Repetto *et al.*, 1987). For some economists and policy-makers sustainable development indicators should be expressed in monetary units, such as Dollars or Pounds, so that the costs of the current unsustainable development paths can be integrated into national accounts. Some of the developments in this aspect of research are noted. Other researchers and policy-makers suggest that alternative measures of "wealth" need to be devised rather than *ad hoc* adjustments to Gross National Product (GNP) or other conventional economic measures, so that a truly sustainable development can be measured. Chapters 4 to 7 examine some of the ways in which it is possible to measure sustainable development indicators, drawing upon a wide literature. Included in these chapters are attempts to develop indicators of sustainable economic welfare as well as ideas concerning carrying capacity and ecological footprints. Rather than discuss these different types of measures in an abstract way these chapters present some empirical results from several case studies. In particular, some preliminary results of an empirical study into sustainable development in Scotland are presented based on research funded by the Scottish Office Department of Agriculture and Fisheries and the Scottish Natural Heritage. The methods used in this pilot study can be used by researchers and policy-makers in many other countries who are seriously concerned with measuring indicators of sustainable development.

Chapters 8 and 9 examine the problems concerned with putting the principles and measures of sustainable development into practice. Chapter 8 considers the ways in which it is possible to model sustainable development. In particular, the ethical position adopted in Chapter 3 and some of the measures described in Chapter 4 are brought into play to indicate the ways in which sustainable development can be modelled. The main thrust of this chapter is to use dynamic simulation computer-based models. These models, which have been developed over the last decade, allow model builders to describe the past pattern of economic and ecological development for a variety of nations. More importantly, the models also allow model builders and decision-makers to examine the various ways in which policies can be implemented so that we can use various policy levers to move the current unsustainable paths of development onto a sustainable course. Obviously, much more detailed modelling remains to be undertaken. In particular, the ways in which ecological–economic systems interact in both space and time need further attention. Similarly, careful thought needs to be given to the ways in which we can educate ourselves, decision-makers, and the general public into adopting alternative lifestyles. These alternative sustainable lifestyles are adopted by a small minority of people in various nations, but to bring about a major cultural and attitudinal shift for the majority of the population without making life uncomfortable for current and future generations, requires more than mathematical modelling. Nevertheless, the models described in Chapter 8 do lay bare some ways in which policies can be implemented now to move us all towards a sustainable world. They do, however, imply a particular ideological position and an underlying set of ethical values which need to be spelt out explicitly.

These values are then described in Chapter 9 which presents a vision of a "Green Society" as discerned in a wide political literature. Whilst any description of a society different from the one in which we now live can be thought of as utopian, such visions should not be dismissed as idle dreamings. In fact there are three major reasons why such utopias are important to those who wish to move the current unsustainable path of economic and social change onto a sustainable trajectory. First, the vision represents, in stark outline, the difference between the contemporary world, dominated by the world market, and a more diverse and culturally richer one. Next, the utopian description is not some unachievable dream, like More's utopian vision (More, 1910), but indicates, in a general way, which changes can be implemented to bring about an alternative and, for the majority of people, better world in which basic needs are satisfied and a higher quality of dignified living can take place. At the time of writing one in four people in the world – some 1 500 000 000 individuals – do not even have these minimum standards for human sustenance and dignity. Third, it is accepted that different societies will no doubt decide to develop along their own paths – all of which are sustainable. The utopian vision is not, therefore, a blueprint for all societies to follow slavishly but a general guide indicating some of the problems that will have to be overcome if we are individually and collectively to move towards development which is sustainable. Chapter 10 then draws together some of the main points of the argument as a statement of what we have achieved and where we now need to direct further effort.

CHAPTER 2

THE EVOLUTION OF THE SUSTAINABLE DEVELOPMENT DEBATE

INTRODUCTION: The need for sustainable development

Since the emergence of the world market-based economy it has become very clear that our particular socio-economic system can produce, distribute, and consume vast amounts of commodities. A cursory examination of the goods available in any large supermarket reveals commodities brought from almost every corner of the earth: exotic fruits and vegetables are available in downtown shops in the cities of the rich OECD countries; huge developments in mass transport are constructed in complex forms, such as the Channel Tunnel linking Great Britain with continental Europe. These and many other signs are, for the affluent, indications of great material progress that comes with the aggressive workings of the market system. Yet, despite the quantities of material produce which are enjoyed by a small minority of the world's people, the very productive power of the global market system is putting increasing strains on the resource-base and life-support systems of the planet and many of its species, including the growing ranks of poor people. As the *Global 2000* report noted, "if present trends continue . . . serious stresses involving population, resources and environment are clearly visible ahead. Despite the greater material output, the world's people will be poorer in many ways than they are today" (Barney, 1980). Furthermore, the very signs and symbols of material progress are breaking up both the traditional ways of life and resource use of contemporary aboriginal societies and, paradoxically, causing increasing strains on the social, economic and environmental fabric of the wealthy industrialised nations. Clearly, recognition that the global market system is putting major strains on the socio-economic and ecological systems of the planet has resulted in calls for sustainable forms of development (Clark and Munn, 1986). Sustainable development can be defined as meeting the basic needs of all, and extending to all, the opportunity to satisfy their aspirations for a better life without compromising the ability of future generations to meet their own needs (WCED, 1987).

There have, of course, been several attempts to examine the growing awareness of environmental concern at international, national and local levels. Hence, attempts to "reclaim paradise" have been charted by international environmental movements (McCormick, 1989). At the national level the growth

7

of environmental groups – often portrayed as an upper middle class social movement – are quite well documented for some countries (Cotgrove, 1982). Similarly, attempts to explore substantive global environmental problems, such as the Greenhouse Effect and its impact on states and territories in Australia have been made (Henderson-Sellers and Blong, 1989). In this chapter, however, attention is directed towards tracing the evolution of the growing awareness of the need for sustainable development from a global perspective. The evolution of this concept is interesting in its own right as it has emerged as the result of public pressure and mass-media coverage, as well as conferences examining substantive environmental problems at international, national and local levels.

THE EARLY YEARS OF ECODEVELOPMENT

Prior to the United Nations *Stockholm Conference on the Human Environment*, held in 1972, there had been some international co-operation in examining ecological problems from a scientific perspective. In particular, the role of the *International Biological Programme* (IBP) and its successor, the International Geosphere Biosphere Programme (IGBP) needs to be emphasised. The IBP was established in 1964 with the avowed aim to examine the biological basis of productivity and human welfare. This interest in ecological dimensions of world natural productivity was a direct result of the then perceived threats to natural ecosystems from economic development. The *modus operandi* of the IBP and its successor, the IGBP was to define a problem, bring together a team of competent specialists, set up an action plan, put the plan into practice and then assess the results. Despite the problems of funding – the IBP had $(US) 1.88 million from 1962–1974 (McCormick, 1989) – it produced substantial work on international environmental issues.

Perhaps the most important meeting to try and link ecological conservation with economic development was the *Stockholm Conference* (1972). As a result of two earlier preparatory meetings held in Founex, Switzerland and Canberra, Australia, Maurice Strong as Secretary-General-designate of the *Stockholm Conference* was able to draw up an agenda. He noted that the representations from the Less-Developed Countries made it clear that "they thought that under-development and poverty constituted the most acute and immediate threat to the environment of their peoples" (Strong, 1977). One of the results of the behind-the-scene negotiations was the establishment of a broad agenda to include soil erosion and loss, desertification, tropical ecosystem management, water supply and human settlements. In a sense, the agenda of the *Stockholm Conference* demonstrated an awareness that economic development without proper regard to environmental constraints was both wasteful and unsustainable (Ward and Dubois, 1972).

The *Stockholm Conference* produced a declaration, a set of principles, and an action plan. The declaration was not meant to be a legal document (Sohn,

1974), but was rather a statement to put on the record the essential arguments of human environmentalism as an inspiration to the more detailed principles and action plan. Twenty-six principles produced at Stockholm can be broken down into five main groups (Table 1).

Included in these principles was the need to reaffirm that whilst nations had the right to exploit their own resources, they were responsible also for ensuring that this did not cause damage to other countries. Accompanying the set of principles, an action plan was produced. It has been summarised as a set of internationally-coordinated activities aimed first at increasing knowledge of environmental trends and their effects on man and resources, and secondly, at protecting and improving the quality of the environment and the productivity of resources by integrated planning and management (Sandbrook, 1983). This plan contained over one-hundred-and-nine separate recommendations.

Two years after the *Stockholm Conference* another meeting was organised in Bucharest to examine the inter-relationships between population growth, resource use, environmental problems and economic development. Until the *Stockholm Conference* the issues of population growth and resource use in economic development tended to be treated as separate issues. While there was some merit in keeping these issues separate, even if it were only to keep these international meetings to a reasonable size, it was clear that many of the problems addressed in separate meetings were interconnected in a close, causal manner. The 1974 conference broke new ground in that it suggested the need for an integrated approach which attempted to take into account the inter-relationships between population, resources, environment and economic development.

Table 1   The Stockholm environmental principles

1	Natural resources should be safeguarded and conserved, the earth's capacity to produce renewable resources should be maintained, and non-renewable resources should be shared.
2	Each country should establish its own standards of environmental management and exploit resources as they wished, without endangering other states. There should be international cooperation aimed at improving the environment.
3	Pollution should not exceed the capacity of the environment to clean itself, and oceanic pollution should be prevented.
4	Science, technology, education and research should all be used to promote environmental protection.
5	Development and environmental concern should go together, and less developed countries should be given every assistance and incentive to promote rational management. (This group was designed to reassure the LDCs.)

(After McCormick, 1989)

9

Some of the aims of the *Stockholm Conference* and the Bucharest meetings were addressed, at least in part, by the *Man and the Biosphere* (MAB) project. This project, under the United Nations Educational, Scientific and Cultural Organisation (UNESCO), was designed to be interdisciplinary and examined fourteen themes, including the role of urban areas as ecological systems (Boyden, 1981), and the impact of human interactions on ecosystems. The MAB programme has four main aims: to identify and assess changes in the biosphere resulting from human activities; to ascertain the effects of these on mankind; to encourage greater global coherence in environmental research; to develop reliable measures so that environmental monitoring could take place. It was hoped that this would lead to better rational management of the resource-base. Finally, it was anticipated that part of the MAB programme would study the inter-relationships between natural ecosystems and socio-economic processes.

It was from the emphasis on the latter theme that the concept of ecodevelopment emerged (Riddell, 1981) as a planning concept in the United Nations Environmental Programme (UNEP, 1975). At first the concept was an attempt to acknowledge that, at the regional and local level, social groups and their immediate environment provide some of the needs for economic and social development, often using appropriate technology. This was to be radically re-defined by some people working in developing countries to acknowledge the role of international affairs as they impinge on apparently local scale development.

In 1981 the ecodevelopment concept was re-defined as the concern "to conserve renewable resources, to pace or regulate the rate of exploitation of non-renewable resources and to control the discharge of residuals" (Riddell, 1981). In a sense many of the ideas expressed within the ecodevelopment framework were precursors to sustainable development. Riddell notes eleven guiding macro-principles which could be used to promote ecodevelopment (Table 2). He suggests that individuals should follow the ideal of ecodevelopment action "with its national emphasis upon economic equality, social harmony and environmental balance in the local pursuit of individual fulfilment, household self-sufficiency and community self-reliance" (Riddell, 1981). Likewise for Sachs (1984), international structures and a moral commitment needed fundamental changes before ecodevelopment could actually work. In a similar argument, Farvar and Glaeser (1979) conclude that even when fundamental approaches, like land reform and restructuring of the relations of production, have been considered in the agenda of development, many of the real issues are hidden or swept aside in the debate over environmental compatibility. As they stated, "naive statements on needs, participation and environmental compatibility are espoused in many papers . . . but whose needs are going to be met and whose are not; who will participate and who will not; and which lobbies, interests groups and economic and political entities will be hurt by environmental compatibility?" Clearly, under the work of several people, the ecodevelopment

Table 2 The eleven macro principles of ecodevelopment

1	Establish an ideological commitment to ecodevelopment
2	Increase social equity
3	Attain international parity
4	Alleviate hunger and poverty
5	Eradicate disease and misery
6	Reduce arms
7	Move closer towards self sufficiency
8	Clean up urban squalor
9	Balance human numbers with resources
10	Conserve resources
11	Protect the environment

(After Riddell, 1981)

theory was radically transformed from a planning concept to a potential weapon in the fight against social injustice, economic exploitation and ecologically- and technologically-inappropriate development. Unfortunately, this very radicalisation of the ecodevelopment concept went too far for those in control of political and economic power. The failure to commit politicians and leading industrialists to promote ecodevelopment resulted in, as Redclift (1987) notes, "advocating ecodevelopment in principle (which) does not commit governments or international organisations to list achievements in practice".

One of the positive results stemming from the theory of ecodevelopment and from the Stockholm and Bucharest conferences was that sustainable development became considered as an alternative way of organising socio-economic development in a way which would, as far as possible, result in less harmful environmental practices. Like the parable of the sower, many seeds of these ideas fell on barren ground; some were cultivated as ideological blue or red blooms, and, fortunately, one or two seeds were able to flourish, as in the case of the national responses to the *World Conservation Strategy* and in the *Brundtland Report*.

THE WORLD CONSERVATION STRATEGY AND NATIONAL RESPONSES

The central tennet of the *World Conservation Strategy* is given as follows:

... the combined destructive impacts of the poor majority struggling to stay alive and an affluent minority consuming most of the world's resources are undermining the very means by which all people can survive and flourish (IUCN,1980).

11

In less-developed countries there are obvious signs of ecological destruction. These include the clearance of forests, soil erosion, overgrazing, the lack of potable water and sewerage systems, the absence of adequate medical facilities, and poor communications. Hence, for the majority of humankind there is an urgent need to re-align ecological conservation with economic development in order to provide the basic essentials for survival, as well as to contemplate longer-term economic and ecological stability.

In the more developed countries the case for the *World Conservation Strategy* is less obvious. For many of the affluent, living in the rich nations, the market appears to provide many of the necessities and luxuries of life. The standard of living and, for many, the quality of life has improved. Some economists suggest that while the market may have its imperfections and externalities all that is required is the application of market forces to resolve the problems which it has created (Edel, 1973). However, the growth of environmental movements in the advanced industrial nations is indicative of a growing awareness that political action is required to prevent further deterioration of the planet's life-support systems. This action, they maintain, is essential as the impersonal workings of market forces by the invisible hand of Adam Smith (Smith, 1976) are, by themselves, insufficient to prevent unsustainable forms of development from continuing.

It is clear that increases in various forms of pollution are damaging the life-support systems of the planet. Water pollution is causing major disruptions to the ecology of estuaries, lakes and even seas, as witnessed in the studies of the North Sea and of the Great Lakes of North America. Similarly, atmospheric pollution is contributing to the impact of acid precipitation over the forests of Europe and North America. Furthermore, global climatic change has been caused by increased CO_2, CFC and other gases being discharged into the atmosphere. These individual emissions at the local level are difficult to control, yet they are clearly contributing to the enhanced Greenhouse Effect at the global scale. While the contribution of industrial nations is well-documented it is clear that it is much easier to talk about global environmental problems than it is to tackle the root causes of these problems at the international, national and local level.

At the global level, the *World Conservation Strategy* has three primary aims, namely to maintain essential ecological processes and life-support systems, to preserve genetic diversity, and to ensure sustainable utilisation of species and ecosystems. While the aims of the *World Conservation Strategy* are well-known the response to it has been mixed. At the grass roots level the *World Conservation Strategy* did not involve or engage the 'average citizen'. When the strategy was released, it was aimed at government policy-makers, conservationists and developers. Little wonder that the *World Conservation Strategy* failed in its attempt to produce a transformation of public attitudes, in the sense that there has been no popular demand for fundamental change in the destructively exploitative relationship of mainstream economies to the land, or more generally, the biosphere.

One positive aspect of the *World Conservation Strategy*, however, was the suggestion that individual countries should prepare national strategies to review their own priorities and obstacles to effective action. The idea of developing a national response to environmental problems is not new. In 1972, for example, the "Blueprint for Survival" (The Ecologist, 1972) produced within Britain listed numerous actions that an ecologically concerned government would adopt as part of its commitment to a greener planet. However, it was the scale of the response to the *World Conservation Strategy* that was impressive, with at least forty countries making a commitment to it (McNeely, 1990). Some, like the United Kingdom, have produced their own reports as a series of recommendations in an attempt to create a conservation-orientated society rather than one of mass consumerism (WWF, 1983). Whether these attempts at creating new forms of development are based on a conservation ethic, or are merely cosmetic changes to exploitation remains in doubt. In geographically larger nations, such as Canada and Australia, the national response to the *World Conservation Strategy* has been to get the Federal governments to act as co-ordinators for individual states and territories to produce their own state/territory conservation strategies to try and promote sustainable development in their own backyard.

Unfortunately, some of the early attempts to produce lists of what is required to produce a "new Jerusalem" from the dark satanic mills of industrial dereliction, were quite naive. So, too were calls to change the motor of economic development by accepting a new environmental ethic. Rather than respond to these calls in a positive way, governments either ignored them or attempted to shift responsibility for pollution to industrialists, in an attempt to distract the environmental lobby from pressing for national legislation or other forms of pollution control. As Dempsey and Power (1972) note, by choosing the occasional scapegoat as a serious polluter the government may placate "some of those who have wrapped themselves in blanket lists of reforms. A blanket, after all, can make you feel warm and sleepy, no matter how unpleasant it may be outside". Fortunately, for the environment and the societies which ultimately depend on the earth's resources, some politicians – at least on the international and national stage – were eager to be seen to take seriously the issues of environmental conservation and pollution.

In Austalia, the Federal Government can, and does, play an important role in attempting to promote the ideas of the *World Conservation Strategy*. First, it called upon a working party to produce a National Conservation Strategy. The National Conservation Strategy for Australia accepted the three aims of the global strategy, and also highlighted, as a fourth objective, the need to maintain and enhance environmental qualities (DHAE, 1983). Next, it requested that every state and territory produce their own documents which, to some extent, reflect the basic philosophy underpinning the *World Conservation Strategy*. This request was strengthened by the Federal Government acting directly in areas in which it had sole control. For example, in certain sectoral areas, such as forestry or national soil conservation or the designation of National Parks, such as Kakadu, the Commonwealth government has taken a leading role. Furthermore, the use of seabed and marine and land areas which it administers as Commonwealth property could be managed in accordance with the principles proposed by the *World Conservation Strategy*. Included in this role the Federal Government could, for example, introduce taxation on the polluters, as well as setting up legislation and national standards on emissions of pollution. Finally, the Federal government could act indirectly by encouraging more research into environmental topics, broader education at school and tertiary levels, and by monitoring the national state of the environment. This would leave individual state/territory governments with the responsibility for enforcing environmental control within their own borders.

By 1983 four of the six states and the Northern Territory had endorsed the National Conservation Strategy of Australia (NCSA); Queensland and Tasmania accepted the NCSA as a broad statement of the philosophies relevant to the conservation and development of living resources (Selman, 1985; Selman, 1987). At the level of specific states/territory the responses varied, with Western Australia taking the lead in producing its own State response (Western Australia, 1987); subsequently the Victorian government produced a document which contained a set of priority programmes (Table 3), more detailed than the National Conservation Strategy.

Each programme area is described in terms of issues, objective governmental action to date, and proposals for the future. Included in the State's response have been guidelines to establish regional plans, for example to re-establish forests in Victoria. Selman (1985) notes that, whilst the Victorian response has been cited as exemplary, it was in accord with the then Cain government's strategic approach. Although it has carried the support of the strong green network in the State it missed the opportunity to challenge consumerism in the area.

Table 3   Priority Programmes for Victoria, Australia

1	Restoring the land
2	Flora and fauna to ensure a biodiverse future
3	Protecting the forests
4	Reviving rivers, coasts and wetlands
5	The wise use of resources
6	Enhancing the built environment
7	Controlling pollution and other hazardous chemicals
8	Environmental education and community involvement

(After Ministry for Planning & Environment, Victoria, 1984)

The responses of the other States and the Northern Territory were less enthusiastic. The then Tasmanian and Queensland Liberal governments were wary of aligning themselves too closely to Federal Government's initiatives. In the case of Queensland it was stated that the State Government was already committed to sound land management and there was no need for further endorsement.

THE BRUNDTLAND REPORT AND ITS AFTERMATH

The Brundtland Commission, established in 1983 to enquire into a global agenda for change, focussed on four major areas:

(1) to propose long-term environmental strategies for achieving sustainable development by the year 2000 and beyond;

(2) to recommend ways in which concern for the environment could be translated into greater cooperation among developing countries and between countries at different stages of economic and social development. It was hoped that such cooperation could lead to the achievement of common and mutually-supportive objectives that take account of the interrelationships between people, resources, environment and development;

(3) to consider ways and means by which the international community could deal more effectively with environmental concerns and;

(4) to help shared perceptions of long-term environmental issues and the appropriate efforts needed to deal successfully with the problems of protecting and enhancing the environment, a long-term agenda for action during the coming decades, and aspirational goals for the world community (WCED, 1987).

Whatever the merits of the *Brundtland Report* it is quite clear that since its publication many governments and environmental organisations as well as industrialists would not view the environment as an externality to economic matters; instead they are attempting to re-appraise their operations in the context that there are assimilative limits to the functioning of any ecosystem. As Slayter (in WCED, 1987) puts it "sustainable development is development which is consistent with the natural functioning of the biosphere".

In a sense, some of the conclusions of the *Brundtland Report* were already stated in a more contentious way by the "Club of Rome" report on the *"Limits to Growth"* (Forrester, 1971; Meadows *et al.*, 1972; Meadows *et al.*, 1974), which indicated that there were limits to growth in a world of finite resources. Whilst some disputed the idea of limits to growth (Simon and Kahn, 1984), others, from a more radical perspective, argued that the entire debate revolved around ideological misconceptions of development and vague definitions (Cole *et al.*, 1973; Harvey, 1974).

In one sense the Bruntland concept of sustainable development also suffers from a surfeit of vague definitions. In the original text sustainable development was given several definitions including the following:

'sustainable development requires meeting the basic needs of all and extending to all the opportunity to satisfy their aspirations for a better life . . . sustainable development requires the promotion of values that encourage consumption standards that are within the bounds of the ecologically possible and to which all can reasonably aspire . . . at minimum, sustainable development must not endanger the natural systems that support life on Earth: the atmosphere, the waters, the soils, and the living beings' (WCED, 1987).

Later writers have commented on the different definitions of sustainable development given in the *Bruntland Report* and have suggested several others of their own (Brown *et al.*, 1987). One of the longer definitions of sustainable development has been given by Brookfield (1989) who wrote that:

"we need to define this term rather exactly, because we do not equate development with growth, nor do we regard it as possible to sustain a utilised ecosystem in unchanged or 'equilibrium' form. We define 'development' itself from the point of view of people rather than from the point of view of the economy: improvements are required in income and well-being, self-determination and cultural identity, as well as reductions in inequality. Sustainability requires improvements in the quality of human life without the destruction or deterioration of the resource base. The latter is obtainable only if there is a large investment in technology and 'capital' of forms which will preserve – and even enhance – the qualities of the ecological base. Most current technology is quite unsuitable for this purpose, and it has aggravated ecological problems. To improve both the quality of human life, and the qualities of the natural environment on which that life is based is not impossible: it has been done in the past, and is being done in places today. It requires, however, substantial savings from consumption in order to provide investment for the future."

By 1989 thirteen pages of definitions of sustainable development had been produced and this list was by no means exhaustive (Pearce *et al.*, 1989). Clearly, academia had generated a spin-off industry in defining the concept without actually applying it to real world studies. As Clark and Munn (1986) note:

"a major challenge of the coming decades is to learn how long-term large interactions between environment and development can be better managed to increase the prospects for ecologically sustainable improvements in human well-being".

Later Redclift (1987) re-emphasised the point that "unless we pitch our conception of sustainable development at a level which recognises international structures, it is in danger of being yet another discarded development concept". Clearly, researchers who wish to promote sustainable development should note the difficulty in translating a slippery concept into a useful tool – the brief sketch of the ecodevelopment concept vividly illustrates the way in which a potentially radical proposal can fail to be translated into practice.

Fortunately, the lack of an agreed definition of sustainable development has not prevented the Australian Federal Government from actively pursuing ecologically sustainable development. In a Commonwealth discussion paper it is argued that:

> "the crux of the issue in implementing sustainable development is establishing mechanisms that ensure an integration of economic and environmental considerations both now and in the future. Reaching that integration can only be a co-operative process" (CDP, 1990).

Needless to say, this Australian approach to sustainable development has invited and received criticism from several ecological organisations, such as the *Australian Conservation Foundation* and *Greenpeace* (Hare, 1990). In the former's conclusion to its critique of the Australian Government's attempt to promote sustainable development it is argued that the Federal view is too narrowly conceived, that short-term economic incentives are given too high a priority over long-term sustainable development and that:

> "we must make fundamental changes in the way in which we relate to the natural world and the resources upon which we depend...the process of achieving ecological sustainability will involve economic structural adjustment, with some sectors declining in size and even disappearing, while new ones are created and growing. Whilst there are general economic tools which can be used to assist this process, we believe that the process will require an overall direction and goal if it is to be achieved. These goals must protect and enhance social equity, and have full community support (Hare, 1990). The task ahead is to translate these noble sentiments into deeds. In Australia there are encouraging signs that the move towards sustainable development is being taken seriously."

Australia is playing an important role in promoting both a national response to the *World Conservation Strategy* as well as promoting sustainable development (DASETT, 1991; ESD, 1991). Many important sectoral initiatives have been undertaken by government agencies and non-government organisations, including the *National Soil Conservation Strategy Programmes* and the *National Tree Planting Program*, released in 1989. It is hoped that these twin programmes will help to conserve soil resources and contribute to retarding the build up of

CO_2 in the atmosphere, respectively. With regard to the Greenhouse Effect a national response has been developed, supported by strategies at the State and Territory level (Moffatt, 1992a). A programme of community awareness is also being promoted to generate realistic perceptions and accurate understanding of the enhanced greenhouse effect. Similarly, a national response to coastal environmental management is being developed (Standing Committee on Environment, Recreation and the Arts, 1991). The details of this proposal are at present unclear, although the suggestion of developing other marine conservation zones similar to the Great Barrier Reef Marine Park are under consideration. Perhaps the most important move to promote sustainable development in Australia has been the establishment of the nine working groups on ways of implementing ecologically sustainable development (ESD) in Australia (CDP, 1990).

With regard to fresh-water resources, the Murray–Darling Basin Commission, established in 1988, and the Australian Water Resource Research Council are currently investigating the ways in which market-based mechanisms may be applied to reduce water pollution and improve water quality. Several key environmental habitats have been included on the World Heritage list, including Kakadu National Park, Uluru National Park, Australian East Coast Temperate and Sub-Tropical Rainforest parks, Wet Tropics of Queensland and Tasmania Wilderness. In complex and contentious issues, such as the proposal for mining at Coronation Hill, the Resource Assessment Commission (RAC) can investigate broad issues which surround resource use. The role of the RAC is another indication of the importance which the Federal government attaches to promoting sustainable development. Clearly, Australian governmental departments, non-governmental organisations and individuals are actively involved in promoting sustainable development projects throughout the country during the Landcare decade.

SOME CONTEMPORARY RESPONSES AND *AGENDA 21*

Since the publication of *Our Common Future*, often referred to as the *Brundtland Report*, the ambiguous term sustainable development has been placed firmly on the political agenda (WCED, 1987). Many countries have begun to promote sustainable development as a desirable policy. In the UK, for example, sustainable development has been given some prominence as part of a "blueprint for a green economy" (Pearce *et al.*, 1989) and this call has been taken further with reports on sustainable development, such as the Department of the Environment's progress report on implementing sustainable development in the United Kingdom (DoE, 1989) and the recent publication of the UK Sustainable Development Strategy (HMSO, 1994). The Canadian Federal Government has established a task force on Environment and Economy to examine the implications of implementing sustainable development throughout

Canada (Keating, 1989). Similarly, the Australian Federal and State/Territory Governments are actively considering different ways of implementing sustainable development throughout the continent (ESD, 1991; Moffatt, 1992b). Several non-governmental organisations, such as the IUCN and the WWF, have been very positive in their support of the sustainable development concept. Many local authorities within the UK are actively examining ways to implement sustainable development at a local level. Similarly, many industries have pledged a greening of their hitherto environmentally unfriendly activity and now wish to be closely associated with new environmental developments.

Whilst these are welcome changes some environmentalists are suspicious of the intentions of big business and view this activity as putting foxes in charge of the chickens. Despite all this political activity several problems concerning the ways in which sustainable development can be put into practice in specific environments have yet to be resolved. The solutions to these problems depend in part on the underlying ways in which sustainable development is conceptualised; the types of ecological systems affected; the type of data available, as well as on the ethical perspective adopted by the parties involved in actually implementing sustainable development practices.

At the heart of the sustainable development debate is the recognition that current patterns of economic growth and development are seriously damaging the ecology of the planet. Numerous studies have demonstrated that the earth's atmosphere is being damaged by the release of CFCs leading to the breakdown of the ozone layer (Farman *et al.*, 1985). Similarly, the increase in the use of fossil fuels and car transport together with changes in land-use have witnessed a rapid rise in many of the greenhouse gases, such as carbon dioxide and methane. These global environmental problems are well documented and require action at the global, national and local scale if they are to be successfully managed and curtailed. In a sense, the need 'to act locally but think globally' is true but the specific ways of achieving reductions in global pollutants, for example, require policy decision making at a variety of scales.

In the nations of the developed world there is the paradox that in countries of great wealth there are simultaneously clear signs of increasing poverty, deteriorating environmental conditions and poor health. Increasingly, poverty amongst affluence is observed in the streets of many major cities. The plight of homeless people existing in general urban squalor is found in numerous wealthy cities in the developed world. Many areas of wilderness are being put under increasing ecological strain due to the mobility of wealthy inhabitants in the rich nations. Simultaneously, the search for non-renewable energy sources in deep oceans and even in pristine environments such as Antarctica is being pursued in a relentless quest to fuel the engines of unsustainable growth.

In the developing world the growth of population, coupled with desertification, deforestation and soil erosion, are weakening the ecological basis for food and fibre production. The loss and degradation of arable land, shortages of firewood for fuel, coupled with water shortages, are contributing to conditions found in many parts of the developing world. The rural exodus to the squatter settlements of the burgeoning cities and the increasing incidence of disease is part of the spiral of unsustainable development affecting over 80% of humanity and much of the world's land resources.

Clearly, these environmentally damaging activities in both the developed and developing world are increasingly straining the poorest members of societies, the resource-base and assimilative capacities of the ecosphere. Many nations now acknowledge that it is imperative to alter these particular unsustainable trajectories of development. The attempts to resolve these problems raise numerous questions concerning the appropriate scale of intervention, the best methods to be used, and the political will to carry out any proposed alterations to essentially unsustainable activities.

Many of the environmental problems that confront us are global in scale and require international co-operation for their solution. The international agreement, such as the Montreal Protocol to eliminate the production of CFCs, is a welcome reminder that occasionally the international community can agree to act in a concerted way. However, many global environmental problems are still being discussed as part of the ongoing debate and negotiations associated with *Agenda 21* agreed at the Rio Earth Summit. Many of these continuing, delicate negotiations are concerned with questions of equity and international economic and political power. Although, at national and regional levels some agreements have been reached in principle to reduce carbon dioxide and other emissions (Pearman, 1988), an international agreement has proved elusive. Since many international agreements are predicated upon international agreements being signed before unilateral decisions are taken, progress is slow. Clearly, international political negotiations to resolve many global environmental problems are fraught with difficulties.

At national and sub-national levels some environmental problems can be resolved by the use of policy levers. For example, the normal use of legislation concerning environmental quality indicators; economic incentives to make production, distribution and consumption more efficient and therefore less wasteful of resources; land-use zoning, and other forms of planning which can help to protect some aspects of the environment. Whilst these environmental controls can be useful they are only part of the concerted actions required to promote sustainable development. The current work in the UK, Canada and Australia, for example, indicates that the promotion of sustainable development may have to call into question many of our own assumptions and practices (Redclift, 1987). It is this radical path of environmental management which frankly recognises the need for local participation in many environmental issues that is much more difficult to achieve. In a sense, it is not the environment which needs management, but rather our own behaviour as individuals, as individuals within larger institutions, and as members of communities.

It is clear that many environmental problems raise deep ethical issues. In the case of the enhanced Greenhouse Effect, for example, environmental scientists and managers are placed in a difficult ethical dilemma of acting now, on the basis of some theory, to prevent the environmental problem from becoming worse and possibly unmanageable, or waiting to see if the theory is confirmed empirically and then perhaps finding that the environmental system has further deteriorated and is locked into an unmanageable trajectory (Pittock, 1988). In the case of the Greenhouse Effect, the lags in the system will inevitably mean that delaying a positive preventative response now will mean that our actions, inadvertent and deliberate, will only affect the climatic system several decades from now.

This ethical dilemma is even more acute in the case of promoting sustainable development. As noted above, many politicians, scientists, business organisations and members of the community feel that we should attempt to move our environmentally destructive market-based systems onto a sustainable trajectory, rather than continue to damage the life-support features of the planet. A transition to a sustainable way of life means taking steps now to reduce the risk of serious environmental damage and related socio-economic problems. Again, failure to respond positively now could jeopardise, or seriously affect, humans and other species at some future time. Sustainable development, stated succinctly, attempts to ensure that current and future generations have a reasonable prospect of a worthwhile quality of life rather than mere existence; to achieve this, actions must be based on ecologically sound foundations.

Currently, the basic research on many of the critical thresholds beyond which damage to individual species in an ecosystem will occur is poorly understood. It is known that the duration of exposure to specific pollutants can adversely affect plant and animal growth and reproduction, but further research on this topic is required. Similarly, the assimilative capacities of many receiving environments are poorly understood, although it is quite clear that there are limits in any given receiving environment upon which damage to the biotic and abiotic elements of the environment can occur. As one of the aims of both the *World Conservation Strategy* and the *Brundtland Report* is to preserve biodiversity it is obvious that neither the wholesale destruction of ecosystems, such as tropical forests, or the insiduous pollution of other environments is commensurate with these goals. Given the uncertainty which surrounds our knowledge of ecosystem processes and the ways in which these systems respond to stochastic changes in the environment, it is clear that we ought to adopt the precautionary principle as a guide to ensure, as far as possible, that future generations have the pleasure and the products which can emerge from keeping biodiversity as broad as possible.

Many of the world's poor, condemned to eking out a living in already degraded ecosystems and environments, find their own lives and landscapes subjected to further strains. The ethical problems confronting people faced with a stark choice of survival or further damage to the environment, often results in the latter being further eroded. Hence, a vicious cycle of environmental degradation is established which is extremely difficult to break and alter into a sustainable form of development. The resolution to this problem brings in several ethical and political issues. These issues include questions over population control, resource allocation between and within generations, as well as major political issues on the re-negotiation of world trade and international debt. If the concept of sustainable development is to be a useful term, it has to be subjected to rigorous thought (O'Riordan, 1988), and the policies proposed must address social justice and moral and cultural issues (Rawls, 1971; Coombs, 1990), as well as economic and environmental problems. Obviously, the broad nature of the sustainable development concept poses numerous theoretical and practical problems for academics, decision-makers, communities and individuals in different societies.

It is against this background of increasingly serious environmental problems, coupled with an awarenes that economic and environmental issues are often inextricably interwoven, that the *Earth Summit* held at Rio de Janeiro was convened in June 1992. Like earlier environmental conferences, especially the 1972 Stockholm meeting, there was much political lobbying by diverse groups before and during the meeting. One of the concrete results of the Rio meeting was the internationally agreed publication known as *Agenda 21*.

Agenda 21 was intended to set out an international programme of action for achieving sustainable development in the 21st century. It is both comprehensive in its scope, and seeks to integrate economic development and environmental conservation locally, nationally and globally. *Agenda 21* attempts to outline the nature of environmental, economic development problems and then suggests possible approaches and desirable policies. Often both of these items are expressed as generalities and in a non-commital way. The principles underlying the Rio Declaration will be examined in the following chapter. At present, however, it is important to realise that the Rio meeting was not the first attempt at international co-operation to try and resolve some of the many environmental problems that surround us. It was, however, important in that it produced some agreement in principle that the nations would attempt to promote sustainable development in the twenty-first century (UNCED, 1992).

Agenda 21 is a report of over 500 pages and comprising 40 chapters. The report is organised into 4 sections which address areas of political action: social and economic development (Chapters 1–8); natural resources, fragile ecosystems and related human activities, by products of industrialisation (Chapters 9–22); major groups (Chapters 23–32) and means of implementation (Chapters 33–40). In many of the chapters the major problem is addressed and some programmes of action are noted. The programme areas generally follow the same structure: the basis of action addressed; the concerns and the efforts to date to deal with the problem. Then the objectives address the main issues and the general ways in which they can be tackled. This leads to an identification of the activities that specific bodies should undertake. These activites are, by implication, to be undertaken by the organisations noted, such as international organisations, governments, non-governmental organisations and the private sector. The means of implementation is then discussed under a series of headings.

Without going into the details of each chapter, it is clear that *Agenda 21* is a major achievement for identifying the links between economic development and environmental conservation. It shows an appreciation of the complex links and interactions between the environment, the economy and the cultural values held by people in different societies. Furthermore, it represents a remarkable and unique achievement in drawing together the various factions involved in environmental issues and attempting to initiate some programme for action. The United Nations has given a lead by creating a UN Commission on Sustainable Development. There are, however, some questions which were not addressed including the vital issues of population control (addressed in 1994) and the use of nuclear power. Similarly, *Agenda 21* does not have any legal status so governments and other groups need not be guided by it, nor are there any ways of enforcing groups to conform to the suggestions. Some of the problems concerned with the principles for sustainable development, issued as the Rio Declaration, in *Agenda 21* will be discussed in the following chapter.

Nevertheless, *Agenda 21* represents a good start towards promoting sustainable development at different areal scales. By stressing co-operation and a bottom-up rather than a top-down approach to sustainable development, this was a good beginning. The real impact of *Agenda 21* will depend upon the extent to which national governments and all the various groups discussed in the document, from local councils, to trade unions and scientific groups, business and industry, absorb and pursue the recommendations therein, influenced also by the continued efforts of environmental and development groups.

CONCLUDING COMMENT

This chapter has examined the evolution of the concept of sustainable development. The forerunner to the establishment of this concept was the earlier idea of ecodevelopment (Riddell, 1981). While this early concept has much in common with sustainable development, it failed to capture the attention and imagination of individuals. The radical nature of the concept, which required a fundamental re-examination and re-structuring of the world economy, was perceived as threatening to many of the current power structures that support the market system. It was, therefore, not surprising that the concept was unable to influence decision-making bodies, either in the governments or leading industries. Paradoxically, the concept of sustainable development emerged from a similar path of development. The details of this trajectory have been described above, and it is clear that whilst the ecodevelopment concept failed to gain global support the concept of sustainable development is receiving wider recognition and momentum. The too radical proposals of the ecodevelopers failed to engage the governments in a meaningful dialogue, in spite of the need to alter current paths of non-sustainable development.

Despite the enthusiasm with which the concept of sustainable development has been taken up by governments, non-government bodies, industry and academia, there is still no agreed definition of the term. It has been suggested that its very vagueness has meant that different groups could interpret it for their own purposes. Yet, if the concept of sustainable development is to be useful in addressing real problems of promoting economically sound, socially just and ecologically sustainable forms of development, at least a broad consensus of its meaning is required. While the ambiguity which surrounds the term could be useful in the early days of the evolution of the idea it is clearly capable of backfiring onto the people who have such high hopes that the concept could come to address real problems of ecologically-sustainable forms of economic development. Unfortunately, as O'Riordan (1988) points out, the term is now so broad as to run the risk of becoming meaningless. It would, of course, be a retrograde step if sustainable development now became an outworn concept as the exploitation of ecological and economic systems are visible for all to see.

However, currently there is a reason for cautious optimism in attempting to achieve ecologically sustainable forms of development in Australia, the United Kingdom and in many other nations. This optimism derives, in part, from the involvement of the Australian Federal Government as well as a well-organised, articulate and potentially politically-motivated green lobby. Clearly, the political leaders are taking the ideas of environmental conservation seriously. As a former Prime Minister of Australia stated, "This Government continues to endorse these objectives as providing the basis for ecologically sustainable development" (Hawke, 1989). Similarly, in the United Kingdom the recent Sustainable Development Strategy (Anon., 1994) indicates some interest in the topic. Despite the criticisms of the recent white paper on sustainable development (Anon., 1994; CDP, 1990; Hare, 1990) there is a genuine political will to effect an ecologically sustainable programme of economic development in Australia, the United Kingdom and elsewhere.

Clearly, a fundamental reappraisal of the assumptions underlying the concept of sustainable development, and the elaboration of a set of tools, are required in the move towards a just, participatory and sustainable society, living in harmony with each other and the ecosphere (Daly, 1987; Daly and Cobb, 1989). Fortunately, some researchers and practitioners have not given up the challenge of developing methods which may be useful in achieving a world in which sustainable development becomes a reality rather than a pious hope.

CHAPTER 3

DEFINITIONS AND PRINCIPLES OF SUSTAINABLE DEVELOPMENT

INTRODUCTION

Sustainable development has evolved from philosophical concerns about humankind's responsibility for nature (Passmore, 1974), into locally- and nationally-based environmental groups demanding more attention to the environment (Lowe and Goyder, 1983). Throughout the last three decades of this century the individual concerns have grown into fully-fledged international movements, concerned with the the impact that human activities are having on the planet. These ideas, combined with the activities of diverse groups such as Greenpeace and Friends of the Earth as well as the International Union For the Conservation of Nature (IUCN), and World-Wide Fund for Nature (WWF) have gained both global momentum and international recognition. These movements gave expression to their concerns at the 1992 UN *Earth Summit* held at Rio de Janeiro and the agreements signed by Heads of State or their representatives at that meeting.

Included within the *Earth Summit* were a series of agreements which were intended to facilitate the development of a sustainable earth. Several agreements were made including a climatic convention; forestry and biodiversity statements and a set of principles for sustainable development. The climatic agreement continued the momentum of the Montreal and London Protocols which were designed to phase out chlorofluorocarbons (CFCs) and also to consider ways of reducing other greenhouse gases such as carbon dioxide (CO_2), nitrous oxides (N_2O) and methane (CH_4). The Forest convention was also signed and represents an early step towards the careful and sustainable use of the world's forest resources. Such careful husbandry could lead to a more secure future for the local communities which use the forest as a traditional resource, whilst providing a balanced way of cropping this potentially renewable resource for the paper and pulp industries. The conservation of forest is also part of the broader effort required to conserve the biodiversity on this planet (Wilson, 1988). This aspect of conservation is essential for life on earth, in all its manifestations, as well as providing the broadest gene pool, still to be tapped for medical research. Arguably the most important agreement signed at the Rio Summit was the declaration of

Agenda 21 which was designed to guide economic development onto a sustainable path for the 21st century.

This chapter examines and discusses some of the numerous definitions and ethical principles underpinning the concept of sustainable development. These definitions do not, of course, exist in a socio-economic or ethical vacuum but the different definitions do often imply different ethical principles underpinning them. It is argued that many of these definitions can be classified as narrowly economistic, or more broadly, as ecocentric. The problem with the former definitions is that they try to extend the neo-classical economic perspective to embrace sustainable development, whilst the ecocentric are searching for a new paradigm of sustainable development. At present, neither of these two competing views are able to capture the complexity underlying the concept of sustainable development.

In section three the twenty-seven ethical principles of sustainable development agreed within *Agenda 21* at the Rio Earth Summit are summarised and then critically assessed. It will be suggested that these ethical principles can be broadly sub-divided into environmental, economic and socio-economic categories. While there is nothing immutable about this classification, it will be argued that there are inherent contradictions within the principles. In particular, there has been little thought over the implications of these principles as a guide to promote sustainable development. The principles represent an attempt by the global community to embrace an environmental ethic which could guide a more caring use of the planet than hitherto. No doubt earlier conservationists would have approved of these international agreements. Nevertheless, it will be argued that these principles need to be subjected to critical thought if they are to guide us on in our attempts to make development sustainable.

Section four then broadens the argument to consider the rights that we have for the rest of the biotic and abiotic world. This aspect of the work draws upon Taylor's (1986) contribution to the debate, and both widens and deepens our consideration over the biotic and abiotic communities. This is then followed by a more detailed description of the principles by which social justice can be achieved in a just way and still protect all living creatures and their abiotic environment. In particular, the work of Rawls (1971) is used as a guide to making a rationale for sustainable development to be achieved in a socially just and ecologically sound manner. Finally, we discuss the relevance of these philosophical aspects of the sustainable development debate to contribute to the solution of actual environmental problems. The ways in which this broader ethical view can then be brought into play with economic, environmental and socio-economic work will be discussed. This aspect of an essentially philosophical debate will be picked up in later chapters which will be concerned with translating these noble ideas into actual practice.

DEFINITIONS

There are numerous definitions associated with the term sustainable development. At the outset some researchers believe that economic growth is sustainable; others believe that this is not the case, although they suggest that sustainable development is possible. Daly (1987), for example, suggests that we can have growth or development, both, one or neither. Clearly, continued growth on a finite planet is not sustainable; the planet cannot continue to accept the exploitation of its natural resources, or the poisoning of its ecosystems and environmental systems; nor overloading of specific ecosystems assimilative capacity, such as in estuaries, landfill sites, or the atmosphere (Peet, 1992). For some researchers sustainable development is not something that needs to be defined but something which is to be declared as an ethical principle. While one might agree with this view, it is clear that there is a need to define sustainable development before examining the ethical principles underpinning the concept.

In 1980 the term 'sustainable utilization of resources' was noted in the *World Conservation Strategy* which had three principal aims, namely, to maintain essential processes and life support systems, to preserve genetic diversity, and to ensure sustainable utilisation of species and ecosystems (IUCN, 1980). By 1987 the concept of sustainable development gained much more attention in the *Brundtland Report*, entitled *'Our Common Future'*, where sustainable development was defined as meeting 'the needs of, and aspirations of, the present generation without compromising the ability of future generations to meet their needs' (WCED, 1987). Another commonly used definition of sustainable development, and one which has been adopted by the International Union for the Conservation of Nature (IUCN) is that type of development 'which improves the quality of life, within the carrying capacity of the earth's life support system' (IUCN/WWF/UNEP, 1991). Numerous definitions of the concept have been offered; Pearce *et al.*, (1989), for example, documents over 60 definitions and this is a conservative estimate (Moffatt, 1992b).

Allen, writing in 1980 on the *World Conservation Strategy*, suggests that sustainable development is development "that is likely to achieve lasting satisfaction of human needs and improvement of the quality of human life". A more detailed definition, given by Brundtland, is that sustainable development requires four aspects, namely the elimination of poverty and deprivation; the conservation and enhancement of the resource base which alone can ensure that the elimination of the poverty is permanent; a broadening of the concept of development so that it covers not only economic growth but also social and cultural development; and most important, it requires the unification of economics and ecology in decision-making (Brundtland 1986 in a letter to Scott, cited in Pearce *et al.*, 1989). From these definitions it can be observed that sustainable development is a broad concept; despite the breadth of the definition some writers have chosen to view it as a narrow economic concept, whereas others have attempted to keep the subject broad, as an attempt to integrate economic, social and ecological development (Barbier, 1989). This latter view is adopted in this text.

Within the narrower definition of sustainable development several economists have attempted to use the neo-classical paradigm of economics to embrace the problems raised by sustainable development. Pearce (1993) and Pearce and co-workers (1989) have discussed the ideas of sustainability and sustainable development. With regard to the latter the necessary conditions for sustainable development are defined as "constancy of natural capital stock. More strictly, the requirement as for non-negative changes in the stock of natural resources, such as soil and soil quality, ground surface waters and their quality, land biomass, water biomass, and the waste assimilative capacity of the receiving environments". In a detailed exposition of sustainable development, from a neo-classical economic perspective, Pezzey (1989) has defined the latter as "non-declining *per capita* utility – because of its self-evident apppeal as a criterion for intergenerational equity". Many of the issues raised within the neo-classical paradigm will be examined in later chapters (see Chapters 4–7). At present it is important to bear in mind that neo-classical economists are attempting to widen their paradigm to cope with the environment. In some cases, considerable ingenuity has been involved to try and accommodate environmental matters within the strictures of the neo-classical economic paradigm. Some economists feel that a new type of sub-discipline is required and, in the 1990s, ecological economics was proposed as an attempt to address these issues from a variety of economic perspectives rather than from the vantage point of neo-classicism. The attempt to establish ecological economics is one approach to broaden and perhaps fundamentally transform the dominant neo-classical economic paradigm so that sustainable development problems can be solved. To achieve this is a daunting intellectual and social challenge.

When the broader definition of sustainable development is used, the methodological problems associated with this are even more daunting. The broader perspective of sustainable development is given in some of the following definitions. First, from the *Brundtland Report*, "sustainable development is development which meets the needs of the present without compromising the ability of future generations to meet their own needs . . . without damaging the life-support systems of the planet" (WCED, 1987). One of the ideas underlying this broad definition is the need to have equity between generations, since pursuing policies that imperil the welfare of future generations, who are unrepresented in any political or economic forum, is unfair. A second feature of the broad definition is that ecological constraints must be acknowledged and economic activity must also be kept within these limits. As Turner (1988) notes, adopting this perspective implies that, "conservation becomes the sole basis for defining a criterion with which to judge the desirability of alternative allocations of natural resources". A third feature of sustainable development is that the mix of economic activities must be constrained so that any environmental service or waste discharged has a limit which must not be exceeded. It is obvious that this limit is difficult to measure for many ecosystems as we know relatively little of the ways in which pollutants move through pathways. Furthermore, our knowledge of the combined interactions of biogeochemical cycles is even further limited, despite the fact that we are probably more knowledgeable of these complex interactions now than in the past.

At a broad conceptual level then, it is relatively easy to picture the economic systems as acting beyond some notional environmental set of constraints. For sustainable development to be realised it is essential that the economic system operates well within these ecologically possible limits. By the same token if economic activity is operating beyond these sustainable bounds then sooner or later the economic and ecological systems will become unsustainable and both will collapse. Jacobs (1991) suggests that currently the global economy is operating well outside these sustainability bounds, and that the purpose of current Brundtland-inspired policies is to ensure that economic activity does not violate sustainability constraints. The reason for moving economic activity well within sustainable development limits is to acknowledge the importance of the precautionary principle and to be rather humble about our knowledge of the way we interact with the planet and the rest of its inhabitants.

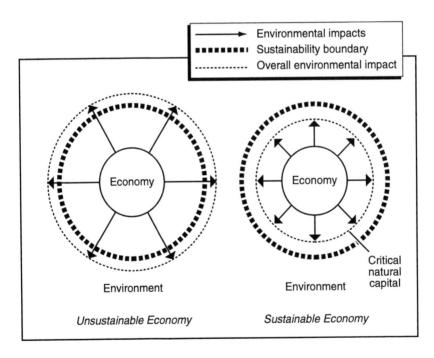

Figure 1 Environmental impacts, welfare and the sustainability boundary (after Jacobs, 1991)

Clearly, developing a paradigm for resolving the multitude of problems which are brought together by the broad definition of sustainable development is an immense intellectual task. There are, however, some guidelines which can be adopted to promote sustainable development by the use of careful policy levers, including economic instruments, such as polluter pay methods, use of best technology for pollution control, as well as legislation. Daly (1977), for example, has been instrumental in attempting to advocate a movement from current unsustainable patterns of economic activity to one which is sustainable. His ideas on the steady-state economy, which draw upon Mill's work (Mill, 1867), represents a new way of thinking about economic impacts on the environment. In particular, Daly suggests that there are several rules which we can use to move our current unsustainable economic systems on to a sustainable path. He suggests that by cutting down on the through put of energy and materials waste production can be reduced, enhancing resource conservation and achieving sustainable development. He also argues the need for population policy to cut back on the amount of energy and material resources used in the economic systems.

While not all economists and environmental scientists will subscribe to Daly's ideas of a steady state the alternative of business as usual is rather disconcerting. The growing number of environmental problems shown in the mass media ranging from bush fires threatening Australian cities, desertification of the lands in Africa and Southern Europe, the concerns over the rights of animals within the UK, the attempts to move from a nuclear energy policy to an environmentally-benign renewable energy resource use, as in Sweden, tropical deforestation and global climatic change, all suggest that we are trying to live beyond the earth's ecological means of support. Underlying these outward manifestations of several ecological crises is the belief that the invisible hand of Smith's Wealth of Nations (Smith, 1976) is becoming all too visible. For some ecologists and economists these externalities can be kept in control by the application of economic measures, derived from within the neo-classical economic paradigm; for others it is the uncritical acceptance of the workings of the capitalist-run global market forces that are the primary cause for many of the environmental problems that beset us. While some economists may question the assumption that neo-classical economics can provide the tools to ensure a more sustainable future, most would agree that State socialist systems, e.g. in Eastern Europe, were also very damaging to their environment. The recent "experiment" in China to have a capitalist system within State socialism is, at present, no better at maintaining the environment than the two "pure" forms.

The different definitions of sustainable development all carry inferences concerning the scales at which a particular project is ascertained to be sustainable. From a temporal perspective the time-scales considered in the sustainable development debate can extend as long as the earth survives as a planet (*circa* another 5000 million years). Normally, however, sustainable development operates on a shorter time-scale and attempts to conserve the environment, alleviate poverty, and leave numerous options open for current and future generations. One group of researchers have argued that as the world's population is growing rapidly while the resources are being consumed and pollution generated at a rapidly growing rate, then we have less than 40 years to move our current wasteful practices of economic development onto a sustainable trajectory (Vitousek *et al.*, 1986). This implies that decisions taken today are set in the context of a long but definite future, generally over three or four decades, rather than the current shorter term decision-making time horizons (1–4 years), as observed in the patterns of political and business cycle behaviour. Similarly, the spatial scales at which ecological processes operate need to be considered. Hollings (1994) argues that to understand ecological systems both the short- and long-term dynamics need to be considered if we hope to effectively promote ecological sustainability.

This debate over the correct diagnoses of the world's environmental problems can be traced back to ideas such as the tragedy of the commons argument. In 1968 Hardin published his essay on the *'Tragedy of the Commons'*. Succinctly stated, he argued that if a group of herdsmen continue to use the common land for their grazing then it is in the interests of each herder to maximise their profits by adding extra cattle to their herd. As the total stock of cattle increases, greater demands on a limited food supply for the cattle are made, so that, sooner or later, overgrazing occurs. The obvious result of this individually rational action is ruinous. As Hardin (1968) notes, "Each man (*sic*) is locked into a system that compels him to increase his herd without limit – in a world which is limited. Ruin is the destination toward which all men rush, each pursuing his own best interest in a society that believes in the freedom of the commons, freedom of the commons brings ruin to us all".

Hardin suggests that there are solutions to this problem. First, he suggests that a certain maximum stock of cattle *per capita* must be agreed by the herdsmen. Any additional cattle above the *per capita* limit must, of course, be slaughtered (culled). This upper limit is the carrying capacity of the ecosystem (commons). The major problem associated with this solution is that the people affected must agree to this policy by mutual coercion. This is one policy suggested by Hardin (1968), but this policy also presupposes a human population policy to limit the number of herdsmen, otherwise the tragedy would only be delayed.

Hardin also favours the privatisation of the commons. Such a policy would, in Hardin's view, simply reproduce the tragedy of the 'commons' for each private landowner. A dynamic simulation of this scenario can result in a steady state (Moffatt, 1984a) and allows some large landowners to have more cattle and other herdsman to starve. Hardin obviously approves of this option. He wrote that, "we must admit that our legal system of private property plus inheritance is unjust – but we put up with it because we are not convinced, at the moment, that anyone has invented a better system. The alternative to the commons is too horrifying to contemplate. Injustice is preferred to total ruin" (Hardin,1968).

Hardin's essay has been criticised on a number of grounds as ahistorical. Societies which use the commons do not pursue individual profits at the expense of the rest of their society. Traditional resource managers often find the use of the resources is closely tied to immediate use of the resources for consumption without damaging the environment and the reproduction of the species on which the traditional group survive. The use of resources is carefully collected and is managed, in part, by carrying out socially produced rules which respect other parts of nature. These socially produced rules form part of the complex pattern of resource use often passed on to current and future generations by the oral tradition practiced within a specific culture. One may question how long such sustainable practices of resource use may continue under the attack from global market forces. Nevertheless, traditional resource managers are not so stupid as to devour the land that feeds them.

From a purely neo-classical economic perspective Dasgupta (1982), for example, has given a devastating critique of Hardin's arguments based on the ways in which market-based mechanisms would be used to manage the commons rather than ruin it. But for the purpose of this chapter, it is clear that the central debate between population change and environmental resource use can result in a whole host of solutions to the problem. Each of these solutions has its positive and negative attributes, but they all depend upon alternatives being underpinned by different ethical positions regarding important issues over the the ways in which resources are used. It can be argued that the interest in sustainable development stems from a realisation that under the current market-based system, and the command economic systems of the former USSR, the current patterns of resource use are unsustainable. One way of viewing the debate over sustainable development is to see it as a means of achieving an emancipatory, just, participatory and sustainable society living in harmony with each other and the environment of the planet. Clearly, if this interpretation of the ongoing debate over sustainable development is right, then environmental managers who are genuinely concerned with promoting sustainable development, will need to pay much closer attention to the ethical principles and political practices involved in maintaining the maximum evolutionary potential of the biosphere. In the next section these ethical principles for sustainable development will be explored.

ETHICAL PRINCIPLES AND THE RIO DECLARATION

Implicit in the above definitions of sustainable development is the moral conviction and ethical desirability that the current generation should pass on their inheritance of natural and cultural wealth, not unchanged, but undiminished in potential, to support future generations. The basic ethical position adopted in this study, and in most sustainable development literature, is that all life is valuable; this implies maintaining ecosystems so that all living creatures can exist in their naturally changing habitats. As a point of ethical principle both the *Brundtland Report* and *Agenda 21* take it as an imperative not to destroy the diversity of natural and cultural life on earth. From an anthropocentric perspective, the general definition of sustainable development adopted in this study is that every future generation must have the option of being as well off as its predecessor. For people living in poverty or in less 'well off' circumstances a second ethical point is that there must be a redistribution of wealth so that in any generation the differences in wealth are reduced to, at least, a socially acceptable minimum standard. Ideally we would hope for a higher level than this for all people. This does, of course, imply that the tragedy of the commons is not reproduced at local or greater spatio-temporal scales. This also raises several major problems including the definition of human needs.

Maslow (1968) has suggested that the concept of individual human need can be subsumed under a hierarchy of human needs. At the basic level are the physiological needs of air, water, food and shelter. Higher material needs include safety and security. Several social needs are also identified, such as a sense of community and self-esteem. Higher moral needs, such as justice, are also noted (Figure 2). It should be noted that this hierarchy of needs was developed nearly

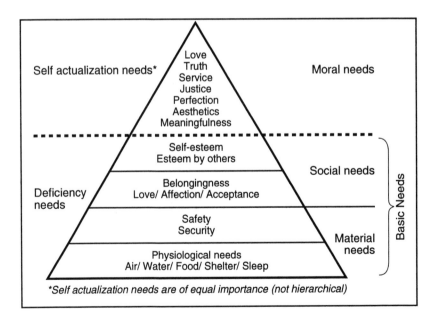

Figure 2   A hierarchy of human needs (after Maslow, 1968)

thirty years ago and is predicated upon ensuring that the environment is capable of supporting all these human activities. It should also be noted that the concept of sustainable development embraces the concepts of material needs met by a sustainable economy and ecology, the socio-economic needs and the need for social justice in the allocation of resources. The hierarchy of needs, first described by Maslow, reflects a hierarchy of values which cannot be reduced to a single dimension. In a sense sustainable development imperatives represent high order needs and values which ultimately depend on a diverse and resilient environment (Turner, 1995). Attempting to develop one or more indicators of sustainable development which could actually be used to indicate whether or not these ideals are being met, is an exceedingly difficult task. This aspect of developing indicators and other measures of sustainable development will be discussed in Part Two of this text.

In 1992 Ekins and Max-Neef suggested that the integration of ecological, economic, socio-political and ethical considerations can be described conceptually as a regular tetrahedron with the four keywords at its corners (Figure 3). There is no implied hierarchy in the figure – each apex is equally important. Any point inside this tetrahedron represents the various degrees of strength

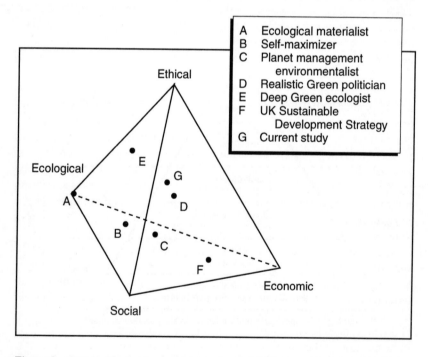

Figure 3 Sustainable development tetrahedron (after Ekins and Max-Neef, 1992)

associated with the four dimensions. The closer a point is to, say the economics apex, the greater the weight of economic factors is given in studying the problem of sustainability. If we concentrated attention on the throughput of energy and materials in an ecosystem then our work would be located at A. Such an ecological study would ignore economic, socio-political and ethical considerations. Ekins suggests that studies located at A represent an ecological materialist; points B to E represent self-maximiser, planet management environmentalist, pragmatic green politician and deep ecologist, respectively. The recent UK sustainable development strategy (Anon., 1994a) could arguably be located at F – with its emphasis on economics rather than a broader and more balanced perspective being adopted – whilst this study is located at G and stresses that we need to examine ethical, economic, ecological and socio-political aspects of the complex concept called 'sustainable development' as a whole (Ekins and Max-Neef, 1992).

The higher-order needs and values embedded in the sustainable development concept have been recognised and acknowledged in several international meetings convened to address environmental and economic development issues, such as the *Stockholm Conference* (1972) and the more recent *Earth Summit* at Rio de Janeiro (1992). In these, and several other international endeavours, the British Government has offered support to the WCS, the *Brundtland Report* and the so-called *Earth Summit* at Rio de Janeiro meetings by actively developing national responses to these international fora. At present, however, it is important that attention is turned to the ethical principles involved in sustainable development. It is felt that these ethical principles have a prior position and underpin any detailed study of sustainable development.

The Rio meeting produced a set of twenty-seven principles on the environment and development (Table 4). These twenty-seven principles recognise the integral and interdependent nature of the Earth, our home. Furthermore, the Rio Declaration has as its goal the establishment of a new and equitable global partnership through the creation of new levels of co-operation among States, key sectors of societies and people. The Rio meeting, building upon the agreements made at the 1972 *Stockholm Conference*, was also working towards international agreements which respect the interests of all, and protect the integrity of the global environmental and developmental system. The twenty-seven principles are described and discussed below (UNCED, 1992).

The first principle states that "human beings are at the centre of concerns for sustainable development. They are entitled to a healthy and productive life in harmony with nature". This principle is little more than an assertion that, in order to survive and flourish, human beings need both a good quality environment and a socio-economic system to satisfy higher needs. For some of the deep Green movement sustainable development is too anthropocentric and gives too little attention to the rights of other species or landscapes. These contentious issues will be discussed later in this chapter. The idea of harmony with nature is

Table 4   The twenty-seven principles on environment and development

Environmental Principles

1) Human beings are at the centre of concerns for sustainable development. They are entitled to a healthy and productive life in harmony with nature.

2) States have, in accordance with the Charter of the United Nations and the principles of international law, the sovereign right to exploit their own resources pursuant to their own environmental and developmental policies, and the responsibility to ensure that activities within their jurisdiction or control do not cause damage to the environment of other States or of areas beyond the limits of national jurisdiction.

4) In order to achieve sustainable development, environmental protection shall constitute an integral part of the development process and cannot be considered in isolation from it.

10) Environmental issues are best handled with the participation of all concerned citizens, at the relevant level. At the national level, each individual shall have appropriate access to information concerning the environment that is held by public authorities, including information on hazardous materials and activities in their communities, and the opportunity to participate in decision-making processes. States shall facilitate and encourage public awareness and participation by making information widely available. Effective access to judicial and administrative proceedings, including redress and remedy, shall be provided.

11) States shall enact effective environmental legislation. Environmental standards, management objectives and priorities should reflect the environmental and developmental context to which they apply. Standards applied by some countries may be inappropriate and of unwarranted economic and social cost to other countries, in particular developing countries.

13) States shall develop national law regarding liability and compensation for the victims of pollution and other environmental damage. States shall also cooperate in an expeditious and more determined manner to develop further international law regarding liability and compensation for adverse effects of environmental damage caused by activities within their jurisdiction or control to areas beyond their jurisdiction.

14) States should effectively cooperate to discourage or prevent the relocation and transfer of any activities and substances that may cause severe environmental degradation or are found to be harmful to human health.

15) In order to protect the environment, the precautionary approach shall be widely applied by States according to their capabilities. Where there are threats of serious or irreversible damage, lack of full scientific certainty shall not be used as a reason for postponing cost-effective measures to prevent environmental degradation.

17) Environmental impact assessment, as a national instrument, shall be undertaken for proposed activities that are likely to have a significant adverse impact on the environment and are subject to a decision of a competent national authority.

18) States shall immediately notify other States of any natural disasters or other emergencies that are likely to produce sudden harmful effects on the environment of those States. Every effort shall be made by the international community to help States so afflicted.

19) States shall provide prior and timely notification and relevant information to potentially affected States on activities that may have a significant adverse transboundary environmental effect and shall consult with those States at an early stage and in good faith.

23) The environment and natural resources of people under oppression, domination and occupation shall be protected.

(NB. The numbers refer to the 27 Principles listed at the Earth Summit meeting at Rio de Janeiro, 1992)

Table 4 Continued

Economic Principles

3) The right to development must be fulfilled so as to equitably meet developmental and environmental needs of present and future generations.

5) All States and all people shall cooperate in the essential task of eradicating poverty as an indispensable requirement for sustainable development, in order to decrease the disparities in standards of living and better meet the needs of the majority of the people of the world.

6) The special situation and needs of developing countries, particularly the least developed and those most environmentally vulnerable, shall be given special priority. International actions in the field of environment and development should also address the interests and needs of all countries.

7) States shall cooperate in a spirit of global partnership to conserve, protect and restore the health and integrity of the Earth's ecosystem. In view of the different contributions to global environmental degradation, States have common but differentiated responsibilities. The developed countries acknowledge the responsibility that they bear in the International pursuit of sustainable development in view of the pressures their societies place on the global environment and of the technologies and financial resources they command.

8) To achieve sustainable development and a higher quality of life for all people, States should reduce and eliminate unsustainable patterns of production and consumption and promote appropriate demographic policies.

9) States should cooperate to strengthen endogenous capacity-building for sustainable development by improving scientific understanding through exchanges of scientific and technological knowledge, and by enhancing the development adaptation, diffusion and transfer of technologies, including new and innovative technologies.

12) States should cooperate to promote a supportive and open international economic system that would lead to economic growth and sustainable development in all countries, to better address the problems of environmental degradation. Trade policy measures for environmental purposes should not constitute a means of arbitrary or unjustifiable discrimination or a disguised restriction on international trade. Unilateral actions to deal with environmental challenges outside the jurisdiction of the importing country should be avoided. Environmental measures addressing transboundary or global environmental problems should, as far as possible, be based on an international consensus.

16) National authorities should endeavour to promote the internalisation of environmental costs and the use of economic instruments, taking into account the approach that the polluter should, in principle, bear the cost of pollution, with due regard to the public interest and without distorting international trade and investment.

Social Principles

20) Women have a vital role in environmental management and development. Their full participation is therefore essential to achieve sustainable development.

21) The creativity, ideals and courage of the youth of the world should be mobilised to forge a global partnership in order to achieve sustainable development and ensure a better future for all.

22) Indigenous people and their communities, and other local communities, have a vital role in environmental management and development because of their knowledge and traditional practices. States should recognise and duly support their identity, culture and interest and enable their effective participation in the achievement of sustainable development.

Peace Principles

24) Warfare is inherently destructive of sustainable development. States shall therefore respect international law providing protection for the environment in times of armed conflict and cooperate in its further development, as necessary.

25) Peace, development and environmental protection are interdependent and indivisible.

26) States shall resolve all their environmental disputes peacefully and by appropriate means in accordance with the Charter of the United Nations.

27) States and people shall cooperate in good faith and in a spirit of partnership in the fulfilment of the principles embodied in this Declaration and in the further development of international law in the field of sustainable development.

rather more difficult to define as animals can show both conflicting (nature being red in tooth and claw) as well as co-operative behaviour. Presumably all living things are entitled to a healthy and productive life.

The other twenty-six principles can be grouped into four broad classes: environmental, economic, social, and peace. These four broad classes are not mutually exclusive but do indicate some of the inconsistencies within the principles. These inconsistencies often confuse principles with methods of resolving unsustainable practices, as well as conflating broad ethical principles with legal obligations. Given that the *Earth Summit* was an extension of the 1970s *Stockholm Conference* on the human environment it is not surprising that the vast majority of the principles of sustainable development are concerned with environmental issues.

The environmental principles acknowledge, in Principle 2, that States have the sovereign right to exploit their own resources pursuant to their own environmental and developmental policies. It also acknowledges the need for states not to cause damage to the environment of other states or areas beyond the limits of national jurisdiction. This principle is important to prevent trans-national pollution boundary problems. These would include the diffusion of sulfur dioxide from, for example, the UK, to add to the acidification problems in the lakes and forests of Scandinavia. Furthermore, the inclusion of areas beyond the national jurisdiction is important, as a principle, for preventing damage to the global commons. The protection of areas from overfishing in international waters for the conservation of wandering species which do not recognise political frontiers, is imporant. Similarly, the conservation of Antarctica from resource exploitation is an important consideration which could be supported by this principle as no one state governs Antarctica, which many people believe should be made into a World Conservation area, and prevent any direct environmentally-damaging impacts by people.

The remainder of the environmental principles are concerned with environmental protection, as distinct from resource use. Principle 4, for example, notes that in order to achieve sustainable development environmental protection shall constitute an integral part of the development process and cannot be considered in isolation from it. Hence, Principle 17 notes that environmental impact assessment, as a national instrument, shall be undertaken for proposed activities that are likely to have a significant, adverse impact on the environment and are subject to the decision of a competent national authority. Principle 4 is also supported by Principle 11 which notes that states should enact effective environmental legislation, including environmental standards, management objectives and priorities. Further, support for Principle 4 is given in Principle 13 which requests that States develop laws regarding the liability and compensation for the victims of pollution and other environmental damage. This 13th Principle also includes the further development of international law for transboundary disputes, and to cover damage to areas beyond their direct jurisdiction. Principle 14 notes that states should effectively co-operate to prevent the relocation and transfer to other states of any activities and substances that cause severe environmental degradation or are found to be harmful to human health.

Principles 18 and 19 are concerned with the transboundary consequences of natural disasters or other emergencies likely to produce sudden harmful effects on the environment of other states. This will include the prior and timely notification of transboundary problems. The case of the nuclear explosion at Chernobyl on the 26 April 1986 resulted in little information being given to other states by the former Soviet Union. Clearly, if Principles 18 and 19 had been stated and applied then the international community could have had earlier warning about the disaster at Chernobyl. Obviously, moving to a sustainable renewable energy source such as wind power would, by definition, relieve current and future generations of the burdens of nuclear energy's economic and environmental costs. In the UK, for example, the cost of dismantling and disposing of redundant nuclear installations is estimated at £20 billion. The sites for the "safe disposal" of radioactive waste products pose enormous political, economic, social and environmental problems (Elliott, 1994). Principle 15 stresses the precautionary principle. In many cases the lack of full scientific certainty shall not be used as a reason for postponing cost-effective measures to prevent environmental degradation. In the case of nuclear power no scientific solutions to the safe disposal of long-lasting high grade nuclear waste have been found, so it would be prudent to explore other safer ways to produce energy. Environmental damage prevention is better than attempting to find a cure for nuclear waste.

Principle 10 noted the importance of participation of all concerned citizens at the relevant level. This includes having access to information on the environment and the opportunity to participate in decision-making processes, including effective access to judicial and administrative proceedings, including redress and remedy.

Perhaps the most difficult environmental Principle is number 23 which states that the environment and natural resources of people under oppression, domination and occupation shall be protected. This is an unusual way of asking for environmental protection, as people enduring such unspecified oppression might feel that they had a prior claim to justice rather than demanding that their environment be protected, whilst their socio-economic fabric is made intolerable. The delegates from the United States of America were unable to agree to this Principle partly because of the loose wording adopted. What for example, is a fair interpretation of domination and oppression? Are many working people and their environments not dominated by the oppressive workings of unbridled market forces in the world economy? Similarly, the lack of agreement over conditions for work in the UK, within the European Union, could also be represented as forms of domination and oppression. What is good for capitalism may not be good for the exploited (working classes) or the environment or both.

Obviously, economic activities and environmental problems are intricately interlinked. The use of any resource will inevitably bring both advantages and disadvantages to people and the rest of the environment from which the resource is used. Several of the twenty-seven Principles can be broadly classified as economic although this classification realises that economic activities often have direct or indirect environmental consequences. Principle 3 notes that "the right to development must be fulfilled so as to equitably meet the developmental and environmental needs of current and future generations". While this is an admirable Principle it has major difficulties in its operation as some resources, once used, cannot be used again. The fossil fuels, for example, would have to remain untouched forever if we are to maintain the stock of resources intact for future generations. Similarly, the use of non-renewable metalliferous ores could remain unused if this Principle was carried out to the letter.

Some economists have argued that Principle 3 is not very sound as it is possible to substitute some forms of non-renewable resources (part of nature's capital) for human-made capital (Turner, 1995). There are, of course, several problems associated with this strategy. These problems are acknowledged by many economists and include the problem of determining critical natural capital, and the problems of attempting to define suitable substitutes for non-renewable resources. Some of these issues will be addressed in Part Two of this book. At present, however, it is sufficient to note that this Principle has its problems when attempts are made to put it into practice. Several environmental economists have attempted to circumvent this problem by examining the potential of using renewable resources, such as forestry and other forms of biomass, instead of non-renewable resources. They have argued for maximum sustainable yield as a measure of the rate of extraction and regrowth of these potentially renewable resources (Costanza, 1991).

Economic Principles 5 to 9 are primarily concerned with the relationship between the rich "northern" nations and the rest of the "southern" or developing nations. Principle 5, for example, is concerned with all states co-operating to eradicate poverty as an indispensable requirement to promote sustainable development. This eradication of poverty is vital if we are to better meet the needs of the majority of the people of the world. Principle 6 notes that the least developed countries and those that are most environmentally sensitive shall be given special priority although all nations' needs should be addressed.

In an attempt to apply Principles 5 and 6, Principles 7, 8 and 9 are invoked. These three Principles note that all states, especially the developed nations, have a moral obligation to conserve, protect and restore the health and integrity of the earth's ecosystems. Principle 8 suggests that, to achieve sustainable development and a higher quality of life for all people, states should reduce and eliminate unsustainable patterns of production and consumption and promote demographic policies. Principle 9 suggests that the transfer of scientific understanding, and technological knowledge, including new innovative technologies, can help in the quest to produce sustainable development. Similarly, Principle 12 suggests that further opening of world trade would promote economic growth and sustainable development. Principle 16 suggests that the use of economic instruments to internalise economic costs of environmental damage should be included. These internal costs would incorporate the polluter pays principle.

It should be clear that these economic principles recognise the disparity between rich and poor nations. Hence, the rich nations, because of their impact on the globe, acknowledge the responsibility that they bear in the international pursuit of sustainable development. It should be noted that acknowledging one's responsibility to nature and the rest of humanity does not tie one to do anything about it. The terms of trade and aid appear, on balance, to benefit the wealthy banks and their shareholders rather than the countries and their populations they are trying to help! (Harvey, 1982). Little wonder that at Rio many of the non-governmental organisations criticised the trade liberalisation principles. In a sense the need for a change in the direction of trade so that the less-developed countries can actually benefit substantially from trade flows has not made much progress since the *Brandt Commission* (Brandt Commission, 1980).

Principles 20 to 22 can be broadly interpreted as social. Principle 20 notes the vital role that women play in environmental management and development and also notes that their full participation is important to achieve sustainable development. Similarly, in Principle 21, youth are encouraged to use their creativity, ideals and courage to ensure sustainable development and a better future for all. The 22nd Principle notes that indigenous peoples and their communities have a vital role in environmental management because of their knowledge and traditional practices. The same principle notes that states should recognise and support their identity, culture, and interests, and enable effective participation in the achievement of sustainable development.

Obviously, these social principles are to be encouraged – but they do appear to represent the lobbying of different groups such as feminists, indigenous and young people at the meeting rather than represent a coherent ethical position on sustainable development. It is somewhat ironic for indigenous peoples to be told that they have a vital role in sustainable development when the *Brundtland Report* noted that many of the first people's cultures and environments were being destroyed by global market forces. The role of women, as we shall see later, is often under-represented in the global economic systems, especially in the case of unpaid domestic labour (see Chapter 6). The elderly, with their wisdom, may take offence that only the youth are to be encouraged to help promote a better world. Clearly, the principle that all people have a role in this task regardless of age, gender, sexual orientation, religion or ethnicity would be a more appropriate principle.

Principles 24 through to 27 are designed to promote peace between nations. Principle 24 states that warfare is inherently destructive of sustainable development; States shall therefore respect international law providing for the environment in times of armed conflict and co-operate in its further development as necessary. This Principle is odd insofar as it appears to put environmental protection above the protection of human lives. Obviously, no right-minded person would want to use defoliants or other aspects of nuclear, chemical or biological warfare in the attempt to settle disputes as attempted in the Vietnam war, or in the recent attack by terrorists on the public in Japan, or the nuclear bombing of Hiroshima and Nagasaki in the Second World War. Both human life and the rest of the environment is of equal concern and a stronger principle claiming that war is an obscenity and that the abolition of war and the vast supplies of armaments for the carrying out of war could have been made. Some calculations have suggested that to carry out the ideals of sustainable development for the period 1995–2000 would cost approximately $(US)200 billion, roughly 4% of the global arms budget for the same period (O'Riordan, 1995).

Principles 25 to 27 state that peace, development and environmental protection are inter-dependent and indivisible (Principle 25). That states shall resolve all their environmental disputes peacefully and by appropriate means in accordance with the Charter of the United Nations (Principle 26). Finally, Principle 27 states that people shall co-operate in good faith and in a spirit of partnership in the fulfillment of the principles embodied in this declaration and in the further development of international law in the field of sustainable development. This last Principle implies that international law for sustainable development has been made, or is in the process of being made.

It could be argued that the Principles agreed at Rio are little more than a face-saving exercise by the representatives of the various groups at the meeting. Less cynically, the Principles represent a basis for more detailed examination of the ethical underpinnings of the concept of sustainable development. Nevertheless, they raise problems concerning the correct (i.e. just) way of allocating resources within and between generations. For some of the neo-classical economists this type of problem can be resolved by use of the Pareto optimum distribution (Pearce *et al.*, 1989). This 'solution' ensures that no one is made worse off – but the distribution of resource use is still unchallenged. This implies the wealthy remain wealthy and the poor no worse off, but still poor.

If the narrow economic perspective of sustainable development is adopted then there is no need to explore the ethical underpinnings of the concept. From the narrow, neo-classical perspective it is possible to argue that the market is the final arbiter on the needs of peoples. Equitable distributions are met when the conditions of Pareto optimality are reached. Preservation of the environment will only occur when every aspect of the environment is expressed in monetary units and is embraced as part of the global market system.

There are, however, numerous counter-arguments against the primacy of the neo-classical perspective. These include the questionable mechanistic and atomistic assumptions underpinning this paradigm: the use of money as the measure of value of a good; the difficulty in defining utility, and the uncritical acceptance of the distribution of wealth in society (Costanza, 1991). Often this latter aspect is defended by suggesting that a Pareto optimum solution, whereby no one is made worse off even if some are made better off, can be used. There are, however, several difficulties with such an approach. First, a Pareto optimum solution is strongly supportive of the *status quo*. Next, the Pareto optimum solution to the problem pre-supposes an efficient free market. Third, that it is concerned with efficiency rather than justice. Clearly, the equitable allocation of scarce resources is important in the discussion of sustainable development but its resolution is not easy.

Whilst the Rio Declaration is a statement of principles, these are not necessarily based on a consistent ethical basis, nor do they necessarily give a good guide to action. It is therefore essential to delve a little deeper in an attempt to provide a coherent ethical basis for sustainable development principles, rather than just to restate those agreed at Rio. These deeper philosphical problems are explored in the rest of this chapter.

ENVIRONMENTAL ETHICS AND THE RIGHTS OF NATURE

The twenty-seven Principles, which make up the Rio Declaration on Environment and Development, open up a potentially huge debate over the ethical rights of humankind for nature (Brennan, 1988). A convenient way of examining the literature on the rights of biotic organisms and abiotic landscapes is to probe into the question of whether or not there are any principles which can guide our sustainable use of the world's resources. It is taken as axiomatic that, in order to survive, any organism must interact with, use and abuse, the immediate environment. People, as moral agents, may recognise the obligation to respect the life and autonomy of all living things as well as respect non-living landscapes, yet we must use some aspects of the living and abiotic world in order to survive and enjoy life. The question before us then, is not whether we should use resources, but rather to ask what moral principles we can use to guide us in an ethically- and ecologically-sound and socially responsible way of making this planet sustainable?

Given that sustainable development can be interpreted in a broad manner, then it is clear that several different ethical positions can be found in the literature. Pearce (1993), following O'Riordan (1981), for example, has tabulated these as a sustainability spectrum ranging from the Technocentric Cornucopian perspective to the Ecocentric Deep Ecology perspective. Different ethical underpinnings for these positions can be found in the sustainability spectrum. Again, these range from the support for the rights and interests of contemporary individual humans, through to the acceptance of bioethics, with its concerns for the rights of all non-human species and even the abiotic parts of the environment (Table 5). These different ethical perspectives imply both different ways to measure the economic–ecological interactions as well as different management strategies to promote sustainability. Clearly, then, ethical positions concerning the principles upon which sustainable development should be erected are vitally important. Furthermore, it has been argued that the ethical principles announced at Rio are only a first step but need to be subjected to deeper critical analysis if they are to provide some of the ethical principles underpinning sustainable development.

One solution to this problem is to recognise, as some religions do, that all life and landscapes are worthy of our respect and care (Engel and Engel, 1990). Although some people find their religious views important (so important that they can wage "holy wars" on each other) these metaphysical views need not concern us here. What is important, however, is attempting to develop a set of ethical principles which give us guidance when considering the environment and all living organisms. This amounts to developing an ethical code of practice for the rights of nature, which includes humanity. If this view accords with the ethics in one or more religions then, on this point, environmentalists and some religious groups can agree, but the metaphysical speculation concerning the belief in deities, which necessarily surround all religions, is not a hypothesis warranted further consideration in this study (Smart, 1989; Park, 1994).

A theory of environmental ethics is an attempt to establish the rational grounds for a system of moral principles by which human treatment of ecosystems (biotic and abiotic) ought to be guided. In pursuing this line of reasoning our presently held beliefs and attitudes may need to be questioned, and our prejudice towards an anthropogenic view of morals may need to be suspended. To explore a new theory of environmental ethics requires a certain detachment from our immediate intuitions so that we can consider these new ethical principles for sustainable development without prejudice. The results of such an enquiry may lead to a radical transformation in our outlook and behaviour with regard to the ways in which people interact with the rest of the environment.

Taylor suggests five conditions for any set of rules and standards which would constitute the basis for a valid normative ethical system. These five conditions are as follows: the rules should be general in form, they must be considered universally applicable to all moral agents, they must be applied disinterestedly, they must be advocated as normative principles for all to adopt, and they must be taken as overriding all non-moral norms. Clearly, these five conditions may not be accepted by post-modernists who appear to uncritically accept current social practice (almost anything goes) and do not like universalistic arguments. But they have to justify why the views they accept for their behaviour towards the planet are morally just rather than mere hedonistic pleasure.

In the context of the sustainable development debate it is clear that humans often conflict with other biotic communities and abiotic elements in ecosystems.

Table 5 The sustainability spectrum

	Technocentric		Ecocentric	
	Cornucopian	*Accommodating*	*Communalist*	*Deep ecology*
Green labels	Resource exploitative, growth orientated position	Resource conservationist & 'managerial' appeal	Resource preservationist position	Extreme preservationist position
Type of economy	Anti-green economy, unfettered free markets	Green economy, green markets guided by economic incentive instruments (Els) (eg. pollution charges etc.)	Deep green economy, steady-state economy regulated by macro-environmental standards & supplemented by Els	Very deep green economy, heavily regulated to minimise 'resource-take'
Management strategies	Primary economic policy objective, maximise economic growth (Gross National Product [GNP])	Modified economic growth (adjusted green accounting to measure GNP)	Zero economic growth; zero population growth	Reduced scale of economy & population
	Taken as axiomatic that unfettered free markets in conjunction with technical progress will ensure infinite substitute possibilities capable of mitigating all 'scarcity/limits' constraints (environmental sources and sinks)	Decoupling important but infinite substitution rejected. Sustainability rules: constant capital rule	Decoupling plus no increase in scale. 'Systems perspective - 'health' of whole ecosystems very important; Gaia hypothesis & implications	Scale reduction imperative; at the extreme for some there is a literal interpretation of Gaia as a personalised agent to which moral obligations are owed
Ethics	Support for traditional ethical reasoning: rights & interests of contemporary individual humans; instrumental value (ie. of recognised value to humans) in nature	Extension of ethical reasoning: 'caring for others' motive - intragenerational & intergenerational equity (ie. contemporary poor & future people); instrumental value in nature	Further extension of ethical reasoning: interests of the collective take precedence over those of the individual; primary value of ecosystems & secondary value of component functions & services	Acceptance of bioethics (ie. moral rights/interests conferred on all non-human species & even the abiotic parts of the environment); intrinsic value in nature (ie. valuable in its own right regardless of human experience)

(After Pearce, 1993)

Economic activities, such as removing a hillside for quarrying or strip-mining, the dredging of an estuarine environment to build a yacht marina, the destruction of forests for building or paper production, are examples of conflicts with "nature". In these and numerous other activities humans have competing claims with other aspects of the environment. Taylor suggests a set of ethically sound priority principles for resolving these conflicts between humans and non-humans which do not assign greater inherent worth to humans, but consider all parties to have the same worth. This is a fundamental requirement of species – impartiality – so that a fair or just resolution of such human–nature conflicts can be resolved.

In fact Taylor suggests a set of five principles that can be used to develop an environmental ethic which gives due respect to nature. The five priority principles are: self-defence, proportionality, minimum wrong, distributive justice and restitutive principle (Taylor, 1986). These principles do not yield a neat solution to every conceivable conflict but they cover all the major ways of adjudicating fairly among competing claims arising from clashes of human ethics and those of biocentric ethics. The self-defence principle states that it is permissible for moral agents to protect themselves against a dangerous or harmful organism by destroying it. This principle is only to be used after every effort has been made to prevent the "attacking" organism harming the moral agent, by avoiding the organism or by preventing it from damaging the environmental conditions required for the survival of the moral agent.

The remaining four priority principles refer to situations where wild animals and plants are harmless to humans but may be in conflict with the latter's "non-basic" or "basic" interests. In the case of the basic interest of harmless plants and animals coming into conflict with non-basic human interests, then the principle of proportionality should be invoked. This principle states that basic interests of one living organism have priority over the non-basic interests of another. This principle prohibits us from allowing non-basic interests of humans to override the basic interests of other living plants or animals.

The principle of minimum wrong allows people who have respect for nature to pursue their non-basic interest even though it conflicts with the basic interest of plants and wild animals. Under this condition it is permissible for people to pursue those values only as long as doing so involves fewer wrongs (violations of duties) than any alternative way of pursuing those values. Taylor gives several examples, such as pollution control, habitat destruction, and direct killing, where the principle of minimum wrong (i.e. the general requirement to do least harm or tread lightly on the earth) can be useful for resolving practical problems.

The fourth priority principle, namely distributive justice, applies when the basic needs of harmless plants and animals are in conflict with basic human needs. As animals and plants have an equal moral worth to human kind, then distributive justice is called upon to provide criteria whereby a solution to the problem must be fair to all. In these circumstances a fair share is an equal share.

Taylor acknowledges that perfect equality of consideration is not wholly realizable. In these cases the fourth principle must be supplemented by another priority principle, that of restitutive justice.

The principle of restitutive justice attempts to restore the balance of justice after a moral subject has been wronged. In the context of "nature", to set aside habitat areas and protect environmental conditions in those areas where wild animals and plants can realise their good is often the most appropriate way of restoring the balance of justice with them. In a sense this principle of restitutive justice returns the favours they do for us by doing something for their sake. The way in which these five principles interact is shown in figure 4.

Taylor's solution to develop a set of ethically-sound priority principles for the rights of nature is not without immediate practical problems. For most of his study consideration of abiotic features of an environment are given little attention. Yet, it is clear that humans do value landscapes for their existence value and often cherish natural or human-made features of the landcapes as icons. Examples, such as Ayers Rock (Uluru) in Australia or St Paul's Cathedral in London, are important landscape facets which can be appreciated from several perspectives. Second, the definition of "basic"/"non-basic" categories is often difficult to demarcate. Similar problems are associated with this type of classification in the economic geography of location. Next, as Norton (1987) notes, in a review of Taylor's seminal work, "in a world where every tuft of grass has inherent worth and is deserving of moral consideration in some sense equal to that given to each human individual, then it is very unlikely that humans

WILD ANIMALS AND PLANTS	Harmful to Humans	Harmless to Humans (or: their harmfulness can reasonably be avoided)		Humans harmful to Humans	HUMANS
		Basic interests	*Basic interests*		
...in conflict with...		...in conflict with...	...in conflict with...		...in conflict with...
		Nonbasic interests	*Basic interests*		
HUMANS		Intrinsically incompatible with respect for nature	Intrinsically compatible with respect for nature, but extrinsically detrimental to wildlife & natural ecosystems		HUMANS
PRIORITY PRINCIPLES	*(1)* *Self-defence*	*(2)* *Proportionality*	*(3)* *Minimum wrong*	*(4)* *Distributive justice* / *(6)* *Social justice*	*(1)* *Self-defence*
		...when (3) or (4) have been applied... (5) *Restitutive justice*			

Figure 4   Five priority principles for the rights of Nature. (Adapted from Taylor, 1986)

could survive in such a world". Clearly, making the fine distinction between our survival and the sustainable use of other living creatures and their abiotic environment is difficult to resolve, as we are all part of complex biogeochemical cycles and ecological food chains. Yet we must resolve this problem of over-use of the resources, as many current economic practices are neither ethically sound nor are they sustainable. Clearly, Taylor's work does give a reasonable and well-argued case for resolving competing claims in our interactions with the rest of "nature". We are, as it were, acting out the tragedy of the commons on a global scale. As argued earlier, there are solutions to this problem but each solution depends on specific ethical underpinnings. Some would suggest we retain market forces and an unjust system of inheritance (Hardin, 1968); others wish for a radical transformation of both the market and command economies which may lead to communal/anarchic solutions. Many of us are unsure what our responses ought to be although we are aware of the need to do something constructive given the current pattern of unsustainable development in the world. Clearly, several of the solutions offered for us to live with respect for nature also invoke different attitudes to social justice.

SOCIAL JUSTICE

The principles outlined in Taylor's *Respect for Nature* represent a deeper level of discussion, and arguably, an improvement on many of the principles declared at the Rio Conference in 1992. Although there are some problems with putting into practice Taylor's priority principles of respecting nature, the principles go some way towards an ethical ordering of the ways in which we both use and respect nature. In a sense the use and respect for nature is similar to some indigenous people's use of nature, when, for example, traditional Aborigines hunt kangaroo for meat they take only sufficient for their immediate needs. This is different from the wholesale slaughtering of animals for markets. How long traditional hunting can be kept in play when contemporary Aborigines in Australia and elsewhere use guns, modern transport and refrigeration for their hunting trips, is also very debatable. Only their ethical code and social practices coupled with an intimate knowledge of their environment, will safeguard nature, but the pressures to move towards a market based system are increasing. In traditional societies not only is nature respected but they divide a specific resource, such as a kangaroo, with other members of their group following traditional norms, based very loosely on status and rank rather than on conscious principles of social justice. Obviously, people acting as moral agents need some way of assessing whether or not their actions are not only caring towards other lives and landscapes but socially just.

The position adopted in this chapter, and throughout the text, is that there are a set of moral principles which can act as a guide to promote sustainable development. These moral principles are a necessary, but not sufficient, condition for sustainable development to be achieved. Furthermore, and more debatable, is the view adopted here that moral principles are universal rather than relativistic. Universal moral principles are said to apply to all humans despite the time and society in which they are located. In contrast moral relativism suggests that the moral codes practised by members of a given society can only be judged by reference to that society. This view is not adopted here as the vast majority of people are unconvinced that, for example, the practice of infanticide can be condoned as a morally correct practice even though this practice may be socially acceptable in some social formations. Without universalistic principles guiding human practices in a just manner then we could end up uncritically accepting a holocaust as just, merely because very few people condemn this barbarity to humanity.

One key way of addressing the problems concerned with social justice is to draw upon the idea of social justice proposed by Rawls (1971). His theory of justice is based on the premise that justice is fairness as distinct from the utilitarian and institutional conceptions of justice, such as the Pareto optimum solution discussed earlier. His concept of social justice is based on a universalistic premise that people as individuals can make a judgement of which society is just if they were to be located into a specific society in any space and time. This represents the 'original position' and, as individuals do not know their position in a hypothetical social formation, they operate behind a veil of ignorance. The main proposition is that in a just society "the liberties of equal citizenship are taken as settled . . . an injustice is tolerable only when it is necessary to avoid a greater injustice". For Rawls, a society is well understood and effectively regulated by a public conception of justice when everyone knows and accepts the same principles of justice and the institutions in society satisfy, and are known to satisfy, these principles of justice.

A key concept in Rawls' work is the original position. This idea is that no one knows his/her place in society, their class or social status, nor does anyone know his/her future in the distribution of national assets or abilities, his/her intelligence, strength and the like. In other words an individual will know if a society is just if his or her position in society is chosen behind a veil of ignorance and they are located anywhere in an original position within society.

Rawls' principles of social justice can be given as follows. The First Principle is that each person is to have an equal right to the most extensive total system of equal basic liberties compatible with a similar system of liberty for all. The Second Principle is concerned with social and economic inequalities which are to be arranged so that they are both: (a) to the greatest benefit of the least advantaged, consistent with the just savings principle, and (b) attached to offices and position open to all under conditions of fair equality of opportunity. These two principles are then followed by two Priority principles ranked in lexical order. The priority of liberty is the first Priority principle. This states that, (a) less extensive liberty must strengthen the total system of liberty for all, and (b) a less equal liberty must be acceptable to those with less liberty. The Second Priority rule which stresses the priority of justice over efficiency and welfare is given as, (a) an inequality of opportunity must enhance the opportunity of those with lesser opportunity, and (b) an excessive rate of saving must, on balance, mitigate the burden of those bearing this hardship. The General Conception of Justice is that "All social primary goods – liberty and opportunity, income and wealth, and the bases of self respect – are to distributed equally unless an unequal distribution of any or all of these goods is to the advantage of the least favoured" (Rawls, 1971).

Whilst Rawls' theory of social justice is difficult to grasp he does attempt to clarify the way in which these principles can operate. In Figure 5 the most advantaged person and the least advantaged person in society are represented by the two axes X and Y, respectively. With suitable scaling, the 45 degree line would represent a perfectly fair or just social distribution of worldly goods between these two people. The principles of social justice are to be operated by the individuals and institutions in society in a just manner so that the least advantaged have, as far as possible, a fair distribution of the social and private goods of that society. Given the idea of the original position then anyone who is

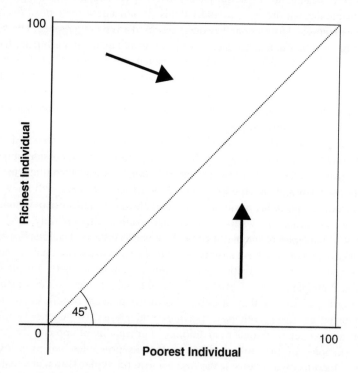

Figure 5   Social justice as equity

located in the society would quickly notice whether or not their location in society was just. Furthermore, members of that society would be able, through their institutions, to ensure that any injustices in the distribution of goods and services would, as far as possible, be fair (Kukathas and Petit, 1992).

Whilst Rawls' work did not address the question of inter-generational equity, it is clear that adopting such a position on justice as fairness could help to underpin the ethical principles underlying sustainable development. In particular, two operational rules for the distribution of resources between generations can be given. First, each generation should maintain the resource base it inherits and leave the next generation with a *per capita* stock that is no less than it inherited. Second, the total stock of renewable resources, resource diversity and assimilative capacity should be maintained through time (Young, 1992).

In a contemporary world where the world's richest 20 per cent of nations absorb over 83 per cent of global income, and where one-in-five of the world's population are without basic needs, there is clearly an unjust distribution of the social goods. Furthermore, when we consider that the human appropriation of the natural resources of the planet are removing the sustenance for all other species, it can be appreciated that things are far from a Rawlsian fair distribution and that a massive task is required to move current practices onto a path of sustainable development.

One of the characteristics of the contemporary world is the growing disparities between individuals and between nations. These disparities include levels of income, education, health care and environmental quality. Clearly, the list is far from exhaustive but indicates that differences in levels of human living and in respect for nature abound. Many different measures have been proposed and used to monitor these changes as witnessed in the level of living indicators (Coates *et al.*, 1977). Similarly, the *Brundtland Report* noted that the increasing patterns of poverty must be addressed if we are to make development sustainable.

This latter problem of poverty has been addressed numerous times in countries within the capitalist system. Some of these studies have been by philanthropists others by government departments and by academics. Harvey (1973), in particular, has addressed the issue of social justice by exploring the Rawlsian ideas of territorial social justice. Using Maslow's (1968) ideas of need, common good and merit as underpinnings of his argument, he suggests three principles of territorial social justice. These three principles are as follows:

(1)   the spatial organisation and the patterns of regional investment should be such as to fulfill the needs of the population. This requires that we first establish socially just methods for determining and measuring needs. The difference between needs and actual allocations provides us with an initial evaluation of the degree of territorial injustice in an existing system.

(2)   A spatial organisation and pattern of territorial resource allocation, which provides extra benefits in the form of need fulfilment (primarily) and

aggregate output (secondarily) in other territories through spillover effects, multiplier effects and the like, is a "better" form of spatial organisation and allocation.

(3)   Deviations in the pattern of territorial investment may be tolerated if they are designed to overcome the specific environmental difficulties which would otherwise prevent the evolution of the system which would meet need or contribute to the common good.

From his examination of the Rawlsian principles of social justice Harvey (1973) then arrived at the sense of territorial social justice as follows:

(1)   The distribution of income should be such that (a) the needs of the population within each territory are met, (b) resources are allocated to maximise inter-territorial multiplier effects, and (c) extra resources are allocated to help overcome special difficulties stemming from the physical and social environment.

(2)   The mechanisms (institutional, organisational, political and economic) should be such that the prospects of the least advantaged are as great as can be.

The Rawlsian ideals of social justice are one way of developing guiding principles that require only a clear mind, rather than a set of religious precepts, as guides to justice. As they stand, however, they still need to be translated into ways of making these guiding principles of social justice operational. No doubt many philosophers will decry such crude operationalisation of these philosophical ideas. The point, however, is not simply to contemplate the world, but to change it in an ecologically sound, economically viable and socially just manner. It is at this juncture that elementary quantitative techniques can be used to ascertain whether or not a pattern of development is just. The criteria of Rawls' theory of justice is not economic efficiency, as beloved by the neo-classical economists and their adherents, but one of equity.

Equitable distribution of resources, for example, can be viewed in terms of Pareto optimality – but only if we see this from a neo-classical perspective. If, however, we wish to develop Rawls' ideals of social justice as equity then we need alternative ways of measuring and implementing, say, the distribution of resources in a just manner. Fortunately, there are simple quantitative methods which can be used to determine whether or not the distribution of, for example, environmental goods and resources, is equitable. These tools include the Lorenz curve and Gini coefficient as well as the coefficient of concentration (Smith, 1975).

In 1994 Smith re-examined the ideas of justice and geography. His study was influenced by Rawls' theory of social justice but also went on to examine some ways of measuring a just distribution. In one example he notes that there is a changing pattern of regional inequality in the Gross Domestic Product (GDP) in the United Kingdom during the 1980s. Using several quantitative techniques, including the coefficient of variation and mean percentage deviation, he confirmed the trend towards greater regional inequality identified by other measures. The general strategy of using different quantitative measures is to establish at least the direction of the trend in regional inequality in the UK. By using both the regional distribution of GDP, as well as the changing distribution of income and wealth in the UK during the 1980s he is able to raise the question of "whether social justice in the UK regressed during the 1980s: by the criterion of justice as equalisation, it did" (Smith, 1994).

When Smith (1975) considers the distribution of inequality in South Africa he asks whether or not income distribution among the four race groups officially recognised until the abolition of apartheid legislation has decreased over the past half century. Using the Lorenz curve and the Gini coefficient, as well as the coefficient of concentration he is able to demonstrate that this has been the case, but he does show that the results of the empirical investigation are sensitive to the measures employed. He also notes that many of the results of equalisation are dependent on the scale of the problem, the quality of the data and the method adopted; he urges the wisdom of using alternative methods, if possible, to get a clear answer to the question of a just distribution.

Rawls' work on justice and the measures suggested by Smith have an immediate applicability for studies in sustainable development. By adopting and adapting the framework we may be able, not only to make our contribution to a sustainable world, but also to monitor whether or not we are moving towards a non-trivial but fair solution to the allocation of resources. Furthermore, we will be able to observe if our actions leading to a sustainable path of development are moving towards a just distribution justly arrived at.

CONCLUDING COMMENT

There are numerous definitions of sustainable development. Each one stresses some aspects of this broad concept and it has been argued that some of the definitions are attempting to extend conventional neo-classical economics to embrace ecological and environmental problems. Some other scholars suggest that these ecological and environmental problems cannot be contained within the straight-jacket of neo-classical economics, and a search for a new paradigm to embrace the world of nature and humankind is underway. These are intellectually exciting times but, to date, ecological economics and co-evolutionary economics and other new approaches have not usurped the neo-classical paradigm from its dominant influential position. There are, however, alternative definitions of sustainable development and whilst these are not predicated upon a particular economic paradigm they do offer different ways of discussing and resolving the fundamental problem of living in harmony with nature, i.e. living in a sustainable manner.

The position adopted in this chapter has been to critically assess the various definitions of sustainable development and then move to a deeper level by examining the principles underpinning the diverse definitions of sustainable development. From the opening statement at the *Agenda 21* meeting there is a consensus that we need to develop a set of ethical principles to achieve sustainable development locally, regionally, nationally and globally. It has been argued that the Rio Declaration Principles are more the result of a mixture of political posturing and compromises, which reflect the conflicting views of the delegates at the meetings, rather than a carefully considered set of ethically sound principles. Whilst the delegates at the Rio conference are to be congratulated in declaring their principles for sustainable development it has been argued that these principles are not carefully thought out.

By drawing upon the work of Taylor and Rawls it has been argued that there is the basis for developing an ethically sound set of principles which are socially just. These principles enrich those listed at Rio and provide one way of using ethical principles as a basis for guiding sustainable development practices including policy making. In a later chapter the ethical principles outlined here will be used as the underpinnings for an operational dynamic simulation model for promoting sustainable development (see Chapter 8). The views developed in this chapter, however, are one contribution to the growing opinion that ethical principles are essential for putting *Agenda 21* in place. If the ideas developed in this chapter are translated into practice they will help to make development ecologically sound, economically worthwhile and socially just. In short these ethical principles can be used to make development sustainable.

PART TWO

Analysis of Sustainable Development

CHAPTER 4

MEASURING SUSTAINABLE DEVELOPMENT INDICATORS

INTRODUCTION

In 1983 the Brundtland Commission was established by the World Commission on Economic Development to enquire into a global agenda for change. A key feature of the agenda was to propose long-term environmental strategies for achieving sustainable development by the year 2000 and beyond (WCED, 1987). The term sustainable development, which appeared earlier in the *World Conservation Strategy* (IUCN, 1980), has many definitions and interpretations including the following: "Sustainable development requires meeting the basic needs of all and extending to all the opportunity to satisfy their aspirations for a better life . . . sustainable development requires the promotion of values that encourage consumption standards that are within the bounds of the ecologically possible and to which all can reasonably aspire . . . at a minimum, sustainable development must not endanger the natural systems that support life on Earth: the atmosphere, the waters, the soil, and living beings" (WCED, 1987). While there are a plethora of definitions surrounding the term (see Chapters 2 and 3) the International Union for the Conservation of Nature, United Nations Environment Programme and World Wide Fund for Nature (1991) have suggested that a society is ecologically sustainable when it conserves the life-support systems and biodiversity, ensures that the uses of renewable resources are sustainable and minimises the depletion of non-renewable resources, and keeps within the carrying capacity of supporting ecosystems. Sustainable development requires carefully managed change to improve environmental and economic conditions and the quality of life for all people and other species.

While there is a continuing discussion over the definition of sustainable development the bulk of the debate has moved on to address the equally difficult problems of conceptualizing the term and deriving indicators and other appropriate measures. From a conceptual perspective sustainable development involves consideration of many issues. These include discussions over problems of inter- and intra-generational resource allocation, problems of ascertaining the assimilative capacity of a receiving environment, methodological issues concerned with critical ecological thresholds, stochasticity and uncertainty in environmental control (Common and Perrings, 1992; Perrings, 1987), as well as the cross-cultural perspectives on population, social justice and the rights of biotic and abiotic phenomena as part of a growing concern into environmental ethics (Engel and Engel, 1990). Some of these important issues have already been addressed in Part One. In Part Two attention is directed at the way in which sustainable development can be measured; in particular Part Two is concerned with the analysis of data to differentiate sustainable from unsustainable forms of development by developing suitable indicators.

The reason for developing indicators is both ethical and pragmatic. From an ethical perspective it is taken as axiomatic that ALL life on earth is to be respected and that human life is to be enjoyed. This enjoyment is not to be some short-term hedonistic delight but must show respect for other living forms and their environment. Furthermore, the ethical problems concerned with the distribution of resources for current and future generations have also to be considered – at least if we are to show any concern for the rights of life. The political implications of these themes will be examined in detail in Part Three. At present, however, it is clear that sustainable development indicators cannot be isolated from the broader ethical questions within which they are embedded.

From a pragmatic perspective it is important for many environmental scientists and decision-makers that some indicators of sustainable development can be produced both as a guide to specific environmental management projects and as a broad strategic guide to evaluating the ways in which a nation's or region's economy and ecology are moving. In some studies empirical data has been used to modify conventional economic measures of economic growth, such as Gross National Product (GNP), in an attempt to account for the destruction of the environment. These modifications of economic measures may be useful in reminding many decision-makers that ultimately all economic activities are based upon the use of the earth's resource base. More sophisticated analyses have attempted to define natural capital as well as 'weak' and 'strong' measures of sustainability (Pearce *et al.*, 1989). Some researchers, however, are beginning to realise the difficulties in attempting to put all the complexities of ecological systems into a common measure, often expressed in monetary units. Distinguished researchers have suggested that the price mechanism is an inappropriate method for attempting to control environmental processes (Common and Perrings, 1992). Other researchers have stressed the need for multi-variate indicators similar to the quality of life indicators (Coates *et al.*, 1977) but used for measuring sustainable development (Daly and Cobb, 1989). Similarly, several writers have noted the need for ecological indicators to be used in measuring sustainable development (Pearce, 1993; Young, 1992).

Despite the importance of the concept many different measures of sustainable development have been proposed. The purpose of this chapter is to critically review the various indicators and measures used in attempts to provide estimates of sustainable development. The following section discusses some of the conceptual issues involved in measuring indicators at a variety of spatio-temporal scales. This is then followed by a detailed, critical study of the various measures of sustainable development. The paucity of relevant empirical studies is noted. Finally, some of the ways in which this major lacuna in environmental data can be infilled are discussed.

ON INDICATORS AND DATA PROBLEMS

In 1980 the *World Conservation Strategy* noted the term 'sustainable utilization of resources' which had three principal aims, namely, to maintain essential processes and life support systems, to preserve genetic diversity and to ensure sustainable utilisation of species and ecosystems (IUCN, 1980). By 1987 the concept of sustainable development had gained much more attention in the *Brundtland Report*, entitled *'Our Common Future'*, where sustainable development was defined as meeting "the needs and aspirations of the present generation without compromising the ability of future generations to meet their needs" (WCED, 1987). Another commonly used definition, and one which has been adopted by the several non-government organisations is that type of development "which improves the quality of life, within the carrying capacity of the earth's life–support system" (IUCN/UNEP,/WWF, 1991).

Sustainable development must also consider the spatial scales for any proposed policies and actions. Whilst it is possible to maintain global sustainability, if population growth and resource consumption are controlled, regrettably there could still be areas of potential unsustainability. At national, regional or local spatial scales it is clear that differences in the geographical distribution of resources, coupled with the differential patterning of economic development, will inevitably mean that some areas, and their populations, are less sustainable than others and more reliant upon a fairer re-distribution of the net global product than relying on their own resources. An obvious human response to such a perception is for the disadvantaged to migrate to another more sustainable area. This may result in degrading a formerly sustainable region. The movement of people in times of famine or war in parts of Africa or in former Yugoslavia are examples of this process. Without a concerted effort to promote sustainable development at local scales, bearing in mind both the natural differences and cultural preferences of indigenous people, then unsustainable practices may be simply relocated and exacerbated.

How can such development strategies be shown to be sustainable? One way of attempting to achieve this goal is to develop a set of sustainable development indicators. Meadows (1990), for example, appeals for an indicator which consists of "simple numbers that can appear on the nightly news along with the GNP and the *Dow-Jones* average. We need indicators that give people an idea of whether or not their environment is getting better or worse". These indicators would also act as signals to decision-makers so that the paths of unsustainable development can be avoided. Whilst the idea of developing sustainable indicators is appealing, it is clear that the concept of sustainable development is broader than the measures used to describe it. This raises the problems of developing suitable indicators and of data availability.

Common to all research into sustainable development indicators is the problem of identifying what to measure, and how. Obviously, the information for the indicators must be available. Similarly, the indicators which are developed must be both informative, (revealing if sustainable development, for example, is being achieved), and act as an effective guide to policy-makers. Anderson (1991) has suggested seven criteria which may constitute a good indicator (Table 6). While these criteria are important for the creation of a sustainable development indicator it is clear that the information for pursuing points 1, 6 and 7 are not always readily available – a point which will be noted in later chapters.

Several other problems are associated with the development of any indicator. These include the problem of selecting the number of dimensions to be used, the relevant scale of measurement, the error terms surrounding the measures, the weighting applied to each measure, and the robustness of the measure, given the variability in most data. Furthermore, most of the definitions of sustainable development imply that it is possible to gather the relevant data so that some unambiguous measure or indicator can be proposed, allowing the monitoring of the contribution of a particular project to sustainable development. It is very clear that the scale and data problems, whilst not insurmountable, are very difficult to overcome. Nevertheless, some researchers suggest that given a major intellectual effort to examine these interrelated problems of scale and data

Table 6   What is a good indicator?

1	The indicator, or the information it is calculated from, should be readily available
2	The indicator should be relatively easy to understand
3	The indicator must be about something which can be measured
4	An indicator should measure something believed to be important or significant in its own right
5	There should only be a short time lag between the state of affairs referred to and the indicator becoming available
6	The indicator should be based on information which can be used to compare different geographical areas
7	International comparability is desirable

(After Anderson, 1991)

economies. In the USA the early work of Zolatos (1981) attempted to show that economic development was not sustainable using information based on detailed census and questionnaire studies. Simpler indicators have attached prices to natural resource use to modify Gross National Product (GNP). At its simplest, the attempts to measure sustainability require that national income be corrected to include all environmental losses. To adjust for these environmental defence expenditures requires a nationally (perhaps internationally) agreed definition of the items for inclusion, as well as agreed methods for calculating the costs of measures sufficient to maintain sustainability. At present, with regard to empirical studies, environmental defence expenditure in the former Federal Republic of Germany and in Japan has been estimated as 1.5% of GNP and anything between 2–10% of GNP, respectively (Leipert and Simonis, 1989; Uno, 1988). It is, of course, a moot point if either of these economies could be thought of as sustainable as their economic growth depends on the use of other countries' resources and labour. Nevertheless, this type of empirical estimate is useful insofar as it acknowledges the role of the environment in economic development, both as a source for raw materials and as a receiving environment for wastes.

In the developing world a more detailed natural resource accounting study undertaken by Repetto and colleagues (1987) for the World Bank represented a pioneering effort to indicate the real ecological and economic costs of economic development for Indonesia. A representative statement of this detailed approach to estimating the economic costs of economic development has been put forward on the lines that "a country could exhaust its mineral resources, cut down its forests, erode its soil, pollute its aquifers, and hunt its wildlife to extinction but measured income would not be affected as these assets disappeared" (Repetto *et al.*, 1987). By attempting to estimate the real costs of economic development they adjusted the Gross Domestic Product (GDP) and Gross Domestic Investments (GDI) figures for quantitative and qualitative changes of the natural resources stock of Indonesia. It was argued that the extraction of crude oil and timber, and the exploitation of soils for crop production were the most important natural resources used in the country's economy. Over the past twenty years (1965–1986) *per capita* growth averaged 4.6%; the GDI rose from 8% of GDP in 1965 to 26% of GDP by 1986. By conventional economic measures the rise in the Indonesian economy was significant, representing 43% of GDP, 55% of the total employment and 83% of exports (Repetto *et al.*, 1987). A new set of figures were derived using a new accounts measure, whereby the growth of GDP at constant prices was linked with the growth of 'net domestic product' (NDP), derived by subtracting estimates of net natural resource depreciation for only three sectors (petroleum, timber and soils). The results of this study are illustrated in Figure 6 and Table 8 where it is clear that the conventionally-measured GDP substantially overstates net income and its growth after accounting for consumption of natural resource capital. As the researchers note, "In fact, while GDP increased at an average annual rate of 7.1% from 1974 to

Table 8 Comparison of gross domestic product (GDP) to net domestic product (NDP) in 1973 Rupiah (billions) showing the net change in natural resource sectors

Year	GDP	Petroleum	Forestry	Soil	Net change	NDP
1971	5545	1527	−312	−89	1126	6671
1972	6067	337	−354	−83	−100	5967
1973	6753	407	−591	−95	−279	6474
1974	7296	3228	−533	−90	2605	9901
1975	7631	−787	−249	−85	−1121	6510
1976	8156	−187	−423	−74	−684	7472
1977	8882	−1225	−405	−81	−1711	7171
1978	9567	−1117	−401	−89	−1607	7960
1979	10 165	−1200	−946	−73	−2219	7946
1980	11 169	−1633	−965	−65	−2663	8505
1981	12 055	−1552	−595	−68	−2215	9840
1982	12 325	−1158	−551	−55	−1764	10 561
1983	12 842	−1825	−974	−71	−2870	9972
1984	13 520	−1765	−493	−76	−2334	11 186
Average annual growth (%)	7.1					4.0

(After Repetto et al. 1989)

1984, the period covered by this case study, our estimate of 'net' domestic product rose by only 4.0% per year. If 1971, a year of significant additions to petroleum reserves, is excluded, the respective growth rates from 1972 to 1984 are 6.9% and 5.4% per year, for gross and net domestic product" (Repetto *et al.*, 1987). It is noted that this measure of national resource accounts is very sensitive to new discoveries of non-renewable resources and to the base year used in the study. Nevertheless, if investments are corrected for depletion and depreciation effects, then they can be shown to fluctuate strongly and even drop below replacement level in 1980.

In Australia Young (1990) has also attempted to derive a crude measure of national natural resource accounting and has shown that such an index is very sensitive to volatile market prices for minerals. The argument from the Indonesian and the Australian case studies suggests that there are benefits from including the use of natural resources in national accounts and furthermore, the benefits of stopping environmental degradation and improving environmental quality may be substantial.

The call for an alteration of national income accounting to include the real ecological and environmental costs of producing the wealth of a nation have been seriously entertained by various countries, such as France and Norway

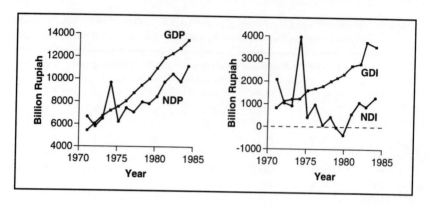

Figure 6 Comparison of (a) gross domestic product (GDP) and 'net domestic product' (NDP) and of (b) gross domestic investment (GDI) and 'net domestic investment' (NDI) for Indonesia. (After Repetto *et al.*, 1987)

(Kuik and Verbruggen, 1991; Young, 1990). Whilst these calls to include natural capital with human capital and capital equipment as part of the balance sheet of a nation's economy are well intentioned they are not without their problems.

First, the so-called measures of sustainable income expressed as Net Domestic Product (NDP), suggested by Repetto *et al.* and Young, may overlook the evaluation problems involved in developing an index or indices of sustainable development. NDP is often expressed in monetary units which may continue to be useful for national accounts but it may ignore the problem of attempting to put a market value upon parts of the ecosystem which have no monetary value. The attempts to place such a value by using contingent valuation and other proxy market variables are not convincing. One economist has already expressed doubts on the usefulness of attempting to do this (Jacobs, 1991). Next, attempting to put all non-marketable environmental assets into monetary units will probably ignore many of the ecological functions which are crucial to the operation of any ecosystem but have no use value to humans. Third, placing all data into a monetary measure may ignore or seriously undervalue other non-monetary aspects of an economy. Visitors viewing Uluru (Ayers Rock) as a tourist attraction, for example, may undervalue its religious significance to local Aboriginal peoples or its value as an icon for Australia. Fourth, many of the natural resource accounting proposals are atheoretical in that they lack any explicitly articulated understanding of the economy–environment interactions. Fifth, many of these approaches are static in their structure and they rarely examine the dynamics of environmental systems.

There have, of course, been several theoretical studies into sustainable development viewed as an extension to the neo-classical economic paradigm (Pezzey, 1989; Barbier, 1989, 1993). In the UK work by Pearce *et al.* (1989)

Table 9   Testing for 'weak' sustainability

Testing for sustainable development: an economy is sustainable if it saves more than the depreciation on its man-made and natural capital. S = gross domestic savings; Y = gross domestic income; δM = value of depreciation of man-made capital; δN = value of depreciation of natural capital; Z = Sustainability Index (= S/Y – $\delta M/N$ – $\delta N/Y$)

Country & type of economy	S/Y	$\delta M/Y$	$\delta N/Y$	Z
Sustainable				
Brazil	20	7	10	+3
Costa Rica	26	3	8	+15
Czechoslovakia	30	10	7	+13
Finland	28	15	2	+11
Germany (pre-unification)	26	12	4	+10
Hungary	26	10	5	+11
Japan	33	14	2	+17
Netherlands	25	10	1	+14
Poland	30	11	3	+16
USA	18	12	3	+3
Zimbabwe	24	10	5	+9
Marginally sustainable				
Mexico	24	12	12	0
Philippines	15	11	4	0
United Kingdom	18	12	6	0
Unsustainable				
Burkino Faso	2	1	10	–9
Ethiopia	3	1	9	–7
Indonesia	20	5	17	–2
Madagascar	8	1	16	–9
Malawi	8	7	4	–3
Mali	–4	4	6	–14
Nigeria	15	3	17	–5
Papua New Guinea	15	9	7	–1

(After Pearce and Atkinson, 1993)

has attempted to define two different criteria for sustainability, namely 'weak' and 'strong' measures. The weak measure of sustainable development assumes the possibility of perfect substitution of natural and man-made capital. This 'weak' measure of sustainability simply states that an economy should save at least as much as the value of depreciation of man-made and natural capital. The indices of sustainable development, often termed Z or PAM, are expressed as percentages or in monetary units (Table 9).

A preliminary empirical study shows that, using the 'weak' measure of sustainability, Costa Rica, Brazil, USA, Japan and Poland are sustainable; Burkino Faso, Mali, Nigeria and Papua New Guinea are unsustainable; the UK,

Mexico and Philippines are marginally sustainable. Whilst the authors suggest that their results using the 'weak' measure of sustainable development (Table 9) should be treated with caution it is clearly a moot point if the economic health of many nations is actually sustainable. Some of the ways in which this aspect of economic work can be integrated with ecological systems will be discussed below (*cf* Chapter 5). A 'strong' indicator of sustainable development would involve identifying and measuring 'critical' natural capital such that any positive depreciation would be a sign of non-sustainability.

(b) Socio-Political studies

Socio-political indicators of development have been developed over many years. These studies are explicitly designed to show how social and physical conditions vary between and within nations so that political initiatives can be put into practice to improve the situation. The early studies were concerned essentially with social phenomena but more recently these ideas have been extended to incorporate environmental, economic and social aspects.

An early study into the quality of life was developed in the 1960s and since then considerable progress has been made in developing socio-economic indicators of sustainable development, some of which include the quality of life. This study developed a prototype index of the quality of life for twenty nations (Drenowski and Scott, 1968). The index was constructed using a system of sliding weights for variables such as nutrition, shelter, health, leisure, security, education and surplus income. A value of zero represents conditions under which human beings are just able to survive and a value of 100 represents 'full satisfaction' of basic and physical and cultural needs. On this scale Uganda had an index of 37 and the USA 171 for *circa* 1960 (Drenowski, 1974). One of the useful aspects of this multivariate scale is that it shows that the correlation between GNP at $US 400 *per capita* is not linear. Japan, Jamaica and Greece, for example, had values at approximately $US 400 but very different levels of living, at 81.9, 49.3 and 80.2, respectively (Coates *et al.*, 1977). One advantage of this type of indicator is that it attempts to give an estimate of the quality of life rather than relying solely on monetary measures such as GNP. Furthermore, it is possible to disaggregate the data so that regional patterns of the quality of life (and by implication sustainable development) can be made. It should, however, be noted again that this early indicator was static while sustainable development indicators are trying to capture a dynamic set of processes operating at different spatial and temporal scales.

A more recent attempt to develop a multi-variate indicator of sustainable development has been proposed as an index of sustainable economic welfare (ISEW) (Daly and Cobb, 1989). This index attempts to include the costs of resource use and pollution in a similar way to that proposed in the Indonesian study (Repetto *et al.*, 1987). The ISEW is calculated by a simple formula:

ISEW = Personal consumption + non-defensive expenditure – defence expenditure + capital formation – costs of environmental damage – depreciation of natural capital.

Most of the terms used to derive this formula are self-evident and clearly explained in an appendix (Daly and Cobb, 1989). The trajectory of ISEW for the USA, 1950–1986, shows that whilst the *per capita* GNP, measured in inflated adjusted units (1972) US dollars, increases, the ISEW tends to stabilise at about $ 5000 for the period 1976–80 and then declines from 1980–1986. A more detailed analysis of the US–ISEW will be given in Chapter 6.

One intepretation of this index is that from 1980 the US economy has entered an unsustainable trajectory. Such an interpretation should, however, be treated with caution as any index is sensitive to the the elements from which it is constructed, and on the base year which is used. If 1951, for example, rather than 1950 is used as the base year, then a different pattern of sustainability can be shown. Also, it can be shown that by omitting unpaid domestic labour the ISEW is changed quite dramatically. One may question whether or not we really want to believe that unpaid domestic labour is more significant for sustainable welfare than non-renewable resource depletion. These results simply highlight the general problem that any index of sustainability is sensitive to the measures incorporated within it as well as the base year chosen for the study (Moffatt, 1984b). Clearly, attempting to incorporate extended market evaluations such as socio-political measures of the resource base of a nation is a delicate and difficult issue. Nevertheless, it is an issue that has to be resolved if we are to explore sustainable trajectories of a region, nation or the world and distinguish these trajectories from essentially unsustainable paths of development.

(c) Ecological studies

Preserving the ecological integrity of many functioning ecosystems is a major message from the *World Conservation Strategy* and the *Brundtland Report* (IUCN, 1980; WCED, 1987). At present, however, the ways in which many ecosystems function are poorly understood and although measures of specific pollutants upon species have improved, the critical thresholds that individual species and ecosystems can tolerate before being destroyed are not well understood. In the absence of any definitive ecological studies it is clear that only limited measures of environmental indicators have been developed for limited areas and over short time periods (Department of Environment, 1992). Even fewer attempts to successfully model ecological–economic interactions for sustainable development have been made. This presumably reflects the fact that this inter-disciplinary subject is in its infancy (see Chapter 8). If we consider ecological measures of sustainable development, as distinct from single measures of environmental quality, such as sulfur dioxide levels in the atmosphere, then at least three measures can be used: Net Primary Production (NPP), Carrying

Capacity (*K*), and Appropriated Carrying Capacity and Ecological Footprints (A*K* and EF). The latter is similar to the environmental space concept.

(A) Net Primary Productivity and Carrying Capacity

A traditional way of measuring the ecological sustainability of an area is to use carrying capacity. Ecologists define carrying capacity (*K*) as the maximal population size of a given species that an area can support without reducing its ability to support the same species in the future. Specifically, carrying capacity is a measure of the amount of renewable resources in the environment in units of the number of organisms these resources can support indefinitely. Carrying capacity is therefore a function of the characteristics of both the area and the organism. A larger area will, *ceteris paribus*, have a higher carrying capacity than a smaller area. This definition of carrying capacity becomes very difficult to use when the social dimensions are introduced. These include aspirations, disparities between private and social costs and the difficulties in making accountable decisions in uncertainty.

One important measure of ecological sustainability is produced by estimating the global net primary production (NPP) and then calculating the amount appropriated by humans. Obviously, there is a limit to photosynthetic resources and, with the growth of the human population and increasing individual patterns of consumption, we are in danger of irreversibly degrading this resource and foreclosing the life-chances of ourselves, future generations and numerous other species.

At the global scale an attempt has been made to determine the link between Net Primary Production (NPP) and carrying capacity (*K*). Net Primary Product is defined as, 'the amount of energy left after subtracting the respiration of primary producers (mostly plants) from the total amount of energy (mostly solar) that is fixed biologically. NPP provides the basis for maintenance, growth and reproduction of all heterotrophs (consumers and decomposers); it is the total food resource on earth' (Vitousek *et al.*, 1986). The units used in the study are petagrams (Pg) of organic matter, equivalent to 10^{15} grams or 10^9 metric tonnes.

The method adopted was to estimate NPP for the earth's major ecosystems using conservative i.e. lower estimates (Table 10). Three calculations were made: a low, intermediate and high estimate of available NPP. The low estimate calculated the amount of NPP co-opted by humans and domestic animals directly; the intermediate estimate included direct use of NPP as well as an estimate of NPP which is destroyed during human land clearing or conversion. The high estimate of NPP used by humans included the low and intermediate classes as well as four major changes in land-use which can cause declines in NPP. These four well-defined changes include, the replacement of natural ecosystems with agricultural systems, the permanent conversion of forest to pasture,

Table 10   Net Primary Productivity of the Earth's major ecosystems

Type	Surface area ($\times 10^6$ km²)	Net primary production (Pg)
Forest	31	48.7
Woodland, grassland & savanna	37	52.1
Deserts	30	3.1
Arctic alpine	25	2.1
Cultivated land	16	15.0
Human area	2	0.4
Other terrestrial: (chaparral, bogs, swamps & marshes)	6	10.7
Subtotal terrestrial	147	132.1
Lakes & streams	2	0.8
Marine	361	91.6
Subtotal aquatic	363	92.4
Total	510	224.5

(After Jones, 1979)

desertification, and the conversion of natural ecosystems to areas of human habitation.

The main conclusion of Vitousek's study is that 'with current patterns of exploitation, distribution and consumption, a substantially larger human population – half again its present size or more – could not be supported without co-opting well over half the terrestrial NPP' (Vitousek *et al.*, 1986). The researchers also note that those observers who believe that the limits to growth are so distant as to be of no consequence for today's decision-makers appear unaware of the biological realities.

(B) Ecological Footprints and Appropriated Carrying Capacity or Environmental Space

The Ecological Footprint concept can be defined as the total area required to maintain indefinitely a given population at an average *per capita* consumption rate. This concept has been introduced and illustrated from work in Canada (Rees and Wackernagel, 1994). In the case of the Vancouver Lower Fraser Valley region of British Columbia, the population in 1990 was 1 700 000 living in an area of 400 000 ha. In order to calculate the ecological footprint the following *per capita* estimates are made: 1.1 ha of land is required for food consumption,

0.5 ha for forest production and 3.5 ha for biomass energy (ethanol); which is the equivalent of current *per capita* fossil fuel energy consumption. The total land required to support these basic human life-support systems is 8 670 000 ha but the valley is only 400 000 ha in extent. Hence, the population has to appropriate or "import" the productive capacity of at least 21-times as much land equivalents to support the current population's consumer lifestyles.

In a similar, but earlier, study Friends of the Earth, Netherlands attempted to indicate the practical implications of sustainable development by using the concept of environmental space in a case study of the Netherlands (Buitenkamp *et al.*, 1992). The key concept underpinning the study is 'environmental space'. This is defined as the world environmental resources divided by the world population and multiplied by the number of inhabitants of a specific country. The resources considered are energy, water, non-renewable resources, agriculture and food, forestry and wood. Even allowing for the generally lower levels of consumption in Western Europe compared to Canada, the Dutch are living well beyond their ecological area. The Netherlands population consumes at least 14-times as much productive land as it contains within its political boundaries (Buitenkamp *et al.*, 1992).

For each of the resource sectors the 'environmental space' is calculated and the proportion of over- or under-use by the inhabitants of the Netherlands is noted. The Netherlands researchers note that in order to achieve sustainable development in the Netherlands changes in consumer behaviour, industrial production and transport are required. The most important changes they suggest are: nearly 100% recycling efficiency and less use of materials, 50% reduction in using fossil fuels, handling materials differently by focusing on improvements in quality and a reduction in the amount of transport, with the bulk of transport being environmentally friendly (Buitenkamp *et al.*, 1992).

The Action Plan for a Sustainable Netherlands also describes the ways in which different political parties would attempt to implement the policies for promoting sustainable development. The Action Plan, which is not an official Government document, clearly indicates that some very difficult policy choices will have to be made if the Government is to pursue seriously sustainable development in the Netherlands. Again, it is a moot point if this could be achieved; for example 100% recycling is unlikely from thermodynamic considerations alone. Nevertheless, the report provides a major impetus to constructive and imaginative thinking about a sustainable future. It compares favourably with the UK sustainable development strategy which has been criticised for being 'too shapeless to be a guide to action . . . and too vague to be refined' (Anon, 1994).

From the above methods of attempting to develop indicators of sustainable development it is clear that no consensus, as yet, exists. This lack of consensus on the most useful indicator(s) of sustainable development is, to some extent, understandable given that sustainable development is a multi-disciplinary problem and different disciplines have their own preferred conceptual frameworks and associated measures. Nevertheless, if sustainable development is to be carried forward into an operational context then it is essential that the twin problems of defining an appropriate theoretical basis for integrating the worlds of nature and society and developing associated measures of sustainable development are addressed.

From Table 7 it is clear that many measures of sustainable development are available. Much of the data may be gleaned from census returns and other relevant information including, where appropriate, images of the landscape including maps. In the economic literature some *ad hoc* adjustments are made for the value of market-valued natural resources to produce indicators of sustainable development. In the socio-political case studies broader indicators are used but there is still no agreement on the "best" set of indicators.

Next, ecological indicators such as Net Primary Productivity and resource accounting methods have been discussed – but these measures need to be related to a body of BOTH economic and ecological theory if we are to indicate ecologically sustainable economic development in a specific country or region. Finally, whatever index or other measures are to be used as indicators of sustainable development it is essential that the difficult problems associated with nature's rights, social justice and the equitable distribution of the earth's resources are addressed. This raises major ethical and political problems in which environmental scientists and managers can make a useful contribution to this ongoing debate.

CONCLUSION

Many countries and non-governmental organisations have accepted that there is a need to move from unsustainable forms of economic growth and development to sustainable trajectories. The idea of promoting this alternative course of development was given a major impetus by the *Brundtland Report* and more recently by the Rio Earth Summit and *Agenda 21*. Whilst these developments are to be welcomed it is clear that difficult conceptual, ethical and operational problems remain to be resolved.

As sustainable development is a multi-disciplinary topic it is clear that a variety of measures can be used. An examination of the literature has suggested several indicators which have been classified as economic, socio-political and ecological. Each of these categories have been broadly interpreted and some form the potential basis for further empirical research. Such empirical research is a necessary part of testing abstract theories of sustainable development and is also an essential part of the policy-making and monitoring framework for ensuring development is sustainable.

Policy-makers need, however, to be given more clear guidance on the types of indicators that can be used in promoting sustainable development. Most of these can be used to indicate past patterns of development and then be applied to monitor and audit the trajectory of various important state variables of the system as we consciously move our patterns of economic development onto a trajectory which is ecologically sustainable. Research pursued along these lines would indicate whether or not our path of economic development is ecologically-sustainable.

Some writers suggest that sustainable development should be collapsed into one indicator like the *Dow-Jones* or the *Financial Times Stock Exchange* (FTSE) indices. Whilst there is some merit in this approach it could, of course, be argued that to collapse a wide range of relevant information into a single indicator of sustainable development may conceal more important aspects of a specific problem than it reveals. It is, therefore, prudent to use multiple indicators and accounting procedures which at least acknowledge the diversity of factors underlying the concept of sustainable development.

This use of several indicators may make decision-making more transparent but can lead to potential conflicts in attempting to give a commensurate measure on some multiple criteria. Unfortunately, for environmental management and strategic environmental policy-making at governmental level, and in the private and public sectors of the economy, there is no agreed set of measures. At present the best practice is to utilise the relevant concepts and measures of sustainable development and also to match these with the available data (Ahmed *et al.*, 1989). From a research perspective this pragmatic approach is far from satisfactory and it has been argued that further research into developing theoretically sound and empirically-useful indicators of sustainable development should be given a high priority – at least if we are to use the environment in a wise and sustainable manner for current and future generations. In the following two chapters some empirical measures of sustainable development indicators for Scotland will be presented.

CHAPTER 5

ECOLOGICAL AND ECONOMIC INDICATORS OF SUSTAINABLE DEVELOPMENT IN SCOTLAND

INTRODUCTION

Sustainable development implies that we pass on to our heirs an overall asset base and productive capacity that is no worse, and presumably, better than our own. One common feature of the various definitions of sustainable development is the recognition that the basis of all human life depends ultimately upon environmental resources. Many non-renewable resources such as coal, gas and oil have been exploited to give present generations in the developed countries both a high standard of living and a good quality of life. Often, these non-renewable resources have been used with little regard to their availability for future generations. Similarly, potentially renewable resources such as timber or fish, have often been harvested at rates well in excess of their natural rate of generation and well beyond their maximum sustainable yield. Similarly, the assimilative capacities of receiving environments such as waterways, the atmosphere, and landfill sites, have been coming under increasing strain and, in some cases, have reached breaking point. The eutrophication of the Murray–Darling River in Australia, the erosion of lands in northern Africa, the acidification of Scottish lochs and numerous other environmental problems bear silent witness to the ways in which we individually and collectively are damaging the environment upon which all species depend and which often impacts directly upon human health and welfare.

Often in modern economies the intricate links between food production, distribution and the consumption of the products of nature go through many transformations and the direct link with the earth is ignored. Similarly, the disposal of waste from individual households must ensure that the assimilative capacities of the environment are not breached locally or at higher spatial scales so that a high quality of air, water and land are available to future generations. Despite our often flagrant misuse of environmental resources it should be stressed that the environment is not simply a productive asset; it also provides the basis of much aesthetic pleasure and enjoyment by simply existing as part of our material and cultural heritage. Even more important, it represents common ground for all other species. It is rather arrogant for some members of the current generation to destroy this world which we should hold in trust for ourselves, future generations and all other living plants and animals – a point acknowledged

73

as an underpinning of the Scottish Natural Heritage and many other environmental organisations (SNH, 1992).

This chapter explores the use of ecological and economic indicators of sustainable development by making a case-study of Scotland. In the next section Net Primary Production (NPP) and Carrying Capacity (K) along with the use of Appropriated Carrying Capacity and Ecological Footprints (ACC/EF) are used at the national scale. Section 5.3 then examines the use of economic indicators of sustainable development. In particular, an Approximated Environmentally-Adjusted Net National Product (AEANNP)and the 'weak' sustainability of sustainable development are used, based on a case study of Scotland. Finally, some of these environmental/ecological indicators are examined to demonstrate their relevance to Scotland and elsewhere.

ECOLOGICAL INDICATORS

As noted in the previous chapter, NPP and carrying capacity have been used to estimate the impact that *Homo sapiens* have upon the ecosphere (Vitousek *et al.*, 1986). The major advantage of using NPP as an indicator of sustainable development is that it provides us with a target to which we can direct our agricultural, afforestation and harvesting requirements of all renewable biotic resources. This argument is predicated on the assumption that we accept that the natural vegetation of an area represents the ultimate natural vegetation development for that site (Jones, 1979).

There are at least four problems associated with using NPP as an indicator of sustainable development. First, many NPP measures only examine vegetation above the surface of the ground. It is exceedingly difficult to calculate the amount of NPP beneath the ground. This has been attempted and in grasslands, for example, grass-root production and root tissue can form as much as 50% of the total NPP of some grassland ecosystems (Struik, 1967). Next, much of the natural vegetation cover has been altered by agricultural and afforestation practices. In the former case NPP from agricultural production is low because it is an annual crop with a pronounced growing season, rather than a perennial cover (Jones, 1979). Third, the use of NPP can only indicate the amount of organic matter (food, fibre and other biological material) available in a given area over a given period – it makes no reference to the amount consumed or destroyed by animal populations including *Homo sapiens*. Fourth, it is exceedingly difficult to obtain good estimates of NPP especially in aquatic environments.

Despite these difficulties involved in using NPP as an indicator of sustainability it is useful to examine NPP and carrying capacity as an indicator of sustainable development in Scotland. This entails making some crude estimates of land cover for a given time and then calculating the amount of biological material (expressed as NPP) available after its exploitation by humankind. The rest of this section offers a preliminary and crude estimate of NPP and carrying capacity, together with the recent Ecological Footprints and Appropriated Carrying Capacity (EF/ACC), in Scotland.

The last Ice Age erased any vegetation cover in Scotland, but once the ice sheet had retreated (11–10 000 BP) and the climate warmed, successive waves of varying mixtures of tree species were able to recolonise Scotland *via* England (Walker and Kirby, 1989). After the Loch Lomond re-advance the glaciated areas of Scotland returned to native vegetation, with the obvious exceptions of the mountain summits which remained as bare rock and a peri-glacial landscape. The predominant vegetation cover of Scotland *circa* 5 000 BP was woodland. The forest zones in approximately 5 000 BP are shown in Figure 7 (Bennett, 1989). The mountain summits remained unforested, as did some of the northern

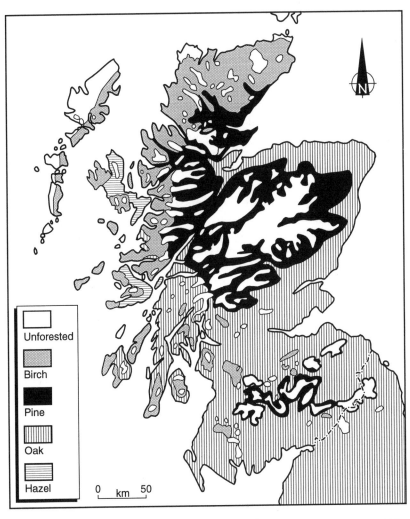

Figure 7   The forest cover of Scotland *circa* 5 000 BP (adapted from Bennett, 1989)

Table 11 A crude estimate of NPP for Scotland 5 000 BP

	%	square km	gm/sq. km	NPP × 10¹²
Treeless	17.5	13 489	140	1.88
Forested	82.5	63 591	600	38.20
	100	77 080		40.08

and western islands. Beneath the unvegetated mountain peaks pine woodlands predominated in the Highlands, probably forming the Great Wood of Caledon (Miles and Jackson, 1991). South of the Great Highland fault and on lower ground, oak dominated the woods – although patches of birch were discernible in the southwest of Scotland. North of the Great Highland fault the forested areas were predominantly birch with some hazel-dominated forests on Skye.

Using Bennett's (1989) map of the forest cover of Scotland *circa* 5 000 BP it is possible to give a crude estimate of NPP in Scotland. The treeless areas of Scotland are given a mean figure of 140 gm/square metre and the forested regions 600 gm/square metre. The area classified as covered by trees or treeless was estimated using the method of squares (Monkhouse and Wilkinson, 1963), to give an estimate of 82.5% forested and 17.5% treeless for Scotland *circa* 5 000 BP. These figures give a crude estimate of NPP in Scotland as 40.08×10^{12} gm (Table 11)

The carrying capacity of Scotland can be estimated, using the method employed by Vitousek and colleagues (1986) by calculating the total amount of organic matter above the surface, and dividing it by the human population consumption. This calculation assumes that all vegetation remains in its natural state and each person consumes the equivalent of 182 500 gm/yr organic matter. The latter figure is derived by using 2 500 kcal/day as a recommended intake per person multiplied by 365 days to yield the yearly figure of 912 500 kcal/yr; a division by 5 converts this unit to gm/yr (Vitousek *et al.*, 1986).

On the basis of this calculation it is clear that if only 25% of the organic matter is consumed or appropriated for human use then the carrying capacity of Scotland is 5 490 000 (Table 12). This is very close to the 1990 estimated population of 5 102 400.

An alternative method of calculating sustainability for Scotland is to use the ecological footprints and appropriated carrying capacity concepts (Rees and Wackernagel, 1994). Simply stated, this measure attempts to determine the amount of land required to support contemporary patterns of energy, food and forestry required by the Scottish population using current patterns of consumption. In the Scottish case the land requirements *per capita* are approximately 1.3 ha for energy using renewable resources only, 0.19 ha for

Table 12   Carrying capacity for Scotland using organic productivity

% Consumed	Carrying capacity	Comment
100	21 961 000	No organic material left
75	16 470 750	
50	10 980 000	
25	5 490 400	

forestry products (excluding energy use), and 0.4 ha for food production. This gives a conservative figure of 1.89 ha per person for these important resources. Using this latter figure the land area required to support Scotland's population in the current (1995) lifestyle is 93 390 square kilometres but the land area is only 77 926 square kilometres. In Scotland 20% more land is required than available. The deficit in land required is made up by using non-renewable resources as well as importing sustainability by using resources from overseas. The latter may exacerbate other countries' sustainable development options.

Obviously, the economic development of Scotland, like many modern economies, has substituted non-renewable resources and imported other people's resources through trade to ensure economic development. The problem of importing resources may, of course, result in the creation of unsustainable resource use in other countries. Essentially, the rise of the contemporary economy in Scotland has used energy substitutions to produce the life-style and comfort that we currently enjoy. This energy substitution is due in part to the use of modern fossil fuel-driven agriculture and the development of modern industries, both based upon fossil fuel substitutes for naturally occurring energy supply locked up in agriculturally-determined NPP and in urban areas which are a major drain on energy supplies. Leach (1976) notes that in the 1970s 17.5 % of all UK fuel was used for food production and this has probably increased in the past twenty years.

In a sense these three calculations of the Net Primary Productivity (NPP), Carrying Capacity (K) and the derivative Ecological Footprint and Appropriated Carrying Capacity (EF/ACC) indicate that Scotland's current population and level of resource use is not sustainable without importing resources from elsewhere – and this is in a country which conventionally is depicted as one with abundant natural resources. It is now interesting to see if the economic measures, described in the previous chapter, are able to give any supporting evidence for these tentative findings.

ECONOMIC INDICATORS

For many economists, working from within the neo-classical paradigm, sustainable development offers the opportunity to extend their methods to address serious environmental issues. As noted in Chapter 4, several methods have been devised to alter the national accounts to ensure that environmental concerns are included in any calculation of sustainable development. For some economists simple alterations of the GNP are seen as administratively efficient – but such a view does not necessarily imply that marginal adjustments to GNP would actually result in the application of conservation methods to the real world. More sophisticated analyses are obviously required and these include alteration of the national accounts or new measures of sustainable development being devised. The alteration of national accounts can take one of two forms. First, the actual quantities of material resources are placed into a statistical appendix of the national accounts, as in Norway. Alternatively, monetary measures are used to estimate the use of resources, including environmental conservation measures, to alter GNP onto a sustainable path. It should be noted that the use of money to combine the world of ecology to that of economics is not without its critics or methodological problems. Many critics of using money as a measure feel that it is an inappropriate way of measuring the value of the environment. Unfortunately, to date, the critics have been unable to provide a better measure – at least in the eyes of economists. If money is used as a measure of sustainable development then some very difficult methodological problems have to be overcome. These include the correct evaluation for non-market goods as well as the delicate task of deciding when the use of money is inappropriate for conserving natural capital (K_n). In this section we examine two economic approaches using money as a numeraire, namely Approximate Environmentally Adjusted Net Natural Product (AEANNP) and the Atkinson and Pearce (1993) (PAM) weak measure of sustainable development.

Within the field of environmental economics, it is now widely recognised that the goal of sustainable development is principally an equity, rather than an efficiency, issue (Howarth and Norgaard, 1992). That is, achieving sustainable development involves achieving equity both within generations (inter-generational equity) and across generations (intra-generational equity). As Asheim (1991) puts it:

> "Sustainable development is a requirement to our generation to manage the resource base such that the average quality of life we ensure ourselves can potentially be shared by all future generations."

Early work in neo-classical growth theory which incorporated natural resource constraints on economic activity (Solow, 1974, 1993) implicitly modelled sustainable development as non-declining consumption over time. This literature led to the development of the Hartwick Rule, explained below. However, given that individuals derive utility directly from the environment, and not just from the consumption goods that are produced partly with natural resources, non-declining consumption has been replaced by non-declining utility as a goal of policy in economic models (Pezzey, 1989). An alternative way of considering sustainable development has been to concentrate on means rather than ends;

since resources are necessary to produce utility, then some constraint of the amount of resources passed forward to future generations seems a possibly desirable goal.

The Solow–Hartwick approach

In 1977 Hartwick proposed a rule for ensuring non-declining consumption through time, in the case where an economy made use of a non-renewable resource (such as oil) in its economic process (Hartwick, 1977). Hartwick showed that so long as the stock of man-made capital did not decline over time, then non-declining consumption was also possible. The stock of man-made capital could be held constant by *re-investing all Hotelling rents from non-renewable resource extraction in man-made capital*. These rents are those resulting from the inter-temporally efficient extraction programme for the non-renewable resource. Thus, as the stock of oil (a type of 'natural' capital) runs down, the stock of man-made capital is built up in replacement. This result has been very important for the development of the economics of sustainable development. It arises in the Hartwick model due to the assumptions employed therein: crucially, that the aggregate production function for consumption goods is of the Cobb–Douglas type. This implies that as the amount remaining of the non-renewable resource goes to zero, its average product goes to infinity (so that even though the natural resource is technically essential for the production of consumption goods, it does not act as a constraint to growth). What is more, man-made and natural capital in this model are assumed to be perfect substitutes for each other (the elasticity of substitution is equal to one).

Criticisms of the Hartwick rule follow three lines. First, that individuals derive utility directly from the environment, and do not view it merely as an input to production. If this is the case, then non-declining consumption is not equivalent to non-declining welfare over time. Second, that the rule depends on the particular functional form chosen for the aggregate production function. Hartwick was able to re-state his rule for a constant elasticity of substitution production function (Hartwick, 1978, 1990), but this function had the property that the elasticity of substitution between the natural resource and man-made capital was greater than one, so that the fixity in supply of the natural resource is actually irrelevant (Common and Perrings, 1992).

The third criticism of the Hartwick rule is that natural resources and man-made capital are not nearly so substitutable as the Solow–Hartwick approach suggests. In what follows it will be useful to compare 'natural' capital with man-made capital. Natural capital may be defined as comprising all gifts of nature: land, animals, fish, plants, non-renewable and renewable energy and mineral resources. Natural capital can be exploited by man, but cannot be created by man (although management might increase breeding rates, for example). According to what might be termed the thermodynamic school (Costanza, 1991), natural capital and man-made capital are in most cases complements rather than substitutes. The various elements of the natural capital stock may be termed "primary inputs", and man-made capital and labour the "agents of transformation". Whilst substitution possibilities are possibly high within each of the two groups (e.g. wood for leather, plastics for copper; or machines for labour), substitution possibilities between the two are very low. Increasing output thus means increasing use of both types of input in most cases.

Non-declining natural capital stock approaches

Rather a different approach to the limited degree of substitutability between natural capital (K_n) and man-made capital (K_m) is that of the London School (Atkinson and Pearce, 1993). Here, the view is taken that whilst some substitution is possible between certain elements of K_n and K_m (for example, better machinery meaning less raw materials are used to produce certain products), many elements of K_n provide non-substitutable services ("keystone processes") to the economy. Examples of such 'critical' natural capital are the processes responsible for regulation of atmospheric composition, the spiritual values provided by wildlife and landscapes, and nutrient cycles. If humans need the services of ecosystems, then it is important to maintain these ecosystems in a functioning state. This in turn means protecting their natural resilience (ability to withstand shocks), which may be achieved by ensuring that certain species ("keystone species") are preserved (Turner, 1995).

If it is necessary to maintain some amount of the natural capital stock constant in order to allow future generations to reach the same level of utility as the average held by this generation, then this becomes a rule for sustainable development. The important question here, however, is how much of K_n should be held constant? Four possible views would be (i) the existing level, (ii) the level consistent with maintaining the critical element of K_n, (iii) some amount inbetween these two, or (iv) increasing K_n by replanting. All four of these alternatives however assume that we can measure the value of K_n at any point in time, in other words that the different elements of K_n can be aggregated in comparable units. For example, should natural capital be measured in physical or monetary units? Physical units confound addition since an oak forest cannot be added to a blue whale. Only if the two types of natural assets are expressed in a common numeraire can they be aggregated, the most obvious unit being money. However, this may be seen as objectionable, since one whale worth £10 million is then equivalent to 1000 whales worth £10 000 each. If natural assets are held constant in physical terms, the level at which the category is defined will become all-important. Consider the maintenance of woodlands in Britain by constant total area. This woodland stock definition might raise the objection that a hectare of Sitka spruce is less valuable than a hectare of native Scots pine or of ancient oak. The category could be disaggregated to hold constant the stock of deciduous trees and the stock of conifers. However, some might wish to go further and define different types of deciduous woodland. Van Pelt (1993) identifies another problem with the constant–natural capital stock concept. This is the problem of spatial aggregation: within which geographic area should we hold stocks constant? If, for example, there was a requirement that, across the whole of Scotland, the total area of woodland was non-declining in any year, then this is consistent with large declines in some localities so long as these are off-set by increases elsewhere. Under such a system, areas with the weakest political power in opposing environmental degradation could suffer systematic, continuing reductions in local environmental quality.

If the natural capital stock cannot be fully aggregated, then it may be necessary to compartmentalise it by sector, and keep each compartment constant. Van Pelt (1993) suggests pollution, renewable resources, biodiversity, pollution assimilation capacity and non-renewable resources as possible categories. To this list might be added the integrity of nutrient recycling processes. However, non-renewable resources, such as oil, are by definition fixed finite stocks which must decline with use. The only ways to maintain a constant economic reserve are for new discoveries to equal extraction, and for costs per unit extracted to decrease with technological progress as quickly as they rise due to cumulative extraction. More strictly, given a finite total abundance of each non-renewable resource, only a zero extraction rate is consistent with a constant natural capital stock unless trade-offs are permitted between renewable and non-renewable resources.

Supposing that the aggregation problem for natural capital can somehow be overcome (perhaps by extensive disaggregation into separate classes and physical quantification), then a rule for sustainable development suggested by the London School is *to prevent reductions in the level of* K_n *below some constraint value* (or series of values for the separate classes). This might appear a heavy restriction on development if the current level of K_n is chosen as the constraint, since it would involve banning all projects/policies having a deleterious effect on K_n. The alternative to this suggested by Pearce *et al.* (1989) involves the use of 'shadow projects'. These are projects/policies designed to produce environmental benefits, in terms of additions to K_n, to exactly off-set reductions in K_n resulting from a specified collection ("portfolio") of projects or policies. For example, such a portfolio could be all public sector investment projects in Scotland in 1992, or the sum total of a company's activities. Neglecting the tremendous data requirements involved in fully operationalizing this procedure for the present, the idea is to impose either a weak or a strong sustainability constraint as a rule for sustainable development.

The Solow–Hartwick approach to sustainability, and 'green' GNP

The general definition of sustainable development adopted here is that every future generation must have the option of being as well-off as its predecessor.

Discounting is compatible with this if the discount rate is less than the rate of technological progress (Solow, 1993). Maintaining a constant potential for wealth creation means maintaining a constant means of production. This includes man-made capital, natural resources, technology and the level of learning. A sustainable path has the characteristic that along it this overall productive capacity is not reduced. What we need to know at each moment in time is how much of this productive base we can use up. This is given by Approximately Environmentally Adjusted Net National Product (AEANNP). Net National Product (NNP) is the conventional concept from the system of national accounts. It comprises total income earned in an economy, less an allowance for depreciation of the economy's man-made capital in that year (since this capital has been 'used up' in the production of goods and services, and must be replaced by investment if the productive capacity of the economy is to be held constant). When is approximately environmentally adjusted NNP (AEANNP) a good measure of sustainable income?: (i) when all elements of NNP are correctly valued in terms of the current economic situation, (ii) when this is true in a forward-looking sense too (prices reflect future scarcity), (iii) when all depreciation of natural capital is similarly allowed for. AEANNP is the annual 'pay-off' from our total (natural plus man-made) capital stock. AEANNP can rise through time if this total capital stock rises, and/or as technology improves. How can the total stock of capital be maintained? By following the Hartwick rule: each year, re-invest the Hotelling rents (price minus marginal cost) from an optimal non-renewable resource extraction plan in new natural or man-made capital. So, the indicator is: **Is AEANNP rising or falling? If AEANNP is falling, then society's sustainable level of income is falling too.**

Pearce and Atkinson (1993) have proposed an indicator of weak sustainability based on the neo-classical assumptions inherent in the Solow–Hartwick approach, in that man-made and natural capital are assumed to be perfect substitutes for each other. This is rather different from the previous approach and is referred to as the "weak" sustainability criterion when shadow projects are available, thus we will refer to the case where the assumption of perfect substitutability is advocated as the Pearce–Atkinson Measure (PAM). The PAM is defined as:

$$PAM = (\frac{S}{Y}) - (\frac{\delta_M}{Y}) - (\frac{\delta_N}{Y})$$

where if PAM > 0, the economy is judged sustainable. The above equation states that PAM will be positive if savings (S) exceed the sum of depreciation on man-made (δ_M) and natural (δ_N) capital and Y represents income. Pearce and Atkinson argue that this is a useful rule, in that if countries fail even this weak test of sustainability, they are unlikely to pass a stronger test (see Table 9). Recently Atkinson and Proops (unpublished) adopted the PAM measure to include imports and exports. They find that the USA becomes less sustainable when trade is included, but that global sustainability is positive. The Middle East becomes more sustainable with trade than without. The high savings rate in Japan makes a large contribution to world sustainability. However, two criticisms may be made of the PAM measure: (i) it assumes perfect substitutability between natural and man-made capital; (ii) in practice, very incomplete estimates of natural capital depreciation are available.

In this section we have considered a number of different economic approaches to the definition and measurement of sustainable development. The neo-classical models of Solow and Hartwick, which have been used as a theoretical basis for both the optimal revisions to NNP and the Pearce–Atkinson measure, are based on the flawed assumption that natural and man-made capital are perfect substitutes. However, these measures are still useful in that:

(i) approximately environmentally-adjusted NNP (AEANNP) gives a better indication of the net returns to environmental exploitation than un-adjusted NNP;

(ii) the Pearce–Atkinson measure gives a minimal test of sustainability, but if a country cannot pass this test it is unlikely to pass a stricter economically-based test.

METHODS AND DATA ANALYSIS

Approximate environmentally-adjusted net national product for Scotland

This section reports on calculations of AEANNP for Scotland for the period 1988–1992. It should be emphasized that these are very preliminary calculations, with many 'holes' in them. They should only be regarded as illustrative, therefore. Nevertheless, the benefit of calculating AEANNP, even with such a 'weak' data set, is that it shows that such calculations can in principle be done – although it should be noted that there are theoretical and practical problems involved in developing this index. These calculations proceed according to the Hartwick model described earlier. We now outline the procedures adopted for each major resource type; full details are given elsewhere (Moffatt *et al.*, 1994).

(i) Non-renewable resources

The non-renewable resources considered here are coal, aggregates, oil and gas from 'Scottish fields' in the North Sea. Barytes and limestone were also considered for inclusion but incomplete data over the 1988–1992 period meant that they had to be omitted. In each case, the correct adjustment is:

(price – marginal cost) × [annual production – new economically-recoverable reserves]

For North Sea oil, an estimate of short-run marginal costs of production over the period in question was obtained from the Economics Department, University of Dundee. The assumption is that technological progress has reduced these costs from 1988 to 1992. No cost data was found for natural gas, so the depreciation figures are over-estimates in this case since costs are not netted out from price. For the remaining minerals, marginal cost data were not available, and in only a minority of cases was average cost data found. New discoveries are also excluded, resulting in *over* adjustments for environmental depreciation (although we also exclude all environmental costs associated with extraction, which means that we *under*-state the necessary adjustments). Moreover, as Hartwick points out, all of these values should be calculated along the optimal decision path; there is no evidence that the pattern of non-renewable extraction in Scotland has followed such an economically-optimal path.

(ii) Renewable resources

The renewable resources included here are the major commercial species of sea fish (cod, haddock, whiting, herring); and coniferous forestry. The optimal adjustment in each case is:

(price − marginal cost) × [change in stock]

The change in the stock for fisheries is approximated from Scottish Office, Agriculture and Fisheries Department Marine Laboratory data. For conifers, the change in the stock is given by [annual production − annual growth in standing stock]; a term might arguably be included for annual re-planting and new planting, but biomass additions from such sources will be very small until the turn of the century. We estimated annual growth by taking an average yield class for Scotland of 8 and multiplying this by the area of mature forest. Marginal costs are unavailable for either fisheries or forests. For the former, some data is available from a small, unrepresentative sample on average costs per boat from the "costs and earnings" survey, using the 70–79.9 feet class of boat. This gives a figure of £373/ton for average (running plus vessel) costs, for example, for cod fishing. For the latter, costs per cubic metre of timber production to the roadside (£11) were provided by Inverness College.

(iii) Pollution

No allowance was made for direct dis-amenity effects. The only data used was defensive expenditure on water pollution control by Regional and Island Councils, which should be deducted from NNP. Data came from the Local Government Statistics unit, and we include both running costs and capital costs. Capital costs for 1991 and 1992 are estimates, as are running costs for 1992.

(iv) Scottish NNP

Scottish GDP is reported in *Regional Trends*. We adjusted this by adding in GDP for the UK continental shelf, to permit deduction of oil/gas depreciation.

Table 13 AEANNP calculations for Scotland, excluding North Sea oil and gas 1988–1992 (all values in £ million.)

Year	NNP	Coal	Aggregate	Cod	Haddock	Whiting	Herring	Conifers	Pollution Abatement
1988	24 501	55.020	113.31	+9.89	15.06	4.22	+20.13	+56.89	127.09
1989	27 036	74.030	139.14	60.35	34.50	+5.93	6.09	+42.96	145.26
1990	30 096	57.312	148.40	19.57	20.37	20.88	4.03	+31.35	174.13
1991	31 215	43.070	145.91	+144.7	+24.99	3.40	3.26	+13.53	197.09
1992	33 852	39.695	138.19	22.94	+40.45	+9.41	6.47	+17.34	223.75

Year	NNP	Net Environmental depreciation	AENNP
1988	24 501	227.79	24 273
1989	27 036	410.48	26 625
1990	30 096	413.34	29 682
1991	31 215	209.51	31 005
1992	33 852	363.84	33 488

Separate results are given when the continental shelf is excluded, but in this case so must depreciation on oil and gas. GDP was converted to GNP and then to NNP using UK ratios. Results for the "North Sea excluded" case are given in Table 13. As may be seen, whilst the sum total of environmental depreciation is quite large (varying from £209 million to £413 million), its effect on NNP is relatively small, with at most a 1.51% decrease from NNP to AEANNP. It should be remembered here that:

(i) many items relevant to total environmental depreciation are not included due to data problems. In particular, no data on private pollution-control expenditure were available, while other relevant environmental damages (such as to wildlife or landscape) have not been included;

(ii) average costs are used rather than marginal costs, this in all probability overstates environmental depreciation;

(iii) for some items (fish in some years, coniferous forests in all years) environmental depreciation is negative, since stocks rose.

For the "North Sea Included" case, results are given in Table 14

Table 14 AEANNP values (£ million) including North Sea oil and gas, 1988–1992

year	Scottish NNP	Continental shelf NNP	Environmental depreciation from Table 13	Oil depreciation	Gas depreciation	AEANNP
1988	24 501	5209	227.79	2119.18	217.32	27 145
1989	27 036	5195	410.48	2415.69	176.71	29 228
1990	30 096	5193	413.34	2924.84	87.00	31 863
1991	31 215	4488	209.51	2857.86	52.68	32 582
1992	33 852	4551	363.84	3159.71	50.32	34 829

Table 15 Total environmental depreciation as a proportion of total NNP, 1988–1992

year	Total Environmental depreciation	as a % of total NNP
1988	2564	9.44
1989	3002	10.27
1990	3425	10.74
1991	3120	9.57
1992	3573	10.25

While oil and gas depreciation clearly add to environmental depreciation, the sum of Scottish plus continental shelf NNP increases total NNP by a greater amount. Total environmental depreciation as a proportion of total NNP is shown in Table 15 and represents on average 10% per year for the period, 1988–1992.

In Figure 8, total NNP and AEANNP for the "North Sea Included" case is illustrated. Both that figure and Table 14 show that the environmental adjustment is relatively greater in this case than in the "North Sea Excluded" case (see Table 13).

The Pearce–Atkinson measure (PAM) for Scotland, 1988–1992

As will be recalled, the PAM involves deducting total depreciation (i.e. of both man-made and natural capital) from savings to arrive at a "weak" sustainability measure. If PAM > 0, then the economy is sustainable on this criteria. Table 16 gives PAM values for Scotland over the period in question. For each year, δ_M is given by (GNP – NNP), including the UK continental shelf; and δ_N is the "total

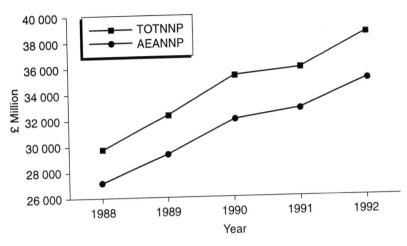

Figure 8 Total NNP and AEANNP: North Sea included

environmental depreciation" given in Table 16. The main problem concerns the savings level, S, since this is not reported for Scotland in official statistics. After consultation with the Scottish Office, this has been estimated as Scottish personal disposable income – Scottish consumers' expenditure. This, however, gives very low figures in our view, leading to the PAM being negative ("weak" unsustainability) in all years.

However, what "savings" should represent is re-investment in man-made capital. This is clearly not so in this case, since some Scottish savings are invested outside Scotland, whilst investment from external (other UK + foreign) sources will account for the bulk of gross Scottish fixed capital formation. In addition, we need to account for re-investment in the North Sea. North Sea investment spending is provided in the *Digest of UK Energy Statistics* (DoEn, 1993). Data on gross investment spending in Scotland for 1988, 1989 and 1990 only are available in

Table 16 PAM calculations for Scotland: savings figures, 1988–1992. (All values in £ million)

year	Savings	δ_M	δ_N	PAM
1988	1419	10 095	2564	−11 240
1989	2007	10 699	3002	−11 694
1990	4018	11 168	3425	−10 575
1991	6482	11 568	3120	−8206
1992	N/A	12 192	3573	−9283

Table 17 PAM calculations for Scotland: investment figures, 1988–1992 (all values, £ million)

year	Scottish gross I	Continental Shelf gross I	δ_M	δ_N	PAM
1988	3785	1970	10 095	2564	–6904
1989	4191	2519	10 699	3002	–6991
1990	4421	3321	11 168	3425	–6851

the most recent edition of *Regional Trends* (RT, 1992 *et seq.*). We thus compute PAM for these three years only. The results are reported in Table 17.

As may be seen, PAM remains negative in all three years. This is primarily because our measure of depreciation of the man-made capital stock (GNP – NNP) greatly exceeds official estimates of gross domestic fixed capital formation. Total investment, however, exceeds depreciation of natural capital in all years.

CONCLUSION

In the sustainable development literature much emphasis has been placed upon maintaining ecological systems and correctly valuing the ecological resources in economic studies. These inter-related problems will be discussed in turn. Obviously, all economic activity ultimately depends on environmental resources as both a supply of raw materials (input) and as a sink for waste products. These environmental resources are fundamental for the creation of wealth and welfare as well as being vital for other species. Hence, it is important that environmental systems be used in an essentially sustainable manner.

Given the importance of environmental systems as life-support systems of the planet there are enormous difficulties involved in attempting to measure and analyse data so that these ecological resources can be sustained. In this chapter several ecological measures have been used, namely Net Primary Production (NPP), carrying capacity (K) and appropriated carrying capacity and ecological footprints. These measures have been used in a detailed case study in Scotland to show their usefulness. Whilst there are problems with the use of any indicator it is clear that Scotland is only marginally sustainable if NPP and carrying capacity, K, are used, and is essentially unsustainable if the ecological footprints measure is used to monitor current economic activity.

When attention is turned to economic measures of sustainable development several options can be used. Again, in this chapter Approximate Environmentally Adjusted Net National Product (AEANNP) and Pearce–Atkinson's "weak" measure of sustainability have been employed. Like the ecological measures, the use of economic measures show conflicting results. The AEANNP measure shows growth whilst the PAM measure shows that Scotland is unsustainable (and negative for the time period considered). Clearly, these results pose major problems for both economic theory and for policy makers who wish to know if Scotland is on an unsustainable trajectory and can be moved onto a path of sustainable development.

An interesting attempt to develop a theoretically sound ecological–economic approach to the problem of sustainable development has been attempted recently (Common and Perrings, 1992). By drawing upon some aspects of neo-classical economics, such as the use of the Hartwick rule (1977, 1990) and Hollings' (1973) notion of resilience and stability in ecosystems, it is possible to reconcile neo-classical economics with ecology on several important issues. In particular, they argue that ecological sustainability requires that the allocation of economic resources should not result in the instability of the economy–environment system as a whole. Also, they emphasise "that an ecological economics of sustainability implies an approach that privileges the requirements of the system above those of the individual" (Common and Perrings, 1992, 32). Furthermore, they suggest that reliance upon consumer behaviour preferences can give the wrong signals for achieving sustainable systems.

Whilst Common and Perrings' model of sustainable development attempts to draw together some aspects of neo-classical economic theory with Hollings' work on the resilience and stability of ecosystems it does raise several interesting problems. First, the empirical question concerning the ways in which the trade-offs between productivity, ecosystem stability and social equity can be determined, need to be discussed. Clearly, these are important topics and research by Conway (1985) into the sustainability in agriculture, which also adopts Hollings' approach to adaptive management with its emphasis on resilience and stability, has attempted to provide a series of measures of agroecosystem sustainability. These measures include inertia, elasticity, amplitude, hysteresis and malleability. Second, further empirical research is required if these ecological measures are to be used more generally in sustainable development studies. Next, the idea of developing ecological–economic models of sustainable development still needs to identify appropriate ecological and economic indicators for empirical work. Fourth, a related theme is that of the scale problem. Obviously, the conservation of species is of prime importance in the *World Conservation Strategy* and it implies the need to maintain and, in many cases, enhance degraded ecosystems so that the potential for evolution can be kept open. Keeping future evolutionary options open is one of the most challenging problems that human-kind has ever encountered. The resolution of this problem requires that careful attention be paid to the spatio-temporal scales upon which the fabric of evolution can be kept intact. Fifth, given the current state of scientific knowledge about the ways in which ecosystems function and our lack of understanding concerning the role of humanity in them, then it would appear sensible and prudent to adopt both the precautionary principle and an attitude

CHAPTER 6

SOCIO-POLITICAL MEASURES: AN INDEX OF SUSTAINABLE ECONOMIC WELFARE FOR SCOTLAND

INTRODUCTION

In the previous chapter some ecological and economic measures of sustainable development were described. This chapter pursues this theme by making an in depth study of a socio-political measure, namely the Index of Sustainable Economic Welfare (ISEW), as applied to Scotland. The original idea of the ISEW was proposed by Daly and Cobb in their study of the ISEW for the coterminus states of the United States of America (Daly and Cobb, 1989; Cobb and Cobb, 1993). The same approach has been adopted by Jackson and Marks (1994) in their recent study of the United Kingdom. This chapter presents a detailed account of applying the ISEW to Scotland (Moffatt and Wilson, 1994).

Fundamental to an understanding of the concept of sustainable development is the need to recognise the fact that the economy is not separate from the environment in which we, and other species, live. There is an interdependence between the environment and the economy because the way we manage the economy impacts on the environment, and the quality of the environment has an impact upon the performance of both the economy and the welfare of its present and future inhabitants (Pearce *et al.*, 1989).

In May 1989, the OECD Council meeting at ministerial level called for a work programme on environmental economics that would integrate environment and economic decision-making more systematically and effectively as a means of contributing to sustainable development (OECD, 1991). In fact a major achievement of the *Earth Summit* held in Rio de Janeiro in 1992 was the creation of a blueprint for global actions to affect the transition to sustainable development. This blueprint, called *Agenda 21* (UNCED, 1992), had as two of its objectives the creation of, and promotion of global use of, indicators of sustainable development. This chapter will consider the development of one such indicator – the index of sustainable economic welfare as applied to Scotland.

In the following section some measures of social, economic and environmental welfare are reviewed with particular attention paid to several earlier studies of developing indices of economic welfare. In the third section the studies of an index of sustainable economic welfare (ISEW) for the USA and the UK are presented. This is then followed by an in depth study of developing an ISEW for Scotland using the revised method of Cobb and Cobb (1993) for the USA and the same method used by Marks and Jackson (1994) for the UK. In the fifth section a discussion of the results and the sensitivity analysis of the ISEW is presented. Finally, some of the paths for future research and their possible policy implications are described.

MEASURING SOCIAL, ECONOMIC AND ENVIRONMENTAL WELFARE

In considering how well current measures of economic welfare reflect sustainable development it is first necessary to understand what the term really means. Probably the most widely used definition appears in the 1987 *Brundtland Report* of the World Commission on Environment and Development which describes it as "development that meets the needs of the present without compromising the ability of future generations to meet their own needs" (WCED, 1987). As noted in Chapter 3 there are numerous definitions of the term sustainable development; nevertheless, according to Jacobs (1991), there exists three elements to its core meaning that remain no matter how it is interpreted. These are, briefly: 1) the integration, in both theory and practice, of environmental and economic policy making; 2) a commitment to global equity *i.e.* the fair distribution of resources both intra- and inter-generational; and 3) the notion that non-financial components be acknowledged when measuring economic welfare. Given these definitions, with their connotations of social as well as economic welfare, do current national account procedures take all these issues into consideration?

Traditionally, the most important measure of economic performance has been the Gross Domestic Product or Gross National Product (GDP or GNP). Their increase, at a national or *per capita* level, is regarded by conventional economists as beneficial, indicating a healthy market which means, for them, a healthy economy; a dropping GNP has connotations of job losses, home repossessions, recession and a government that is not fit to run the country. Since their first publication only 50 years ago they have come to indicate more than was originally intended. At that time, in the period of the Great Depression, Keynesian economists were preoccupied with the business cycle, with explaining how an economy could remain for long periods of time at less than full employment, so they needed to measure aggregate demand (Keynes, 1936). Now GNP has come to be used as a measure of overall national welfare, closely bound up with human welfare, the stronger the economy the greater the contribution. In addition, other countries are applying the same measures, since national accounts have been standardised to the UN system (UN, 1968), direct comparisons can be made.

Over recent years though there has been a gradual acceptance that using GNP as a measure of welfare has its anomalies, particularly with regard to the environment and sustainability. Since GNP is a monetary aggregate it does not distinguish between different types of economic activity, it simply records the total. Within this total will be activities that do contribute to welfare, for example, spending on leisure, foods or perhaps clothing. However, there will also be included expenditure on such things as the loss of amenity, damage to health or other ill effects resulting from pollution, for example. These "defensive expenditures" obviously have a negative effect on overall welfare (as will the pollution itself, of course) but make a positive contribution to GNP, a clear anomaly. To environmentalists a major problem with current national accounting methods relates to what they leave out, natural capital. National accounts do take account of stocks of human-made capital (such as buildings and equipment), subtracting from GNP an allowance for its depreciation. The resulting figure, Net National Product (NNP) then reflects the first principle of accounting, namely that economic success must be measured by the stock of capital as well as the flow of income. This practice recognises that a consumption level maintained by drawing down the stock of capital will exceed the sustainable level of income. In leaving out natural capital from this equation it could be possible for a country to exhaust its mineral resource, cut down its forests, erode its soils, pollute its aquifers and hunt its wildlife and fisheries to extinction, without it affecting the NNP. Here then lies another anomaly, the country's NNP could continue rising on the back of this exploitation and yet it has lost all potential future production.

In summary then, there are three areas in the currently used accounting system that make it unsuitable for measuring sustainable development. They are: 1) defensive expenditure, 2) environmental damage resulting from economic activity and, 3) natural capital. An alternative measure is clearly needed that adequately reflects these three key issues.

Several measures have been proposed which might better reflect national welfare (than GNP). Some measures have been proposed that place their emphasis on social indicators. These include the Potential Life Time (PLT) measure proposed by Meghnad Desai (Desai, 1994) or the earlier Human Development Index (HDI) (UNDP, 1990), which considers purchasing power, life expectancy and literacy. Anderson (1991) has suggested a list of 16 measures as alternatives to standard economic accounting. Only considered here, though, are measures that make some attempt to reflect the points outlined earlier in the definition of the central meaning of sustainable development.

If defensive expenditure and the depreciation of natural capital were deducted from NNP then we would have what Daly and Cobb (1989) have defined as Hicksian Income, a measure of sustainable consumption or true income. Hicks' (1948) thinking was that income calculations were meant to give people an indication of the amount which they could consume without impoverishing themselves, i.e. an amount which could be spent in a time period but still leaving them as well off at the end of it as they were at the beginning. The main objective is to keep capital intact, or in other words sustainable, both human-made and natural.

Although this is an improved measure of income, it is not a measure of social welfare (however, an advantage of using such a measure is that it would not interfere with the current national accounts thus allowing for historical continuity and comparability). There may, however, be a relationship between Hicksian income and economic welfare. Daly and Cobb argue that "Hicksian income (maximum sustainable consumption) is inherently more measurable than economic welfare. Although the aim of Hicksian income is not a measure of welfare, but rather a practical guide to avoid impoverishment by over consumption, the component of sustainable consumption looms large in most welfare indexes. One would therefore expect a significant positive correlation between Hicksian income and most welfare indexes" (Daly and Cobb, 1989).

Twenty years ago there was a consensus among economists that GNP reflected the level of economic welfare. In fact, Nordhaus and Tobin (1973) created an index called the Measure of Economic Welfare (MEW) in an effort to prove it. They labelled this measure "primitive and experimental" as it only recognised the more obvious discrepancies between GNP and economic welfare. The measure involved: "reclassification of GNP expenditures as consumption, investment, and intermediate; imputation for the services of household work; correction for some of the disamenities for urbanisation".

With regard to their reclassification of GNP expenditures the total spent on education and health, both private and public, has been reclassified as capital investments. With consumer durables being treated as capital goods an allowance has been made for the deletion from GNP of their depreciation, along with that for government capital, as is already accomplished in NNP. Nordhaus and Tobin make an important distinction between gross and *per capita* GNP. It is possible, with a rising population, for a rising gross GNP to equate to a falling *per capita* GNP, and it is the (rising) latter which is the welfare objective that can only be achieved if some portion of NNP is reinvested. The capital stock must be growing at the same rate as the population and labour force. This is what they describe as a growth requirement which they subtract from GNP to get a sustainable MEW.

Defensive expenditures, as mentioned previously, have been deducted from this index. In this category Nordhaus and Tobin include the expenditures on commuting to work, police services, sanitation services, road maintenance and national defence. To the index have been added estimates for the services derived from capital, leisure and non-market work. The authors' comment on the exclusion of the latter two factors from standard national accounts is worth repeating, "The omission of leisure and of non-market productive activity from measures of production conveys the impression that economists are blindly materialistic" (Nordhaus and Tobin, 1973).

Table 18   Comparison of GNP and MEW for the US, 1929–1965

	1929	*1935*	*1945*	*1947*	*1954*	*1958*	*1965*
				Year			
Population (m)	121.8	127.3	140.5	144.7	163.0	174.9	194.6
GNP ($ billion)	203.6	169.5	355.2	309.9	407.0	447.3	617.8
GNP *per capita*	1672	1332	2528	2142	2497	2557	3175
% change		–20.3	+89.8	–15.3	+16.6	+2.4	+24.2
MEW	4462	4504	5098	5934	5898	5991	6378
% change		+0.9	+13.2	+16.4	–0.6	+1.6	+6.5

Nordhaus and Tobin close their discussion on this index by suggesting that although the growth of *per capita* MEW is lower than *per capita* NNP (1.1% per year for MEW as against 1.7% per year for NNP for the period 1929–65) the figures are sufficiently close to disprove the theory that "conventional national accounts are a myth that evaporates when a welfare-oriented measure is substituted" (Nordhaus and Tobin, 1973). An obvious question here is why do they compare MEW with NNP rather than with GNP? They were attempting to show that conventional national accounts do correlate with a measure of economic welfare, so surely they should have done the comparison with the measure most commonly used, i.e. GNP. In comparing MEW with NNP they are in fact comparing it with a measure that has already taken a "step" towards being a sustainable measure. Table 18, based on Nordhaus and Tobin's own data, takes this into account and compares MEW with GNP rather than NNP. It suggests the rise in MEW is actually 0.997% not 1.1% per year, and that the rise in NNP is equivalent to a rise in *per capita* GNP of 1.8% per year over the full 1929–1965 period.

Daly and Cobb (1989) also take issue with these findings. They have examined different time-frames and have identified several anomalies. For example, from 1935 to 1945, *per capita* GNP rose almost 90%, while *per capita* MEW rose only 13%. During the following time period, 1945–47, *per capita* GNP actually fell by about 15% while MEW rose by over 16%. This was, however, the period immediately after the Second World War so it would be difficult to draw any conclusions from this short-term negative relationship. Clearly, closer inspection has revealed that there is indeed a difference between standard national accounts and a welfare-oriented measure. Daly and Cobb believe that the MEW index does actually shed doubt on the thesis that national income accounts serve as a good proxy measure of economic welfare. Table 18 illustrates more of these differences between the growth rates of GNP and MEW (notice that GNP, not NNP, has been compared here with MEW since this will be used when comparing against other indices later in this study).

The first index to make any allowance for natural resources was that proposed by Xenophon Zolotas (Zolotas, 1981). His index, entitled Economic Aspects of Welfare (EAW), was designed to "depict the direction of change in the effective economic well-being of a society that is already in the stage of advanced industrialism". It follows on from his belief that there exists a relationship between social welfare and economic growth that is directly associated with the stage of development in which a society finds itself. A country passes through three stages as its GNP grows: a society of privation, a period dominated by absolute wants, when each increment in national income leads to a large increase in social welfare; a society of steady improvements, when each increase in national income is matched by an equal increase in social welfare; and a society of declining improvements, when the rate of increase in social welfare drops below that of the national income.

The index takes as its starting point private or personal consumption to which is added or subtracted various factors. The added factors are estimates for the value of: services from the environment, public buildings, consumer durables, household labour and leisure; and health and education contributing to welfare. In the same manner as Nordhaus and Tobin, various defensive expenditures such as the cost of commuting are deducted, as are estimates for the cost of environmental pollution and resource depletion. Unlike the MEW index though capital accumulation and the issue of sustainability have been left out.

The result is an index that starts out in 1950 nearly 1.5 times larger than GNP and remains almost constant up to 1977. Of particular interest though is the fact that EAW rises throughout the study period, albeit slower than GNP. However, Zolotas' figures are not *per capita*. When they are expressed as *per capita* figures there is still a rising EAW (but not as steep) as illustrated in Table 19.

A direct comparison is possible, for the time periods that overlap, with the growth of Nordhaus and Tobin's MEW index. From 1947–65, *per capita* MEW grew by 7.5% for the full period, or 0.4% per year. During the closest comparable period, 1950–65, *per capita* growth of EAW was 8.8%, or 0.56% per year. It is quite remarkable that the figures are so close particularly given the different methods of calculation. In addition, the growth of MEW over this period, at approximately one third of the rise in GNP (2.2% per annum between 1947 and 1965), is matched by a similar one third rise in EAW compared to GNP for the period up to 1977 (EAW rose by 0.6 % per annum between 1950 and 1977).

Neither the Nordhaus and Tobin MEW index or the EAW index of Zolotas, described above, make full provision for natural capital (although they both do to some extent) or defensive expenditures to warrant their use as a measure of sustainable development. The index of Zolotas does not consider sustainability, whereas that of Nordhaus and Tobin, which does take sustainability into account, does not make provision for some environmental issues that have risen in importance over recent years. An alternative needs to be found, a measure that

Table 19   Comparison of GNP and EAW for the US, 1950–1977

	Year				
	1950	*1960*	*1965*	*1970*	*1977*
Population (m)	152.3	180.7	194.6	205.0	220.2
GNP ($ billion)	533.5	736.8	925.9	1075.3	1332.7
GNP *per capita* ($)	3503	4077	4758	5245	6052
% change		+16.4	+16.7	+10.2	+15.4
EAW ($ billion)	795.3	985.5	1105.7	1222.2	1364.5
EAW *per capita* ($)	5222	5454	5682	5962	6197
% change		+4.4	+4.2	+4.9	+3.9

takes full account of natural resources and all of the negative welfare costs associated with economic activity.

The earliest national government to adjust their national accounts to reflect environmental issues was that of Japan. In 1973 they produced a measure called Net National Welfare (NNW), which was based on the index of Nordhaus and Tobin but with several important differences. Included were adjustments for environmental damage and the cost of auto accidents, whereas missing from this index were estimates for household labour. Pearce *et al.* (1989) highlight a problem with the methods used in this index for calculating an adjustment for environmental damage. The Japanese have applied quality standards for each of the main problem areas: water contamination, air pollution and waste disposal. Pearce *et al.* state that "there are three difficulties with this method of correction for environmental pollution. First, the choice of standard is arbitrary, although it may have a political basis. By choosing a low enough standard the costs can be made negligible and by choosing a high enough one they can be made astronomical. Related to this is the second point, which is that we are ignoring the impacts of any residual pollution that is left once the standard has been imposed. Unless this standard is optimal in a rather specific sense, some additional impact should be allowed for. The third point is that the approach ignores totally the impact of defensive expenditure, which should be allowed if a correct measure is to be obtained".

Table 20, using data taken from Uno (1988), illustrates how NNW differs from GNP for the period 1955 to 1985. During this period of extremely rapid growth in the Japanese economy GNP has grown by 730%. Over the same period NNW has grown by 475%, a relatively close association when comparing with the results earlier for the MEW and EAW indices. Daly and Cobb (1989) were at a loss to explain the relatively close agreement with GNP for this Japanese study and the three to one difference in the MEW index. It may be that the theory of Zolotas, described earlier, about a society's position relative to its GNP applies here. It is possible that the US is further along the line as a "society of declining

Table 20 Comparison of GNP and NNW for Japan, 1955–1985

	Year						
	1955	*1960*	*1965*	*1970*	*1975*	*1980*	*1985*
GNP	17 268	26 183	41 591	72 144	93 260	118 105	143 387
% change		+51.6	+58.8	+73.5	+29.3	+26.6	+21.4
NNW	18 036	23 126	32 116	47 548	74 231	90 646	103 781
% change		+28.2	+38.9	+48.1	+56.1	+22.1	+14.5

improvements", where the rate of increase in social welfare relative to increases in income (GNP) is lower than in Japan.

The discussion so far has centred on attempts to incorporate environmental considerations into existing national accounts. There have, however, been efforts to produce separate accounts for a nation's natural and environmental resources. These "satellite" accounts have been produced in both physical and monetary formats, the former by Norway (as early as 1974), France and Canada. The aim of a physical account is to keep track of "stock" changes through consumption, discovery or replenishment and extends the idea of an input–output analysis. There are problems with this approach. A full physical resource account is very costly to undertake, but it can be useful in identifying the links between the environment and economic activity and in forecasting future natural resource demand. In addition, physical accounts do not have a common unit of measure, making comparisons very difficult.

Monetary accounts also have their problems. The biggest is probably how do you put a value on a natural resource. As Repetto (1987) points out, while "a good environment yields a continuing flow of beneficial goods and services, valuing those benefits is complex" (Repetto *et al.*, 1987). Natural resource commodity prices can fluctuate wildly on world markets over a very short time (Moffatt, 1994). This could have a dramatic effect on a monetary account if unrealised capital gains are included within it.

The integration of monetary natural resource accounts into the standard national accounts is an aim of the European Community which has called for the adoption, by the year 2000, of environmentally adjusted national accounts (EC, 1992). In addition, the UN has drafted a provisional handbook (UN, 1990) on this issue and the UK government's Central Statistical Office (ET, various years) has gone so far as to produce a simplified experimental environmental account (ET, 1992), physical as well as monetary, for 1990 based on the UN handbook. The UK government intends to "build on the experimental work published in 1992, to take forward work on UK environmental accounts", and a new working group will be set up to consider environmental indicators (Anon., 1994).

Below is a discussion on an attempt to produce a single indicator of economic welfare, in effect an adjusted GNP, removing items that do not contribute to welfare, adding those that do, and also taking sustainability into account.

INDICES OF SUSTAINABLE ECONOMIC WELFARE (ISEW)

Perhaps the most recent measure of economic welfare centred on sustainable development, is that proposed by Daly and Cobb (1989), the Index of Sustainable Economic Welfare. Throughout their book the authors are pleading for a change in the way economic progress is regarded, questioning what really constitutes economic success. They are seeking changes in deeply ingrained attitudes with the aim of moving towards what they call an economics for community. As these attitudes run so deep they accept this change will not happen overnight but as a step forward they have proposed this index in the belief that "policies directed to improvement as measured by the index of sustainable economic welfare would lead in directions that economics for community calls for".

The Index of Sustainable Economic Welfare (ISEW) has been built around some of the accomplishments of the indices already described above but includes some new elements. As with most indexes, this one starts with personal consumption. However, Daly and Cobb do not add to and subtract from this figure the various elements that make up their index. Instead they first apply an index of income inequality to personal consumption. This is designed to reflect any changes in distributional equity, an issue that the authors regard as very important when measuring economic welfare; they have "implicitly assumed that marginal increases in consumption by the poor are of greater value than marginal increases by the rich" (Daly and Cobb, 1989).

To this weighted personal consumption are added or subtracted nineteen elements that make up the index. Deductions for defensive expenditures include: health and education, advertising, commuting, urbanisation, auto accidents and pollution. Other deductions are for consumer durable expenditure and the costs associated with the depletion of non-renewable resources, long-term environmental damage and the loss of wetlands and farmlands. Additions include: services from household labour, consumer durables and streets and highways; consumption on health and education; net capital growth and change in net international position. The reasoning behind most of these elements is fairly straightforward given that most have appeared in previous indices. However, the last element, change in net international position is included to take into account the source of investment capital. The aim is to measure long-term national self-reliance with the authors believing that borrowing from abroad reflects a weakness in the viability of the economy.

ISEW for the United States of America

Daly and Cobb have calculated their index for the United States with and without estimates for resource depletion and long-term environmental damage; without

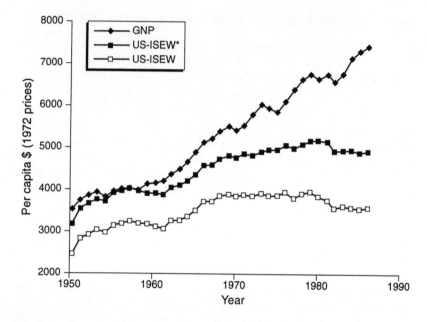

Figure 9 *Per capita* GNP, US–ISEW and US–ISEW*, 1950–1986

them on the grounds that the estimates for these two elements are more speculative than the procedures used for the other estimates and their inclusion may be regarded as controversial. The full results of their US study, from 1950 to 1986, are illustrated in Figure 9. This shows *per capita* GNP, US–ISEW and US–ISEW* (where US–ISEW* excludes resource depletion and long-term environmental damage). Selected results, with their percentage growth rates, are given in Table 21. It can be seen that the pattern of growth up to the early 1970s and then decline from 1980 is matched in both US–ISEW and US–ISEW*. To Daly and Cobb this suggests that the inclusion of the "controversial" estimates for resource depletion and long-term environmental damage have not affected the pattern of economic welfare.

In their conclusion Daly and Cobb have compared the growth of *per capita* ISEW for the period 1951–1986 rather than start at 1950. This is on the grounds that *per capita* ISEW grew more in 1950 than in any other year and was distorting the results. Such a move is defensible if one or more of the contributing elements had "rogue" estimates for 1950. The only element that might fit this description is net capital growth which is a (relatively) high negative number compared to other mostly positive years. However, this "rogue" figure has been estimated in the same manner as other years, being based on five-year moving averages of labour force and net stock of fixed capital (in fact a large increase in the labour force in 1946 is the cause). If the methodology is good enough for

Table 21 Comparison *per capita* GNP with US–ISEW and US–ISEW*, 1950–1986

	Year					
	1950	*1960*	*1965*	*1970*	*1977*	*1986*
GNP ($)	3512	4080	4783	5294	6219	7226
% change		+16.2	+17.2	+10.7	+17.5	+16.2
US–ISEW ($)	2488	3052	3419	3723	3656	3402
% change		+22.7	+12.0	+8.9	–1.8	–6.9
US–ISEW* ($)	3174	3836	4262	4663	4811	4732
% change		+20.9	+11.1	+21.5	+3.2	–1.6

the later years then it is surely good enough for 1950 so the following comparisons will use 1950 as the base year.

The growth in US–ISEW and US–ISEW* for the full 1950–1986 period was 0.9% and 1.1% per year, respectively and contrasts with a GNP rising at virtually double this rate at 2% per year. Looking at the full period though does hide considerable short-term variations. For example, between 1950 and 1960 both US–ISEW and US–ISEW* grew faster at 22.7% and 20.9% respectively than GNP at 16.2%. Towards the end of the study period, between 1977 and 1986, US–ISEW fell by 6.9%, US–ISEW* fell by 1.6% while GNP rose by 16.2%. What is noticeable from the results in Table 21 is the declining growth rates through time of both US–ISEW and US–ISEW*. Also of note is that both of these indexes increase considerably faster, for overlapping time periods, than the overall rises in the other indices described earlier, MEW at 0.4% per year and EAW at 0.6% per year.

ISEW for the United Kingdom

The publication of the Daly and Cobb ISEW index spawned much debate, principally on the methods and assumptions used in calculating the variables. Subsequently, a revised index was produced by Cobb and Cobb (1993), very similar to the original but with a few column changes. These were the deletion of advertising expenditure and the inclusion of expenditures on personal pollution control and ozone depletion. There followed from this the production of an index of sustainable economic welfare for the UK prepared by Jackson and Marks (1994).

The results of the UK–ISEW study by Jackson and Marks are shown in Figure 10. In the same manner as the US results, graphs of *per capita* GNP, ISEW and ISEW* have been illustrated. Of note is the similarity between the US and UK results, with GNP rising and a fall off for both ISEW and ISEW*

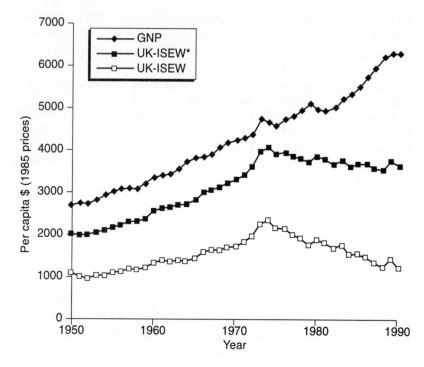

Figure 10   *Per capita* GNP, UK–ISEW and UK–ISEW*, 1950–1990

from the mid-1970s, although the fall off is slightly more marked in the UK study. In fact by 1990 the UK–ISEW has fallen virtually to its 1950 level (£1136 in 1990 compared with £1100 in 1950). As with the US study then, there is a clear difference between the index of sustainable economic welfare and *per capita* GNP. To Jackson and Marks this suggests that: a) as a measure of welfare the UK–ISEW suggests that actual welfare is considerably lower than economic output (as measured by GNP); and b) as an index of welfare UK–ISEW has a considerably different shape to the GNP curve for the period of the study.

AN INDEX OF SUSTAINABLE ECONOMIC WELFARE FOR SCOTLAND

A primary objective of this chapter is to measure the level of sustainable economic welfare in Scotland. To this end the most comprehensive measure found so far, Cobb and Cobb's revised ISEW, will be used. Below is a full description of how the data for each of their indicators were derived and the assumptions that were made. It should be noted that an initial pilot study of five measures of sustainability has already been carried out by Moffatt *et al.* (1994). One of the measures they considered and actually calculated for Scotland was ISEW using 6 out of the 20 indicators. These variables are marked by ** in the descriptions below.

All costs are given in 1985 pounds sterling. This has been achieved by using the 'implied GDP deflator' published in ET (various years). This conversion factor is for the UK as a whole and is calculated by dividing the GDP at current market prices by the GDP at 1985 prices. Unfortunately this deflator is not calculated at the Scotland level.

Column lettering refers to the indicators position in Table 22. In each column efforts have been made to find purely Scottish data. Only as a last resort have UK estimates been scaled on the basis of, for example, GDP, population or number of households. Where this has occurred it is stated in the text.

** *Column A: Year*

The pilot Scottish ISEW by Moffatt *et al* is limited to the period 1984–1990. This has been extended in this study to 1980–1991. Ideally, to allow a fuller comparison with previous studies, this should have been extended back to 1950 but time constraints and data availability mitigated against this. In addition, due to the time taken by the various government agencies to update their records, it has not been possible to go beyond the year 1991.

Table 22   Scottish ISEW, 1980–1991

A	B	C	D	E	H	I–F	J	K
			Weighted personal consumption	Domestic labour	Health & education expenditure	Consumer durables difference	Health & education defensive expenditure	Commuting costs
Year	Consumer expenditure	Distributional inequality	(+)	(+)	(+)	(–)	(–)	(–)
1980	16 548	97.1	17 042	7369	1024	1872	79	453
1981	16 561	98.7	16 780	7651	1035	1847	90	489
1982	16 977	98.7	17 200	7702	1042	2005	99	530
1983	17 895	98.7	18 131	8312	1059	2390	95	517
1984	18 622	100.5	18 529	8243	1082	2427	106	511
1985	18 887	102.2	18 480	8334	1080	2554	120	505
1986	19 554	109.3	17 890	8662	1101	2873	141	518
1987	20 193	116.3	17 363	8485	1164	2963	153	546
1988	21 408	123.4	17 348	8603	1201	3453	172	539
1989	21 329	119.9	17 789	8809	1216	3398	185	553
1990	21 720	126.9	17 116	8954	1238	3256	190	572
1991	21 158	123.4	17 146	9158	1392	3237	184	576

Continued overleaf

Table 22 Continued

A	L	M	N	O	P	Q	R	S
Year	Personal pollution control costs (–)	Automobile accident costs (–)	Water pollution costs (–)	Air pollution costs (–)	Noise pollution costs (–)	Wetland loss (–)	Farmland loss (–)	Depletion of non-renewables (–)
1980	88	100	201	1662	88	159	413	3963
1981	97	97	201	1591	88	161	422	3916
1982	109	96	201	1565	89	162	430	3887
1983	129	92	200	1513	90	163	435	3949
1984	141	98	200	1488	90	165	443	4000
1985	152	102	200	1520	91	166	449	4339
1986	163	104	199	1563	91	167	453	4558
1987	136	102	198	1585	92	169	461	4598
1988	147	106	198	1599	92	170	470	4954
1989	161	115	197	1620	93	171	476	5185
1990	175	114	197	1610	93	173	484	5361
1991	181	104	196	1604	94	174	488	5673

A	T	U	V	W	X	Y	Z	AA
Year	Long term environmental damage (–)	Ozone depletion costs (–)	Net capital growth (+)	Net change in international position (+)	ISEW (sum)	Per capita ISEW	GDP	Per capita GDP
1980	6111	2282	503	0	8468	1643	23 240	4510
1981	6218	2402	205	0	8051	1554	22 920	4425
1982	6321	2532	–230	0	7689	1488	23 419	4532
1983	6422	2662	–699	0	8144	1581	24 302	4719
1984	6522	2729	–1300	0	7635	1484	24 233	4709
1985	6627	2880	–965	0	7226	1407	25 270	4919
1986	6734	3034	–419	0	6635	1296	26 377	5151
1987	6839	3157	–24	0	5990	1172	27 365	5353
1988	6949	3271	398	0	5430	1066	28 238	5543
1989	7060	3412	879	0	6065	1191	28 959	5688
1990	7172	3610	1182	0	5483	1075	30 035	5887
1991	7287	3798	1725	0	5826	1141	29 569	5790

** *Column B: Personal consumption or consumer expenditure*

Consumer expenditure figures are taken directly from Scottish Abstract of Statistics (SAS, various years, Table 11.2). They form the starting point for the index. It should be noted that community charges replaced domestic rates in

Scotland from 1989. Domestic rates are recorded in consumer expenditure whereas community charges are not.

** *Column C: Distributional inequality*

By applying an index of distributional inequality to total consumer expenditure figures it is hoped that account will be taken of changes in relative income between the rich and poor. Such changes could be the result of various income tax reforms. Daly and Cobb's (1989) reasoning for including such an index is based on the assumption that "an additional thousand dollars in income adds more to the welfare of a poor family than it does to a rich family".

This index of income inequality is derived from the commonly used Gini coefficient. The Gini coefficient is a measure of the area above the actual distribution curve divided by the area beneath the perfect distribution (straight) line and can take a value between 0 and 1 with a perfect distribution represented by 0.

Gini coefficients for equivalised disposable income for the UK have been taken directly from Atkinson and Micklewright (1992) and the index used here derived by rebasing the 1950 figure to 100. Unfortunately, it has not been possible to find similar Gini coefficient figures for Scotland. However, Gini coefficients for 1988 have been found for Scottish and UK pre-tax income distributions. These were very similar (0.290 for UK and 0.286 for Scotland), which suggests the UK index may approximate closely to that for Scotland. Since it could be misleading to base such an assumption on close agreement on only one year, further study is required here. Ideally separate Gini coefficients for Scotland, based on income after deductions, i.e. as in the UK based on equivalised disposable income, should be published annually, perhaps in SAS.

** *Column D: Weighted personal consumption*

Weighted personal consumption is simply column B divided by column C, i.e. personal consumption divided by distributional inequality. To this figure will be added or subtracted the financial contribution or burden the following variables make towards sustainable economic welfare.

** *Column E: Services from domestic labour*

This study uses data from Jackson and Marks (1994) to estimate services from domestic or household labour for Scotland. In the absence of reliable Scottish data an assumption has been made that the *per capita* benefits to be derived from domestic labour is the same in Scotland as in the UK; consequently, UK figures have been scaled according to the ratio of UK to Scottish populations.

Since these figures only go up to 1990 an estimate for 1991 has been found by linear extrapolation.

Column F: Services: consumer durable

Daly and Cobb (1989) in their original index kept separate the value of the services that flow from consumer durables and the actual expenditure on consumer durables, adding the former in column F and subtracting the latter in column I. This study combines the results from both columns into one, column I. See that column for a more detailed explanation.

Column G: Services: streets and highways

This column has been omitted from this study on the grounds that government expenditure on roads is primarily financed through a vehicle taxation system and tax on fuel so will already be included in consumer expenditure. Ideally the vehicle tax component of consumer expenditure should be subtracted from the index with the value of the services flowing from this expenditure being added. Unfortunately for Scotland (as in the UK) insufficient data exists to carry this out.

** Column H: Public expenditure on health and education

An important factor here is what proportion of public expenditure on health and education actually contributes to welfare. There are expenditures in both areas that do not contribute to welfare. An example for health, cited by Jackson and Marks (1994), is the cost to the NHS of treating smoking-related diseases (in excess of £600 million per year for the UK). Further examples include the cost of treating road accident casualties or an increased number of asthmatics resulting from worsening atmospheric pollution. These are obviously defensive expenditures and as such should not be included in the index. In line with Cobb and Cobb (1990) and Jackson and Marks (1994) one half of total health expenditure has been regarded as contributing to welfare and can be added to the index.

A similar line of reasoning applies to expenditure on education. The assumption here follows that of Zolotas (1981) who considered that most education is necessary just to maintain the skills of what he calls "human capital". Within this, he classed all primary and secondary education. It is in post-secondary or higher education that Zolotas believed increases in personal welfare were attributable. He assumed that one half of expenditure on higher education is consumption in the sense that it is sought for its own sake rather than to serve another purpose and as such should be added to the index.

Figures on Scotland's expenditure on health have been taken from Scottish Abstract of Statistics (SAS, various years). Data on Scotland's higher education expenditure has been found in a more circuitous manner. It has been possible to

Table 23   Public expenditure on health and education (real at 1985 £m), 1980–1991

	a *NHS* *expenditure*	*b* *Higher Education* *expenditure*	*0.5 ×(a + b)* *Health and* *Education spending*	
			Real	*1985*
1980	1329	139	734	1024
1981	1494	158	826	1035
1982	1623	167	895	1042
1983	1727	187	957	1059
1984	1851	197	1024	1082
1985	1964	197	1080	1080
1986	2082	196	1139	1101
1987	2274	255	1265	1164
1988	2509	272	1390	1201
1989	2728	289	1508	1216
1990	2983	278	1631	1238
1991	3624	282	1953	1392

find the total education expenditure by local *and* central government in graph format only so an allowance should be made for reading accuracy. Expenditure on higher education has been found by reading off the total education expenditure per head from the graphs in *Regional Trends* (RT, various years), multiplying this by the percentage spend on higher education (RT, e.g. 1987) and then multiplying by the population.

Unfortunately, *Regional Trends* only holds this data from 1981 onwards. Estimates for 1980 have therefore been extrapolated. All data and the final figures for use in the index are shown in Table 23. As already described, the contribution to the index is made up of one half of health expenditure plus one half of higher education expenditure.

Column I: Expenditure on consumer durables

As already described, columns F and I have been combined in this study. To calculate the value of the flow of services from and expenditure on consumer durables the method used by Jackson and Marks has been applied here. They used Patterson's (1992) estimates of the total value of services from all consumer expenditure (that is expenditure on non-durables plus services from durables) which they subtracted from total consumer expenditure, thus producing what in Daly and Cobb is column F minus column I.

Results for Scotland have been calculated by scaling Jackson and Marks' figures for Scotland and scaling the UK proportion of consumer expenditure

Table 24 Percentage of households with selected durable goods, 1981 and 1991

	1981		1991	
	UK	*Scotland*	*UK*	*Scotland*
Central heating	58	51	82	80
Home computer	–	–	22	19
Video	–	–	70	69
Television	97	97	98	98
Deep freezer	47	39	84	79
Dishwasher	4	3	15	12
Tumble dryer	22	24	48	49
Washing machine	77	83	87	90
Microwave oven	–	–	57	53

for each year. Since the UK estimates are based on the stocks of various consumer durables this method is defensible if these stocks are equivalent (i.e. per household) in Scotland and the UK (and assuming that the user costs are the same).

Table 24 illustrates that there are some differences in the overall percentages (source: RT, 1994) but is this enough to warrant finding a new estimate for Scotland? The UK average across all consumer durables exceeds the Scottish average by 0.8% in 1981 and by 2.0% in 1991. These differences suggest that an alternative method of calculation may be more appropriate. Further study would be required if this is the case. A further point is that this widening difference in ownership of consumer durables brings into question the efficacy of using UK distributional inequality figures for Scotland (in column C). It may suggest that the distribution of income in Scotland is less even than in the UK as a whole. Again this requires further research.

** *Column J: Defensive private expenditures on health and education*

In estimating the proportion of private expenditure on health and education that contributes to welfare Jackson and Marks used assumptions similar to those used in column H and decided that one half of each category should be deducted from the index as defensive expenditure. This assumption has been applied to this study.

Data on private expenditures on health and education has been derived from the *Family Expenditure Survey* (FES, various years). This provides a breakdown of all household expenditures by UK region. The figures shown here have been found by calculating the percentage of the total weekly expenditure by Scottish households on health and education (under subheadings: medicine and surgical goods; medical, dental and nursing fees and spectacles; and education and training expenses) and applying this percentage to consumer expenditure (column B).

Column K: Costs of commuting

Data on consumer expenditure, by household per week, on car, rail and bus/ coach transport has been obtained from *Scottish Abstract of Statistics* (SAS, various years). Average weekly commuting costs have been found by multiplying these figures by the proportion of passenger miles attributable to commuting (from NTS, 1985). By expressing these costs as a percentage of total household expenditure and applying this percentage to total consumer expenditure overall commuting costs have been calculated.

Expenditure data for cars *excludes* the element of vehicle purchase costs. In excluding such expenditure on a consumer durable this study has avoided the problem of double counting encountered by Jackson and Marks (it will be recalled that expenditure on consumer durables has already been accounted for in column I).

It should be noted that the percentages of miles travelled attributable to commuting are UK estimates. It has been assumed that these percentages will be the same in Scotland. However, commuter rail travel in and around London is likely to contribute a large part to the UK figure of 56% so this should be viewed with some caution in the Scottish context. Since no figures for Scotland are available these are the best and only estimates that can be used.

A further assumption is that within each mode of transport the cost per mile travelled will be the same whatever the reason for the journey. In other words, that the 56% of rail passenger miles attributed to commuting results in 56% of rail passenger expenditure. Given that shorter commuting-type journeys are likely to have a higher cost per mile than longer recreational ones this assumption will result in an underestimate of the total costs of commuting.

No estimate has been made here of the costs associated with the time lost in commuting longer distances to and from work. Zolotas (1981) estimated a year-on-year 2 minute increase in the length of the round trip each day due to worsening traffic conditions and people living at ever greater distances from metropolitan areas. Such an increase would be difficult to defend for Scotland given that the population is concentrated in the central belt of the country.

** *Column L: Costs of personal pollution control*

Little data exists on the personal costs associated with pollution control. The only directly relevant information found so far is from the Department of the Environment who produced a one-off estimate for household environmental expenditure for the UK of £680 million in 1990–91. Jackson and Marks (1994) used this figure to construct time-series data based on an index created for the

Table 25   Costs of personal pollution control at 1985 prices, 1980–1991

	Cost of pollution control UK (source Jackson & Marks)	*Population Scotland (× 1000)*	*Population UK (× 1000)*	*Cost of pollution control Scotland (£ million)*
1980	953	5153	55 945	88
1981	1051	5180	56 352	97
1982	1183	5167	56 306	109
1983	1412	5150	56 347	129
1984	1544	5146	56 460	141
1985	1675	5137	56 618	152
1986	1807	5121	56 763	163
1987	1511	5112	56 930	136
1988	1642	5094	57 065	147
1989	1807	5091	57 236	161
1990	1971	5102	57 411	175
1991	2048	5107	57 801	181

US by Cobb and Cobb (1993) on the assumption that the patterns of environmental awareness and consumer expenditure are similar between the USA and UK. The same method has been applied here.

Data for Scotland (see Table 25) have been derived from this Jackson and Marks time series by scaling it to the relative UK to Scotland population proportions for each year. This time series ends in 1990 so the 1991 figure is an extrapolated estimate.

** Column M: Costs of automobile accidents

On the grounds that the hospital and medical costs associated with road accidents have already been accounted for in column H (public expenditure on health and education), only expenditure on non-injury accidents is included here. Data on the number of non-injury accidents for Scotland have not been found. However, by taking Jackson and Marks' estimate that the number of accidents not involving injury and the number involving injury is in the ratio of 8:1, an estimate for Scotland has been found based on data on injury accidents provided in *Road Accidents Scotland* (RAS, 1992). By taking the cost of each non-injury accident (BRF, 1993) as shown in Table 26 (interpolating for missing years) and applying these to the number of accidents, the total cost of automobile accidents has been derived and is shown in column M.

Column N: Costs of water pollution

Estimates for the costs of water pollution in Scotland have been derived from an index of river, canal and estuary water quality. This index was created by

Table 26   Costs of damage only (i.e. non-injury) road
accidents, 1980–1991

	Costs per damage only road accidents (£ real)
1980	410
1985	620
1990	930
1991	960

taking the reciprocal of the percentages of the total length of rivers which were classified as unpolluted (from SAS, 1993) and applying it to the same percentage of GDP as used for the USA study by Daly and Cobb. A similar method was applied to the UK study by Jackson and Marks but their index was nearly 50% higher for the base year of 1972 (1.53 for UK, 1.05 for Scotland), indicating a significantly lower level of polluted rivers in Scotland. Jackson and Marks estimated UK costs for 1972 of £3.2 billion (in 1985 prices) which is 5.7% of GDP (£56282 million). Applying the same percentage to Scotland's GDP (£4872 million) results in a cost of £277 million. This figure has been applied to the rebased index shown in Table 22.

Jackson and Marks discuss two areas that are excluded from their costs, estuaries and groundwater. The first has been included here but the latter has not. Water extraction from the ground makes up a very small proportion of the total water used in Scotland, yielding in 1990 an average of 112 megalitres per day out of a total yield from all sources of 3846 megalitres (SAS, 1993). Excluding it here, as has been done on the UK–ISEW, does not imply no costs would result from its pollution, more that it would make a relatively small contribution to the overall costs (and would be very difficult to calculate). In excluding it it is probable that the costs shown here for water pollution are a conservative estimate.

Column O: Costs of air pollution

This column is a prime example of the change in calculation method required following an increase in the knowledge base. Daly and Cobb achieved their estimates by creating an index of air pollution based on the sum of the emissions of three pollutants, sulfur dioxide (SO_2), nitrogen oxides (NO_x), and black smoke to which they applied a $30 billion damage cost. Since then, of course, other pollutants have been identified as having a significant effect on air quality. In addition it is now thought more appropriate to base the estimate on the sum of the costs associated with each pollutant rather than summing emissions first.

111

Both these points have been actioned here. This index considers the emissions of carbon monoxide (CO) and volatile organic compounds (VOC) as well as the three pollutants already mentioned, with the costs associated with each one (in £ per tonne) based on those used by Jackson and Marks in their UK index.

Unfortunately, emission figures are not available for Scotland but according to the National Environmental Technology Centre, who have taken over some of the work of the now closed Warren Spring Laboratory, the UK figures were simply based on fuel consumption and transport statistics which would suggest that, if the *per capita* mileage and fuel usage figures were similar, then the UK figures can be scaled according to the populations. In fact fuel consumption is slightly higher in Scotland although this is compensated by a lower *per capita* mileage figure.

Column P: Costs of noise pollution

It has proved very difficult to find data relating to the cost of noise pollution, for the UK as well as for Scotland. Data exists in *Digest of Environmental Protection and Water Statistics* (DoE, 1992) on the number of complaints received by environmental health officers in Scotland. However, it would be difficult to estimate costs based on such information. A further complication is that the complaint procedure is different in Scotland in that the police are usually the first point of contact, with the complaint only reaching environmental health officers (EHO) if they have not resolved the problem so the number reaching EHOs will be lower than actual.

Since very little useful data does exist the figures of Jackson and Marks, who assumed a UK cost of £1 billion in 1985 with a 1% annual increase, have been scaled according to the UK and Scottish populations. There is an argument for further scaling these figures to the population densities given its likely connection with the level of noise complaints. However, this has not been done here.

Column Q: Loss of wetlands

Daly and Cobb's original study for the US contained a column on the costs associated with the loss of wetlands. Given that there are a number of other land types that are under threat in Scotland through urbanisation this column has been expanded to include heathland, moorland and peatland areas. For brevity these will still come under the term wetlands throughout this study.

The only time-series data that has been found for Scotland relates to land cover in selected areas of the Cairngorms and the Central Valley (SES, 1991 and 1993). Since these are each examples of highland and lowland Scotland an index of wetland loss has been created from the average of these two data sets (in the regions wetland cover dropped from 854 km² in 1946 to 718 km² in 1988. As an index this is 1.18 in 1946 and 1.00 in 1988). Equating this index to the national wetland cover in 1988, i.e. 39.6% of 78829 km^2 (GS, 1990), suggests wetland cover in 1946 was 36835 km^2; therefore there has been a loss of 13379 ha/yr. It is recognised that there are dangers in applying such an extrapolation to the whole of Scotland.

A sizeable proportion of this loss is attributable to forestry. It is arguable whether in the long-term forestry has any major effect on the functions of wetlands, such as groundwater storage and purification or storm protection (for examples of the argument see Moffat 1988; Binns 1979), particularly if Forestry Commission guidelines have been adhered to. If it does not effect them then the afforested land has not lost any of its economic value (in terms of wetlands) and it is not appropriate to include wetland lost to forestry in this column. This line of argument has been followed here. It does however, in all probability result in a conservative estimate for the costs of the loss of wetlands. In Scotland the loss of wetlands to forestry makes up 96% of the total and reduces the loss to other changes in land use down to 535 ha per year. Each year's cost (@ £2471 ha) has been added to the accumulated 1950 figure of Jackson and Marks (£367million) scaled according to land area.

** *Column R: Loss of farmlands*

Within this column are costs not only relating to loss of farmland to urbanisation but also estimated costs for the loss of productivity resulting from the erosion and deterioration of soil quality that is attributable to farming practices.

Data on the loss of agricultural land to rural development is available for Scotland in *Scottish Abstract of Statistics* (SAS, 1993). To arrive at a cost for their index Jackson and Marks applied a capitalised value of £3700 a hectare. This value is actually higher (approx. £700 at 1992 prices) than agricultural land prices (in England), but Jackson and Marks reason that the higher value reflects increases in productivity that can be gained by the application of fertilisers and energy.

This study has arrived at a cost for land loss in a different manner. Prices more relevant to Scotland have been found in the *Economic Report on Scottish Agriculture* (SOAFD, 1992). These prices, plus 25% to reflect the value of increases in productivity as outlined above, have been applied to the land loss figures (see Table 27).

In estimating the cost of erosion in Scotland the assumptions of Jackson and Marks have been followed. They have taken a low estimate of erosion costs for the UK of £20 million per annum. To arrive at an annual cost estimate for Scotland this figure has been scaled according to the relative Scotland to UK agricultural land area proportions. This has remained constant over the study period at 0.317 (5 858 000 ha in Scotland divided by 18 498 000 ha in the UK in 1991) and results in an annual cost of erosion in Scotland of just over £6 million per year.

Table 27   Costs of loss of farmland (1985 £s), 1980–1991

	Farmland lost (ha)	Price/ha (1985)	Cost of land lost (£m)	Cost of erosion (£m)	Total (£m)
1980	0	3230	0	413	413
1981	979	2854	3	420	423
1982	1494	2606	4	426	430
1983	838	2723	2	432	435
1984	1994	2122	4	439	443
1985	1877	1960	4	445	449
1986	708	1884	1	451	452
1987	1790	1677	3	458	461
1988	2395	2346	6	464	470
1989	2238	2602	6	470	476
1990	2142	3312	7	477	484
1991	1491	3330	5	483	488

To allow for the costs of the accumulated loss of land and erosion up to 1980 the above land area proportions have been applied to Jackson and Marks' 1980 figure of £1284 million to arrive at an estimate of £413 million. To this has been added each year's land loss and erosion costs (see Table 27).

Column S: Depletion of non-renewable resources

In the manner of Cobb and Cobb a cost escalation factor of 3% per annum has been applied to a £37 (1985 price) replacement cost per barrel equivalent (or 65 pence/therm) on the consumption of each of the non-renewable energy resources, coal, oil, gas and nuclear. This replacement cost is effectively an amount of rent from resource production that should be reinvested in a process to create a perpetual stream of output of a renewable substitute for the non-renewable resource being depleted. The 3% escalation factor has been built in to take account of the increasing costs of supplying each marginal unit of energy.

Data on primary fuel consumption has been found in *Scottish Economics Bulletin* (SEB, 1993). Scotland is in a fortunate position in that a sizeable proportion of its electricity consumption has been satisfied by hydropower, a renewable resource, and as such has been excluded from these estimates.

Column T: Costs of long-term environmental damage

This column is included to take some account of the future damage costs, principally arising from increasing levels of greenhouse gases in the atmosphere, resulting from emissions from energy consumption. On the grounds that it is better to include something rather than "ignore the problem for lack of an acceptable methodology", Daly and Cobb have applied an arbitrarily selected damage cost of $0.50 (1972 prices) per barrel of oil equivalent consumed. They have accumulated these costs reflecting the fact that most greenhouse gases have long atmospheric residence times and so will continue to contribute to environmental damage long after they have been emitted.

The same procedure has been applied here using a damage cost of 1.5 pence per therm (in 1985 prices, and which equates to $0.50 per barrel or £3.73 per tonne of coal equivalent) on data back to 1950 (SAS, various years). An accumulated cost up to 1950 has been taken from Jackson and Marks and scaled according to Scotland and UK GDP ratios. The ratio of GDP has been used since it is an approximate measure of economic activity which in turn is an approximation to fuel consumption.

Column U: Costs of ozone depletion

This is a new column added in the revised study by Cobb and Cobb and is included following scientific findings that ozone depletion is the result of the release of CFCs into the atmosphere. Their argument for using CFC production rather than emission figures is that damage from CFCs sold overseas should also be included in the index. After all, the index should reflect all environmental damage incurred as a result of economic activity, whether or not that damage occurs outside the country. To use CFC production figures for Scotland however, would not be helpful since none is made there. It would appear appropriate, therefore, to use consumption figures instead.

There is a problem though with using consumption figures. Because these CFCs are consumed does not necessarily mean that they have been released into the atmosphere. Considerable efforts are now being made to avoid their destructive release and there could be long time lags between consumption and release. It does however seem likely that most, if not all, of these gases will eventually make their way into the atmosphere.

In view of these considerations the CFC production figures from Jackson and Marks have been used in this study and scaled according to the ratio of Scotland and UK GDPs. An advantage of using these estimates is they take account of the lesser known CFCs, CFC–113, CFC–114 and CFC–115, in addition to the main ones, CFC–11 and CFC–12, thus reflecting the recent switch of production away from the latter.

Column V: Net capital growth

The growth in net capital stock has been calculated by Jackson and Marks *via* changes in the replacement cost of net capital stock and making an allowance

Table 28   An estimate of net capital growth in 1991

Year a	Labour force (000s) b	Change in labour (%) c	Rolling average (%) d	Net stock of fixed capital (£m) e	Rolling average of net stock f	Change in rolling average $f-f_{t-1}$ g	Capital required for labour (£m) $d \times f_{t-1}$ h	Net capital growth (£m) (g–h) i
1985	27 980							
1986	28 087	0.382		785.5				
1987	28 287	0.712		821.2				
1988	28 507	0.777		870.0				
1989	28 690	0.641		912.3				
1990	28 758	0.237	0.550	927.9	863.4			
1991	·28 547	–0.754	0.327	897.6	885.8	22.4	2.8	19.6

for changes in the workforce. Again the relevant information is not calculated at the Scottish level, so the only way to get an estimate would be by scaling the UK figures. The problem is deciding the most representative means by which to do it. If, for example, population was used at say 8% it does not follow that 8% of the capital growth applies to Scotland. On the grounds that this element is a positive contributor to the index the Jackson and Marks figure has been scaled according to the sizes of the workforce. An estimate for 1991, using the methodology of Jackson and Marks and its calculation is shown in Table 28.

Column W: Net change in international position

The net change in international position measures the amount a country invests overseas minus the amount invested by foreigners in that country. This is a difficult variable to quantify given Scotland's position within the UK. Enquiries to the Scottish Office confirm that no data on overseas investment exists at the Scotland level.

The nearest this study has come to obtaining full estimates for inward investment are figures for investments in manufacturing industries by overseas enterprises found in *Scottish Abstract of Statistics* (SAS, 1993). However, in the absence of any outward investment figures these estimates have not been used and this column has been set to zero.

Column X: Index of sustainable economic welfare (ISEW)

The Index of Sustainable Economic Welfare (ISEW) is the sum of the previous columns each of which have been marked by a + or – sign to indicate their positive or negative contribution.

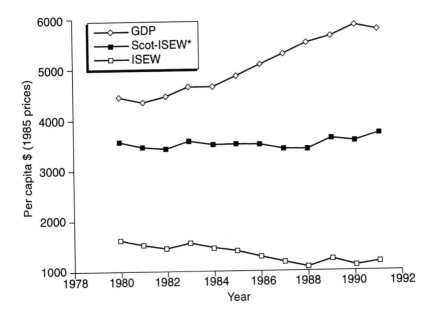

Figure 11   An ISEW for Scotland, 1980–1991

Column Y: Per capita index of sustainable economic welfare

The ISEW sum in column X has been divided by the population each year to produce *per capita* figures. By providing a *per capita* ISEW a more meaningful comparison can be made with results from other studies. Further discussion on such comparisons can be found elsewhere in this chapter. Estimates of Scotland's population have been taken from *Population Trends* (PT, various years).

Column Z: Gross domestic product

It has not been possible to find Scotland's GNP since the country's net property income from abroad is not calculated (this would be deducted from GDP to give GNP). Scotland's Gross Domestic Product (GDP), at current prices, has been taken from *Economic Trends* (ET, various years). These figures were translated to 1985 prices by applying the implied GDP deflator for the UK, also published in *Economic Trends*. It has not been possible to find an equivalent deflator for Scotland.

Column AA: Per capita gross domestic product

The GDP figures in column Z have been divided by the same population estimates used for column Y.

The results of this study give the ISEW *per capita* for Scotland (Figure 11, hereafter results called Scot–ISEW for 1980–1991) which is made up from data found for all the variables described in Cobb and Cobb's methodology. Table 22 shows the contribution each indicator makes to the index (for further details see Wilson, 1994)

Comparing these results with the UK index of Jackson and Marks also shows a great deal of similarity for overlapping time periods. For the period 1980-90 per capita UK-ISEW dropped from £1831 to £1136 (38%) compared to a drop from £1643 to £1075 (35%) in Scotland. UK GNP rose by 27% as opposed to a 30% rise (in GDP) in Scotland.

Sensitivity analysis and discussion

There exists a high level of correlation between the final ISEW figure and some of the contributing variables in both the US and Scottish studies (see Table 29). Of particular interest is the correlation with GNP/GDP, for the US study at 0.926 and for Scotland at –0.949 (using Pearson coefficients). It is perhaps revealing that such a strong negative correlation exists for Scotland, that as GDP increases so our social and economic welfare decreases. Whilst it should be emphasised that this is only over a short period of eleven years, it does suggest that there is no need to collect data for all the indicators, as the index could be simply expressed as a function of GDP! The curve so derived is shown in Figure 12.

It would be dangerous to draw too many conclusions from the correlation coefficients for Scotland because of the limited number of years that have been surveyed. The variable with the highest (negative) coefficient is in fact the distributional inequality multiplier applied to consumer expenditure. The index of distributional inequality is a UK figure (since the equivalent for Scotland does not exist) that changed very little up to the early 1980s and then increased quite rapidly. It suggests that if this study had been extended back beyond 1980 (and assuming the curve of Scot–ISEW was similar to the UK), such a high correlation would no longer exist. Disregarding this anomaly, however, the idea that the level of sustainable economic welfare is linked to the degree of income inequality, may appeal to many people insofar as policies can be directed towards reducing the inequality in income distribution (i.e. imposing socially-just policies) and thereby increase overall sustainable economic welfare. The line of regression in Figure 13 illustrates this linkage.

Looking at the correlations for the US index there are eleven variables with coefficients greater than 0.9, with the highest being the cost of water pollution at 0.99. Using this variable as our simplification produces a regression line as shown in Figure 14 (based on the equation $61.5 \times$ cost of water pollution $- 131.7$).

To make inferences on social and economic welfare based on one indicator could of course be highly dangerous and smacks of environmental determinism.

Table 29 Correlation coefficients for US and Scottish ISEW

	US–ISEW	Scot–ISEW
Distributional inequality	–0.107	–0.973
Weighted consumer expenditure	0.962	0.143
Household labour	0.928	–0.850
Consumer durables (service)	0.878	
Streets and highways	0.977	
Health and education (spend)	0.929	–0.836
Consumer durables (spend)	0.865	–0.945
Health and education (defensive)	0.937	–0.970
Advertising	0.855	
Commuting	0.886	–0.841
Personal pollution		–0.794
Urbanisation	0.846	
Auto accidents	0.946	–0.789
Water pollution	0.990	0.924
Air pollution	0.054	–0.283
Noise pollution	0.974	–0.925
Loss of wetlands	0.976	–0.940
Loss of farmlands	0.937	–0.940
Depletion of non-renewables	0.750	–0.900
Long-term damage	0.909	–0.938
Ozone depletion		–0.927
Net growth	0.079	–0.549
International position	–0.235	
GNP/GDP	0.926	–0.949

Hence, the next step is to attempt to find four or five variables that adequately reflect the result and do not distort it too much as each changes. A stepwise regression analysis on the Scottish data has identified four variables that approximate to Scot–ISEW (with $r^2 = 0.991$): distributional inequality, net capital growth, weighted consumer expenditure, and defensive expenditure on health and education. The regression line is illustrated in Figure 15 and shows a very good approximation to Scot–ISEW.

In terms of the US study a four variable regression (with $r^2 = 0.996$) can be best achieved from: the cost of water pollution; weighted consumer expenditure; services from streets and highways; and expenditure on consumer durables illustrated in Figure 16. Clearly, different indicators contribute to the Scotland and US simplified ISEW curves. Weighted consumer expenditure, however, does appear in both, which is to be expected since it forms the basis for the index and makes the major contribution to the results.

Whenever data for a large number of variables are gathered together in a manner such as this it is always possible that there exist inter-relationships

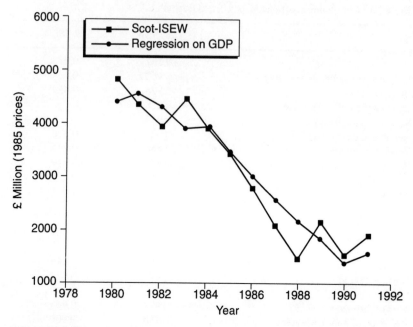

Figure 12 An estimation of Scot–ISEW derived from a regression of GDP, 1980–1991

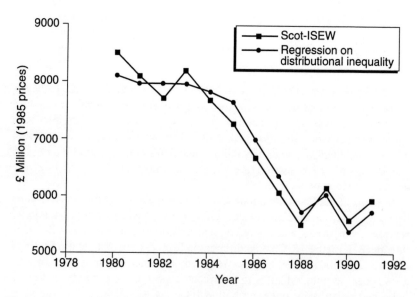

Figure 13 Scot–ISEW derived from the regression of distribution of inequality, 1980–1991

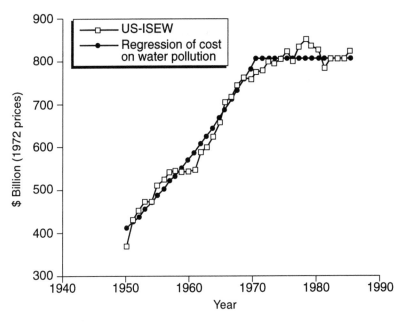

Figure 14   Simplified US–ISEW derived from regression of cost of water pollution, 1950–1986

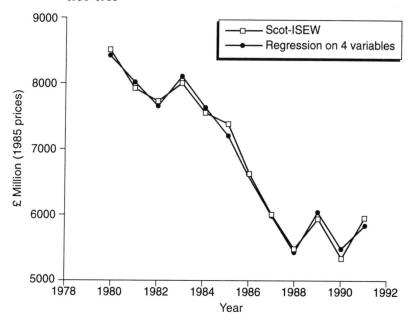

Figure 15   Scot–ISEW derived from a regression of cost of four indicators, 1980–1991

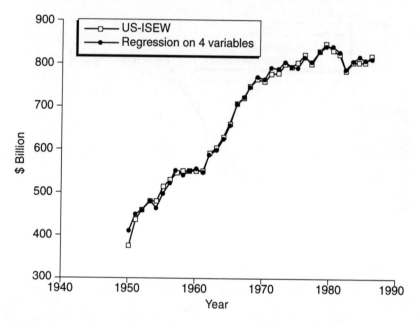

Figure 16   US–ISEW derived from a regression of four indicators, 1950–1986

between some of the variables, that a 'cluster' of inter-related variables could be represented by just one variable or factor. The possibility of such inter-relationships existing has been examined for both the US and Scottish data using principal component analysis. The results, however, are not conclusive and further analysis by other methods has not been carried out. (For details see Wilson, 1994).

A further consideration when deriving an index such as this is that it is highly likely that there will exist one or two indicators that will have a significant impact on the overall result. Consequently it is vital that these variables are accurate and that any assumptions made during their calculation stand up to scrutiny. In addition, the vast difference between GDP and Scot–ISEW also suggests that a closer inspection of the contribution each indicator makes to the index is warranted.

As already outlined, the variable making the largest positive contribution to Scot–ISEW is weighted consumer expenditure which itself is sensitive to changes in the index of distributional inequality (since consumer expenditure is divided by distributional inequality). In fact the effect this multiplier has on the overall index can be seen graphically in Figure 17, which compares *per capita* Scot–ISEW derived with a weighted and unweighted consumer expenditure. Taking out the effect of income inequality turns the graph from a falling to a rising

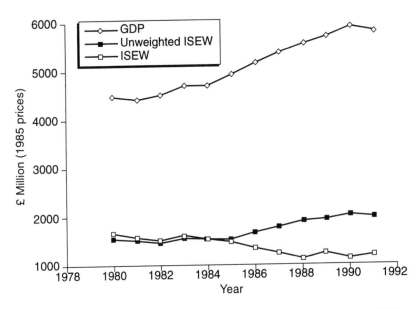

Figure 17 Scot–ISEW with weighted and unweighted consumer expenditure, 1980–1991

curve. Until 1985 however, it has had very little effect with both curves almost matching. Overall, the unweighted Scot–ISEW has risen 24% over the period 1980–91, a considerable difference to the 30% fall with the effects of distributional inequality included. Viewed another way, the unweighted Scot–ISEW in 1991 is 68.6% higher than the weighted Scot–ISEW. Clearly the Scot–ISEW index is sensitive to changes in the index of distributional inequality. It should be noted though that the unweighted curve is still considerably different to the GDP curve.

There are three other variables that make a positive contribution to Scot–ISEW, household labour, expenditure on health and education, and net capital growth. The contribution of the latter two is minimal but household labour makes a sizeable contribution, being around half of weighted consumer expenditure (see column D of Table 22). The assumptions made in the calculation of services from household labour could clearly have some effect on the index. It will be recalled that this indicator was derived by scaling (by population) the UK estimate of Jackson and Marks who themselves made assumptions about the shadow wage rate in deriving their figures. It follows that the index could be sensitive to assumptions made on shadow wage rates (it would obviously be helpful if these could be found at the Scottish rather than UK level). Returning to the positive contributors to the index it is perhaps significant that only one of these positive contributors rises at or above the rate of increase of GDP and that is a variable with a relatively small contribution: health and education spending.

Of the indicators that make a negative contribution to Scot–ISEW by far the largest are long-term environmental damage and depletion of non-renewable resources. Given the concern already expressed about the assumptions used in their calculation, an index has already been created without them in Scot–ISEW*. This and the original Scot–ISEW graph illustrate the sensitivity of the index to these variables. Since the slope of the curve is unaltered there is little sensitivity if ISEW is to be used as an *index*, but as there is a large gap between the curves then ISEW *is* sensitive to these indicators if it is to be used as a *measure*.

Overall then, there are several indicators to which Scotland's index of sustainable economic welfare is particularly sensitive. These are distributional inequality, consumer expenditure, services from household labour, depletion of non-renewable resources and long-term environmental damage. The reliability of the index will rely to a large extent on the accuracy of the data used in these indicators.

A major objective of an index such as this is that it should provide a solid basis for decision-making at all levels. The index should be able to highlight areas in which sustainable development objectives are not being met, allowing for the development of compensating environmental management policies. A measure of the suitability of ISEW for Scotland will be the number of such areas for policy development that can be identified from the results of this study.

A look at Table 22 reveals that there are in fact several possible areas for policy development. The first relates to distributional inequality. Factors such as income tax changes in the mid 1980s and rising unemployment raised the index of distributional inequality and this has, as already described, had a profound effect on ISEW. The identification of actual policies that will rectify the problems found here is beyond the scope of this study. Clearly, the policies required to reduce income inequality are related to the factors that caused its increase in the first place: unemployment and income tax.

Key areas for policy development are within indicators that are making increasing negative contributions to the index. The three largest are: depletion of non-renewable resources; long-term environmental damage; and ozone depletion costs. Clearly there are huge benefits to be gained by reducing these influences. Equally, there will also be benefits to be gained if policies can be directed at increasing the effects of the positive contributors to the index. The results suggest that this should be targeted at health and education spending and net capital growth.

CONCLUSION

The creation of any measure of sustainable development has problems. The ISEW measure proposed by Daly and Cobb (1989) and later revised by Cobb and Cobb (1993) probably comes closest to fulfilling the objectives of contributing to policies to promoting sustainable development. The index proposed by Zolotas (1981) does not consider sustainability whereas that proposed by Nordhaus and Tobin (1973) does not consider environmental issues that have become increasingly important in the years since they published their work. The work (NNP) by leading Japanese economists that followed the ideas of Nordhaus and Tobin did take environmental issues into consideration but did not make any allowance for non-monetary activities such as household labour or leisure.

In applying the index of sustainable economic welfare to Scotland several problems have been encountered. The biggest relates to data availability; estimates for too many of the indicators (seven) have had to be found by scaling the UK estimates of Jackson and Marks. This is unsatisfactory, however plausible the assumptions made during scaling. If the government is serious about achieving the objectives laid out at the *Earth Summit* and as outlined in the UK Sustainable Development Strategy (Anon., 1994) then it is vital that the means by which the relevant economic and environmental data can be recorded must be put in place as soon as possible.

Results for Scotland indicate a widening gap between the measure of sustainability and the more usual measure of economic development, GDP. It is perhaps significant that of the indicators that make a positive contribution to the Scottish index only one actually rises as fast as GDP during the study period 1980–1991. This is spending on health and education which only makes a small contribution to the index. All the negative influences on the index have increased with the exception of the cost of water pollution that has dropped slightly, perhaps reflecting River Purification Boards efforts in targeting their water quality improvements at the most polluted rivers.

The Scottish index is particularly sensitive to changes in some of the indicators. These have been identified as distributional inequality, household labour, long-term environmental damage and depletion of non-renewable resources. Some indicators have been identified from the results as areas in which policy developments should be directed. These are distributional inequality, net capital growth, long-term environmental damage, depletion of non-renewable resources and ozone depletion. A problem however is that even if policies were put in place to stop further increases in costs for the last three listed indicators (which is not likely anyway), they would still exert a strong influence in years to come because of their cumulative nature. Given the influence some of the indicators have on the index it is important that the final index is not considered in isolation. The full results should also be viewed, i.e. Table 22, with an eye to identifying areas for policy development. It should be recognised though that in this case it has proved difficult to identify areas for policy changes from a study limited to an eleven-year period. Ideally the

Table 30   Additional ISEW data for Scotland

Year	Population Scotland	Population UK	Household labour, UK	NHS spending	Higher Education spending	Personal pollution control J + M, UK	Non-injury accident	Cost of non-injury accident
			1985	r	r		r	
1980	5153	55 945	80 005	1329	139.0	953	174 304	410
1981	5180	56 352	83 238	1494	157.5	1051	171 880	452
1982	5167	56 306	83 931	1623	167.2	1183	166 800	494
1983	5150	56 347	90 943	1727	187.0	1412	155 472	536
1984	5146	56 460	90 439	1851	197.0	1544	159 792	578
1985	5137	56 618	91 851	1964	196.6	1675	165 152	620
1986	5121	56 763	96 012	2082	196.3	1807	158 544	682
1987	5112	56 930	94 489	2274	255.0	1511	149 256	744
1988	5094	57 065	96 373	2509	271.9	1642	152 760	806
1989	5091	57 236	99 031	2728	288.8	1807	164 864	868
1990	5102	57 411	10 0753	2983	278.3	1971	161 336	930
1991	5107	57 801		3624	282.3	2048	152 072	960

Year	J + M columns l–F	Car 0.35	Rail 0.56	Bus 0.39	Weekly expenditure	Cost of communi- cations	Water pollution index	Re-based to 1972 0.69	Ozone depletion UK
	1985				r	r			1985
1980	22152	6.06	0.47	1.71	111.56	325	1.054	0.726	31 740
1981	21865	7.91	0.46	1.74	125.54	390	1.053	0.725	33 486
1982	23387	8.89	0.57	1.71	131.19	455	1.051	0.724	35 127
1983	27643	8.45	0.61	1.67	136.64	468	1.050	0.723	36 897
1984	27491	9.20	0.60	1.61	152.47	483	1.048	0.722	38 797
1985	29607	9.26	0.64	1.66	158.80	505	1.047	0.721	40 721
1986	34231	9.16	0.60	1.90	161.80	536	1.043	0.719	42 769
1987	36074	10.34	0.63	1.80	172.78	593	1.040	0.717	44 976
1988	42602	11.23	0.50	1.87	196.27	624	1.037	0.714	47 157
1989	43475	12.27	0.79	1.87	210.69	686	1.034	0.712	49 023
1990	41184	13.60	0.62	1.74	219.56	754	1.031	0.710	50 292
1991	41184	14.52	0.79	1.67	226.79	808	1.027.	0.708	52 515

study should be extended, perhaps back to 1950, to allow better comparison with US and UK studies.

Included here is data used in the ISEW index that has not been published elsewhere. It has been included for completeness and should allow the reader to find where and how the results in Table 22 were derived (see also Table 30).

Table 30 continued

Year	Inflation	Farmland lost (ha)	Real price/ha	Price/ha in 1985	Value of land lost	Cost of erosion	Total farmland lost	UK consumer spending
				1985	1985	1985	1985	1985
1980	0.717	0	1853	3230	0	413	413	195 825
1981	0.798	979	1822	2854	3	420	422	196 011
1982	0.859	1494	1791	2606	4	426	430	197 980
1983	0.904	838	1969	2723	2	432	435	206 932
1984	0.946	1995	1606	2122	4	439	443	210 959
1985	1.000	1877	1568	1960	4	445	449	218 947
1986	1.035	708	1560	1884	1	451	453	232 996
1987	1.086	1790	1457	1677	3	458	461	245 823
1988	1.158	2395	2173	2346	6	464	470	264 096
1989	1.240	2238	2581	2602	6	470	476	272 917
1990	1.317	2142	3489	3312	7	477	484	274 744
1991	1.403	1491	3738	3330	5	483	488	269 218

Year	GDP UK	Energy consumption Mtherm 0.62	Wetland loss	Noise cost UK	Air pollution UK	Net growth UK	Workforce Scotland	Workforce UK
	r			1985	1985	1985		
1980	23 1772	7443	1	951	18 048	5512	2439	26 748
1981	25 4927	7134	1	961	17 312	2251	2421	26 603
1982	27 9041	6869	1	970	17 052	−2536	2416	26 609
1983	30 4456	6770	1	980	16 550	−7795	2403	26 792
1984	32 5852	6651	1	990	16 328	−14 673	2433	27 459
1985	35 7344	6998	1	1000	16 750	−10 934	2470	27 980
1986	38 4843	7138	1	1010	17 325	−4772	2468	28 087
1987	42 3381	6990	1	1020	17 649	−271	2454	28 287
1988	47 1430	7312	1	1031	17 918	4600	2466	28 507
1989	51 5957	7431	1	1041	18 217	10 163	2480	28 690
1990	55 1118	7459	1	1052	18 121	13 764	2470	28 758
1991	57 3645	7663	1	1063	18 157	19 600	2513	28 547

Up to now all major policy changes have been geared to the increase of GDP regardless of the issue of sustainability or the growing gap between rich and poor. It is to be hoped that the creation around the world of indices like ISEW will help identify some of the problem areas and may in turn lead to the development of policies that will improve people's social and economic welfare. Despite the methodology and data problems associated with the development of any index of sustainable development it has been demonstrated that an index can be created for Scotland. If such indices can be created for Scotland on limited resources then there can be few excuses if central government cannot achieve the objectives outlined in chapter 40 of *Agenda 21*, i.e. the creation of, and promotion of global use of, indicators of sustainable development.

CHAPTER 7

INDICATORS OF SUSTAINABLE DEVELOPMENT: SOME LESSONS FROM SCOTLAND

INTRODUCTION

The previous three chapters have examined the economic, ecological and socio-political indicators for sustainable development at a variety of spatial and temporal scales. The Scottish case study has demonstrated that there are problems in both collecting the relevant data for some of these indicators and in using an indicator or set of indicators for attempting to monitor current and future human activities so that they can be managed in an essentially sustainable manner. This chapter draws together some of the threads of our argument to present a set of indicators of sustainable development for Scotland and it is suggested that these findings may be applicable elsewhere.

In the following section the results of the Scottish case-study are presented. This includes an appraisal of the economic, ecological and socio-political measures of sustainable development. Next, some of the problems in classifying the indicators of sustainable development are presented. In particular it acknowledges the self-evident fact that an indicator of sustainable development for say an industrial urban area may be addressing different problems than those associated with upland rural activities. This classification is hierarchical and recognises the variety and diversity of the Scottish environment. Finally, we speculate on the ways in which such a set of indicators can be efficiently organised in a hierarchical manner to help promote sustainable development at the national and community scale in Scotland.

RESULTS FROM SCOTLAND AND AN APPRAISAL

The results of the Scottish case-study are given in Table 31. First, the economic measures indicate that the AEANNP for Scotland as a whole is sustainable. Paradoxically, when the 'weak' economic measure of sustainable development (PAM) is used for Scotland the use of this economic indicator shows that Scotland is not sustainable. The differences between these two diametrically opposed patterns clearly call for further detailed research.

Next, the ecological measures using NPP and K indicate that Scotland is very close to its carrying capacity. This result is based on the absolute use of

129

Table 31 Is Scotland sustainable?

Indicator	Measure	Sustainable	Marginal	Unsustainable
AEANNP	£millions	Yes	–	No
PAM	£millions	No	–	Yes
NNP/K	kcal/capita	–	Yes	–
EF/ACC	ha/capita	No	–	Yes
ISEW	£millions	–	Yes	–

organic resources as a proxy for using 25% of the primary land-based ecological food chains per year. When the alternative ecological measure, namely the ecological footprint and appropriated carrying capacity (EF/ACC), is used then it is clear that Scotland, with its present patterns of energy and food consumption, is unsustainable. It should, of course, be noted that these two ecological measures add further support to the argument that Scotland is unsustainable if current patterns of resource use continue. This tentative conclusion is further reinforced by the use of the ISEW, based on Scottish data, for the period 1984–1990. The pattern suggests that economic welfare has declined during this period – but the actual shape of the curve is not declining as rapidly as in the case of the USA (Daly and Cobb, 1989) or as in the case of England and Wales (Jackson and Marks, 1994).

The economic, ecological and socio-political indicators described in the previous chapters are measuring different aspects of the 'real world' and it may be tempting to see if a classification of them is useful. From the ecological study using NPP and *K* it has been shown that Scotland is very near its carrying capacity. It should be noted that these simple calculations avoid reference to imports and fossil fuel energy subsidies. Using the EF/ACC concept it is clear that many people in Scotland, like many other technologically advanced countries, are living well, but also well beyond their means of ecological support. To ensure that future generations can have a life at least as good as their parents would imply that we must cut back on the amount of energy and goods that we consume. This would imply a more efficient use of resources and the implementation of a careful conservation strategy throughout Scotland, and by implication any other country.

When neo-classical economic analyses are employed using the AEANNP, for example, the pattern of resource use is observed to be growing in Scotland. Even when suitable measures of environmental protection are taken into account there is still an upward trend in the use of resources. Whilst this may reassure some economists the question of how long this can continue can be raised.

There are, however, some problems concerning the use of AENP (and by implication our cruder AEANNP). Jacobs (1991), for example, has made a damning critique of the adjusted environmental net national product AENP measure. He notes that if environmental degradation is likely to get worse then this will be reflected by a growing divergence between GNP and environmentally adjusted environmental NNP. More important, however, is the observation that "sustainable income itself can grow *even if degradation increases*. This will occur if in any year growth of GNP is greater than growth of depreciation, that is, if the 'environmental efficiency' of GNP is rising, but not by enough actually to cause environmental improvement" (Jacobs, 1991, italics in the original). To illustrate his argument Jacobs describes a situation where GNP grows at 5% per annum and depreciation of human capital remains constant at 10% of GNP. Environmental degradation starts at 10% of GNP and gets worse at a rate of 2% per year.

He wrote that "the problem here is that sustainable income takes environmental degradation into account only after it has measured GNP. It is therefore at least as influenced by changes in GNP as it is by changes in environmental quality: if the former are larger, they will have a bigger impact on it. Sustainable income is thus not an environmental indicator: its movement does not show environmental quality to be improving or declining. Even less is it a measure of sustainability, since an economy can be unsustainable – *and moving away from sustainability* – even while AENP rises . . . If we wish to measure environmental performance or sustainability, however, we shall have to look elsewhere" (Jacobs, 1991).

Obviously, if Jacobs' critique of AENP is valid, then we are forced to look elsewhere for a measure of sustainability. Perhaps one of the best candidates for an economic measure of sustainability is Pearce and Atkinson's 'weak' sustainability measure (Pearce and Atkinson, 1993; Pearce, 1993). The case study of the UK has shown that the UK is marginally sustainable using the weak measure. Certainly, the use of Pearce's 'weak' measure of sustainability shows that Scotland's economy is unsustainable – but it should be appreciated that many of these measures are very sensitive to the use of non-renewable resource data and to import and export data. Further, research into the sensitivity of these calculations on a firmer factual base is required.

The ISEW developed for Scotland differs slightly from the pioneering USA study. Nevertheless, the results show that the pattern of the ISEW has declined less steeply than that of either USA or England and Wales. The analysis, using simplified data obtained by means of sensitivity tests using linear regression, revealed no common predictor of the ISEW pattern in the USA, England and Wales or Scottish data. Clearly, the results show that the ISEW is merely an *ad hoc* adjustment of GNP. Whilst the ISEW might be more useful than GNP as a measure of sustainable development there is a need to develop a firm theoretical basis for this measure if it is to be useful for measuring whether or not a path of development is sustainable.

The overall results of all three studies reveal a conflicting pattern. The AEANNP for Scotland has shown an increase during the period (1981–1991) and this result runs counter to both the NPP/K of sustainable development and the EF/ACC measure which suggest that Scotland is not on a sustainable trajectory. The AEANNP measure contradicts the PAM measure, but if Jacobs' critique of AENP is applicable then the 'weak' measure also shows that Scotland is not on a sustainable trajectory; or at best, one which is marginally sustainable.

It is clear that there is no theoretical basis for the economic and socio-political measures used as indicators of sustainable development. In these instances the measures are merely *ad hoc* adjustments to GNP. Some economists may take solace from this finding but does GNP have a robust theoretical basis or is it just a socially accepted measure of economic activity? Clearly, the task of devising suitable economic and socio-political measures of sustainable development must continue. It would be useful if these new measures, if and when they are devised, are based on a sound theoretical base rather than being merely *ad hoc* alterations to GNP or other empirically derived measures.

SOME PROBLEMS INVOLVED IN DEVELOPING SUSTAINABLE DEVELOPMENT INDICATORS

Chapters 4 through to 6 have described and adopted several specific indicators of sustainable development. It should now be clear that at present no universal agreement on a specific sustainable development index has been made. For some this finding is comforting, as Miles (1985) notes, "Insurmountable difficulties are posed by the search for a single composite measure of welfare or quality of life. Perhaps we should be glad that human life remains too rich to be represented in one-dimensional terms" (Miles, 1985 quoted in Ekins, 1990). For others, however, the lack of a single composite index or useful set of indices poses great difficulties in attempting to monitor whether or not a particular trajectory of an environmental system is on a course of sustainable development or not. Clearly, the lack of suitable indicator(s) of sustainable development would place decision-makers, scientists and the concerned citizen in a quandary of indecision. It is, therefore, useful to examine some of the problems involved in developing indicators of sustainable development.

The use of various economic, ecological and socio-political indicators is a first step towards developing ecologically useful indicators of sustainable development. There are, however, various problems associated with the indicators currently used. These problems can be described as crude empiricism, incommensurate measures, the weighting problem and critical thresholds. The problems associated with each of these are discussed below.

Obviously, for detailed scientific research and monitoring of the environment it is essential that we have quantitative as well as qualitative estimates of environmental quality. In several publications some measures of atmospheric pollution have been presented (GSS, various years). These measures can give an indication of the temporal trend in say, air quality, but need to be combined spatially to illustrate the geographical variation across the country. Equally important, however, is the fact that these measures of individual pollutants do not really inform us of the possibility of ecological systems crossing critical thresholds and hence preventing former ecological activities from being sustained. The determination of critical loads is very difficult and is currently being examined as part of the on-going debate into evolutionary ecology and environmental stress (Calow and Berry, 1989).

Whilst there have been major advances in collecting data on a consistent basis across the UK, as witnessed for example in the 1990 Countryside Survey (DoE, 1990), it is clear that more high quality environmental and ecological data is required for comparative studies. Even if all this data were collected, collated as a set of large relational data bases, and freely available for both research and public consultation, there is still the difficult problem of weighting the various measures. The use of weighting of environmental or other measures is to acknowledge their relative importance. Three different methods of weighting can be identified in the literature namely expert opinion, public opinion and use of numerical scaling.

The use of expert opinion to weigh the importance of one variable against another is questionable as it lays the whole operation of 'expert opinion' open to the charge that it is not objective. Also there are the problems of identifying the expert and acknowledging the fact that expert opinion changes. These problems bedevil aspects of the creation of empirically verifiable expert systems for environmental management (Moffatt, 1990). As an alternative to expert weighting some researchers have advocated the use of public opinion as a way of subjectively weighing up the importance of environmental and other measures (Hope *et al.*, 1992). This is also a suspect method of weighing up the relative importance of environmental or other indicators. The public may be ignorant of important environmental indicators; public opinion is very fickle and may reflect the importance of mass media coverage rather than the intrinsic importance of the problem under scrutiny. Even more damning is the fact that public subjective perception of environmental quality may not be related to objective environmental conditions. Wall (1974), for example, notes that in a study of air pollution in Sheffield the inhabitants did not regard it as a serious problem, placing it low on their order of priorities; this conclusion was in a city which, at that time, had one of the highest levels of sulfur dioxide pollution in England (Moffatt, 1984b). A useful method of developing weighted indexes is to use the raw data for each measure to ascertain the maximum and minimum values to represent the range of observations. The range is then ranked on a scale from 0 (good quality) to 100 (bad quality) for each of the various environmental indicators. It is important to stress that the original data must be retained in the data base as ranked data is a very crude form of measurement. It should also be noted that economic aggregation procedures use weightings based on the revealed preferences of individuals, and are subject to the "lack of information" criticism raised above.

The idea that critical thresholds are present in most ecological systems is taken as axiomatic. Nevertheless, if a critical threshold is breached then ecological damage may not be irreversible. In some cases, such as eutrophication in a loch, an increase in precipitation and through flow may help the loch to revert to its pre-eutrophic state. Undoubtedly, fish kills and loss of genetic diversity at this specific site may arise. If rare or unique species are located in this loch alone then this may result in extinction of that species. In many other cases, however, this event is unlikely to arise and careful monitoring of the ecological systems could give early warning of the onset of changes in the environmental system before a specific critical threshold is reached. In some cases, such as the acidification of Scottish lochs and Swedish lakes, a quick fix by liming has been adopted. It is now clear that this quick fix approach is not suitable and can often cause more serious damage to the ecosystem it was meant to repair (Roberts, 1994). In particular, the application of certain chemicals such as lime or, in the past DDT, have been likened to a biological time bomb (Stigilani and Salomons, 1993). After a period of the ecological fuse smouldering away undetected the release of say, heavy metals from surrounding soils in the catchment can occur suddenly and unexpectedly. More important, however, is the possibility of irreversible changes occurring due to critical thresholds being breached. Clearly, more research is required into the critical thresholds of acidification in Scottish lochs and other biological and environmental 'time bombs' before we can ensure that management strategies are able to prevent an irreversible environmental catastrophe from occurring.

From the literature several economic, ecological and socio-political indicators of sustainable development have been noted. These indicators are all attempting to provide useful information to indicate whether or not a country is sustainable. At present all the indicators used in the study suffer from problems of empiricism, incommensurability, weighting, and critical thresholds. On balance the results indicate that Scotland is, at best, marginally sustainable; and two out of the five measures indicate that Scotland's economy and ecology is unsustainable. It should be stressed that these results are tentative and further detailed research is required. At present, however, these tentative results should not be a reason for complacency nor one of over reaction. Nevertheless, if an area or a nation is not sustainable then obviously policies would have to be introduced to ensure, as far as possible, that the action could be moved on to an ecologically sound, socially just, and economically viable future path.

CONCLUSION

Obviously, the results presented in the Scottish case-study are tentative. The methods employed may be reworked with better quality data. Nevertheless, the

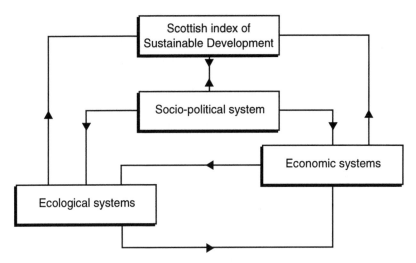

Figure 18   Toward an index of sustainable development

preliminary results indicate that from an economic, ecological and socio-political perspective there is a need to implement a clear set of sustainable development policies as soon as possible; any delay will make it even more difficult for policies to succeed.

It is therefore tempting to speculate on the possibility of developing a Scottish Index of Sustainable Development (SISD) based on some form of integration of the indices used in the three case studies. This new index would probably be hierarchical to show the importance of ecology, economy and socio-political welfare for people and their environment in Scotland. The base of the hierarchy would be represented by NPP as a basis for the continuance of life in Scotland; the economic indicator would show how far the economic activity is depleting or adding to the stock of natural capital; and the ISEW would act as an indicator to show the way in which the economy and ecology are contributing together in promoting sustainable development for human welfare in Scotland (Figure 18). This SISD could act like a barometer to show the pressures on the Scottish environment, economy and the welfare of local communities and act as an indicator for policy makers and other interested people.

Clearly, separate indicators of economic, ecological and socio-political welfare are required as a guide to achieve sustainable development. Equally, clear is the need to put these indicators into a lexical order with the most basic being the base ecological measures. Without conserving and protecting natural capital and the functioning of ecosystems then other higher order needs (Maslow, 1968) such as economic provision and economic welfare, cannot be provided for in a sustainable way. Next, given a sound functioning ecosphere then there is need for efficient economic activities which cut down the amount of waste and the throughput of energy and materials. If the market system is left alone then this is unlikely to achieve either ecological stability or decent social provision for all people. Hence, a third level is required so that the least advantaged people in society do not suffer in the quest for sustainable development.

Three important areas of future research can be suggested. First, there is a need for further detailed theoretical and empirical work examining the ISEW as well as the 'weak' and 'strong' sustainable development in Scotland. Next, there is a need to have more detailed studies to collect the relevant data such as NPP and other ecological data across Scotland. These finer measures would refine the work outlined earlier. Thirdly, there is a need for integrating models of land-use with sustainable development. In particular by interfacing a GIS and suitable process-based models it will be possible to gain a better understanding of our current use of biophysical resources as well as exploring possible scenarios for future paths of sustainable development under enhanced greenhouse warming scenarios. These tasks are still to be undertaken as part of a new research programme and may offer some further answers to the problems. Nevertheless, the tentative results of this study show it is possible to develop some useful indicators which could be applied in strategic environmental management and planning. It is now time to move from this analysis of sustainable development indicators to consider the ways in which we can contribute to policies which could promote sustainable development.

PART THREE

Sustainable development: policy implications

CHAPTER 8

MODELLING SUSTAINABLE DEVELOPMENT

INTRODUCTION

So far the earlier chapters have described the principles and definitions which surround the concept of sustainable development. These chapters were then followed by a series of case-studies attempting to measure sustainable development in terms of indicators. It was shown that in the Scottish case-study some of the indicators were suggesting, at best, that Scotland is marginally sustainable given the current patterns of population growth and consumption. Other indicators demonstrated that Scotland had already exceeded a sustainable level of development. These preliminary results indicate that the ecological systems of Scotland are being put under strain and, if present use continues, they could severely restrict the socio-economic systems surviving and flourishing in a sustainable manner. It is therefore important to try to alter this situation by demonstrating the feasibility of moving any marginally or unsustainable pattern of development onto a sustainable course. One way of demonstrating this possibility is by use of dynamic simulation modelling.

In this chapter we move on to consider the way in which sustainable development can be modelled. By modelling we mean making a simple representation of a system so that the basic causal processes can be made clear and that the simulated output is similar to the observed behaviour of the system. Once a reasonable, empirically verified model is produced then it can be used to explore scenarios of different policies which, if implemented, could illustrate whether or not one scenario is more or less sustainable than the current unsustainable pattern of development.

There are numerous approaches to model building and the basic feature of any approach is to simplify a real world system so that we can understand the way in which it functions. Such understanding, if used wisely, may help us contribute to promoting sustainable development. At present there are very few models which attempt to integrate ecological, social and economic activity in a just manner – which we have argued is a major part of sustainable development. (*cf* Part 1). Perhaps the most promising approach to understanding and managing the transition to a sustainable future is to develop systems-based models using energy to underpin the modelling effort. The methodological problems associated with modelling are described in the following section. This is followed by a discussion of some of the ways in which energy modelling has been used to describe sustainable development. It will be argued that by using a systems approach, with energy as its underpinning, it is possible to develop useful models of sustainable development for examining the ways in which it is possible to move a nation, or an area, onto a sustainable trajectory. The third section provides some examples of this approach from a variety of case studies taken from work in Australia and Scotland. The fourth section then discusses the ways in which energy-based systems models can be interconnected with GIS and expert systems to support further research into and to aid the development of policies, promoting sustainable development globally, nationally and locally.

METHODOLOGICAL PROBLEMS ASSOCIATED WITH MODELLING

There are two obvious ways of enquiring into a possible future, namely to extrapolate current empirical trends or, alternatively, to model the processes so that they mimic the historical path of unsustainable development and then examine various policies which may lead to a trajectory of sustainable development being realised. The extrapolation of current trends is very simple but not without its problems. A time-series of a data set is plotted on a graph and then standard statistical functions, such as linear or non-linear regression, are used to determine the predicted or future path. This extrapolation of data assumes several things. First, the data exists and is important for the time-series to be graphed. Second, and more subtly, it is implied that the future will be a continuation of the past trends. Third, there is the assumption that there is little we can do to alter such a trajectory into the future. Whilst we have to concede the first point it does not follow that we need to accept the second and third restrictions on empirical extrapolation.

In the case of the growth in greenhouse gases, for example, numerous empirical studies have shown the upward trend of CO_2, CFCs, NO_2 and CH_4 (Pearman, 1988). If business as usual continues into an unrestricted future then by 2025 AD the enhanced greenhouse gases would be approximately twice their 1987 level. Clearly, such anthropogenic increases would be unprecedented and would probably increase the earth's mean surface temperature by between 1.2 and 2.5°C (IPCC, 1990). Obviously, linear extrapolation of past trends can lead to an uncomfortable feeling that continuing business as usual is not really sensible. In the case of certain greenhouse gases, such as the CFC family, the international community have agreed *via* the Montreal Protocol to cease production, distribution and release of these gases into the atmosphere. In this specific case empirical research has shown that they damage the stratospheric ozone as well as contributing to global warming. Furthermore, policies to curb the continued growth in the production and distribution of this family of gases have been implemented to reduce emissions to zero, by 1995. Obviously, in the case of other greenhouse gases, such as CO_2 and CH_4, reductions to zero are not possible. Nevertheless, this example illustrates the need to make judgements over whether or not we collectively feel that environmental problems are worth preventing NOW rather than waiting until the problems become so difficult that it locks us onto a tragic trajectory.

An alternative approach to empirical extrapolation of the growth of greenhouse gases is to model the ways in which the gases move through the atmosphere. Several Atmospheric Global Circulation Models (AGCMs) are currently being refined and used to predict the possibility of climatic change due to enhanced greenhouse warming (Moffatt, 1992a). Despite the reservations expressed by some scientists, the accepted scientific view is that a doubling of greenhouse gases could result in a rise in mean global temperature between 1.2 and 2.5°C (IPCC, 1990). Such a change would have important impacts on the geographical distribution of temperature and precipitation. Furthermore, several texts have outlined the likely impact on farming, water supplies, urbanisation and the spread of diseases caused by anthropogenically-generated changes in the global climate (Henderson-Sellers and Blong, 1989).

Whilst AGCMs are very sophisticated we must always remind ourselves that they are just models. The assumptions upon which they are based, the accuracy of data, the numerical values of the parameters and the ways in which the algorithms are used to solve the equations, all affect the output of the model. In addition to the technical problems which surround model building there are also the normative problems associated with the ways of tackling the problem. For example, is the problem important and who says so? Does the choice of state variables and hypothesised relations pre-suppose a specific world view or paradigm? What value judgements underpin the model? Are these value judgements explicit to the model user? Does the model builder realise the values implicit in the model or are we prisoners of a way of seeing? Can the values be made explicit so at least others will know the normative aspects which are incorporated into the structure of the model? Any model is a simplification of reality and it is unlikely that we will ever be able to rely solely on computer simulation models to solve all complex problems associated with climatic change or with the broader topic of sustainable development. Nevertheless, modelling is one way in which we can attempt to understand the ways in which a complex system functions and allows us to explore alternative future scenarios for that modelled system.

These general considerations reside at the heart of any model building effort especially those which are trying to interface ecological–economic models. At least five technical questions also need to be addressed before using models. These are the problem of simplification, boundary problem, the scale problem, the handling of uncertainty, and the ethics of modelling and managing complex systems.

The problem of simplification is paradoxically difficult. Obviously, any model is based on certain simplifications of some aspect of the real world so that the latter may become intelligible. This requires some artistic, creative thought to ensure that the major influences in the model are captured within the structure of the system. Even in relatively simple mathematical models with non-linear feedback loops there are complex dynamics including oscillating behaviour and chaotic dynamics (May, 1976). The former may be predictable (but could be ultimately unsustainable) whilst the latter, by definition, is unpredictable. As all model building requires simplification it is obvious that various real conditions may be excluded by the analyst, unless further detailed research is continued. Such research may lead to a better understanding of the system and would need to be explained clearly to the intelligent layperson and policy-makers.

Closely, associated with simplification is the need to demarcate the boundary between those items incorporated within the system – usually the major state variables – and those parts of the real world (the bulk of it) which reside outside the system of interest. Even when we consider the elements within a model of a system the demarcation lines between one aspect of the system and another may be unclear. When, for example, does nitrate percolating through a soil act like water and when does it act as a chemical agent? More important is the fact that when dealing with broad issues of sustainable development one cannot reduce nature or society to a single process, and this may lead to awkwardly large and unmanageable models, even if all the boundary issues can be resolved.

The question of suitable scales for building models also needs to be addressed. In the case of many ecological and environmental models temporal scales ranging from seconds through to thousands of years are found in the literature. Economic models, however, rarely move beyond a few simulated years, with the exception of economic long-wave models which, by definition, are based on smoothed data representing important aspects of the economy over 70 or even 100 years. Furthermore, some scientists have argued that the development of ecological systems depends crucially upon the differential rate of change in a specific ecosystem. The faster dynamics show change whilst the slower changes give rise to the evolutionary aspects of the system (Hollings, 1994). Clearly, trying to capture these diverse processes operating over different time-scales for sustainable development is exceedingly difficult.

A similar scale problem arises when consideration is given to the spatial scales for examining the pattern of sustainable development. Obviously, spatial scales can range from a mosaic of small areas (< 1 square metre) through to the entire ecosphere with a gradation from regions to continents. Further complications ensue when the data is collected at different spatial or areal units of collection and the data needs to be collated. Using sophisticated GIS does not overcome these problems although it may at first sight disguise them.

Problems such as the ecological fallacy and the modifiable areal unit can occur and there are currently attempts to use Artificial Neural Networks to resolve these problems, and whilst they show promise, to date they have not succeeded (Openshaw, 1995).

Even when relationships between variables are quite well known and the boundary and scale problems have been overcome, many models will still be surrounded by areas of uncertainty and risk. Technically, the areas of uncertainty and risk can be handled by the model builder, but very often either at the expense of accuracy, or to the detriment of the adequacy of the model's results in the eyes of the user. As Opschoor (1991) notes, "In practice many of these issues mentioned will be resolved by opting for relatively simple, aggregated models, highlighting main features – but main features only – of the system involved. Such aggregated models, however, are often felt to be inadequately gross simplifications of reality".

In the case of sustainable development we have a similar problem associated with the level of aggregation at global, national and local scales as well as the time horizon to be used. Nevertheless, it is possible that if current trends continue then we may be unable to shift current unsustainable practices onto a sustainable path or paths. To explore possible future paths, computer modelling is a useful method. Despite the limitations associated with modelling it is clear that computer simulation models do offer the unique opportunity to explore alternative policies concerned with making development sustainable and, in this role, they are an indispensable aid to those who wish to promote sustainable development on simulations of the real world before translating these policies into real-world practice. In the rest of this chapter simulations of sustainable paths will be investigated.

ECOLOGICAL–ECONOMIC MODELLING

There is a basic mutualism between nature and society: economic goods and services for human welfare ultimately originate from two sources, nature and labour, merged in the processes of production. These complex interactions between nature and the labour process can be interconnected by considering the role of energy in ecological–economic modelling.

Energy, as the first law of thermodynamics informs us, can neither be created or destroyed, but only converted from one form to another. The most important implication of this law for our purposes, is that when energy is converted from one form to another the total amount of energy remains constant. For modelling sustainable development another implication of the first law of thermodynamics is that all energy used in a system can be accounted for by using suitable measurements. The energy accounts always balance; to date no exceptions have ever been noted. If, for example, we choose to burn coal in a fire then the amount of energy stored in the coal can be released as heat together with smoke, particulate matter and, when the fire dies out as the coal's energy is exhausted as ash. If we were able to measure all the energy in this operation then we would find that the total energy is conserved.

The second law of thermodynamics – the entropy law – states that all physical processes proceed in such a way that the availability of the energy involved decreases. For any natural or human-made closed system, the total energy available to do work must decrease. Eventually, any closed system runs out of available energy and comes to a stop. It could, of course, be argued that closed systems do not exist outside laboratory conditions – most of us live in open systems. Unfortunately, even the Solar System, which as a first approximation can be thought of as a closed system, must die when the radioactive combustion in the Sun is spent. Closer to home, it is obvious that the input of solar radiation acts as the prime source of energy, with the non-renewable resources being, geologically-speaking, a short-term bonus for our use. Environmental systems will cease to function without the vital inputs of solar energy.

At an individual level the well intentioned attempts to repair, reuse and recycle materials can only prolong the life of the raw materials being used; ultimately they will decay, no matter how noble the sentiments and practice of recycling. This is yet another reminder of the inexorable workings of the second law of thermodynamics (Georgescu-Roegen, 1971).

The most important implication of the second law of thermodynamics is that the material economy *necessarily* and *unavoidably* degrades the resources which sustain it. The increasing resource scarcity on the one hand and the increasing levels of pollution on the other are results of this unvarying one-way sequence of material consumption and depletion. In order to determine the flow of energy through an economic process or economic system several methods have been developed. These methods include process studies and input–output work.

Process analysis studies the inputs and outputs from a specific process and then adds up all the energy involved to produce a commodity. Obviously, even in the production of relatively simple goods like a refrigerator the amount of energy used is difficult to monitor. Nevertheless, if we are interested in determining the total energy content used in say, the production of fridges, then process analysis is useful. Energy analysis of this type can also be used in estimating the amount of energy used in agricultural production. It has been estimated that the British-produced potato is 50% crude oil – at least from an energy analysis perspective (Leach, 1976).

When attention is turned to the economy as a whole rather than individual components of it then input–output analysis is used. Specifically input–output addresses the production part of the economy, with explicit accounting for the energy inputs required to maintain the economy. It is possible, at least in theory, to account for all energy sources (i.e. direct and indirect), energy requirements of production, distribution, and consumption of goods, for any given economy.

As a generalisation, process analysis is appropriate for the study of specific economic activities such as fridge manufacturing or farming. Input–output analysis is more useful when a study is undertaken to examine the effects of resource use for an entire economy although it can also be used at a local level of the whole farm or industry. It should be noted that it is possible to develop dynamic input–output models which explicitly incorporate processes. This will be described below. The underpinning of these two approaches are the laws of thermodynamics. It should also be noted that thermodynamics is primarily concerned with the energetic properties of systems not of the things themselves. As Peet (1992) notes, in energy analysis the expenditure of energy and time to do work is a linking mechanism between the natural environmental system and the human socio-economic system. The link may enable a unified, more complete analysis of the combined environment–economy system to be carried out. This is attempted in the rest of this section.

The early ideas of energy analysis applied to economic matters have been studied by several scholars (Georgescu-Roegen, 1971). Unfortunately, their writings have, by and large, been ignored by conventional economists, who appear to accept that thermodynamics has little to offer in the arena of human activity and policy. Yet, it has been argued that energy is an important underpinning of any sensible discussion as to the ways in which ecosystems function. More important is the view that any discussion of sustainable development which does not take on board the importance of energy is more likely to fail than succeed. This section develops this theme by using energy as the basis of simulation models of sustainable development. We begin by describing a simple input–output model of a hypothetical society which has to adapt to a changing environment in order to survive. Next, this description is developed as a simple dynamic simulation model of sustainable development.

The relationship between economic activity, environmental conditions and nature's (including human) welfare is not very well understood. One way of viewing this relationship is to assume that economic development is a process which is essentially about the adaptation to a changing environment, while itself being an important source of environmental change.

The concept of economic development as an adaptive process to a changing environment has been put forward by Wilkinson in 1973 and later developed as an input–output numerical illustration in 1988 by Common. Wilkinson, for example, wrote that, "Looking at economic development in its ecological setting we see that it is a process of solving a succession of problems which from time to time threaten the productive system and the sufficiency of subsistence. In effect human societies out of ecological equilibrium have to run to keep up; their development does not necessarily imply any long-term improvements in the quality of human life" (Wilkinson, 1973). Common explores this theme by means of a numerical example presented as an input–output framework (Common, 1988).

In this illustration society is in ecological equilibrium with its surroundings in that its population is constant and adjusted to the carrying capacity of its ecological niche. Initially, the population uses renewable resources, for which the maximum sustainable yield is 100 units. The subsistence requirements, meeting Maslow's basic needs criteria (see Part One), for 100 individuals are 55 units of food and 30 units of clothing, requiring primary inputs of 260 units of labour and 100 units of resource R1. In a sense this hypothetical society is in ecological equilibrium: its size is the maximum that its niche can support on a sustainable basis.

A rupture to the ecological system through various mechanisms such as a breakdown in the cultural system for controlling population growth or a decrease in the potentially sustainable resource yield leads to a new situation whereby the new population cannot survive solely in terms of its use of R1 and its technology. The society has to adapt or perish.

Common suggests an adaptation by technological change using a non-renewable resource R2 as a "fuel". The input requirements of R1 per unit of food and clothing output are reduced. With subsistence for 110 individuals the deliveries of final demand of 60.5 units of food and 33 units of clothing, the primary input requirements are 91.6 units of R1, 25.4 units of R2 and 322.9 units of labour. With a population of 110 individuals the least-cost sustainable method of providing subsistence requires the input of 2.935 units of labour *per capita*, compared with 2.6 in the original situation. The society is, therefore, worse off than formerly. This deterioration would prompt an interest in labour saving technological innovation.

Assuming that such labour saving technological innovation can be found, that the population size remains constant, and that there are no adverse environmental changes, economic welfare improves. In his illustrative example Common notes that "if, for example, labour saving innovations can be found which involves the use of no additional quantities of commodities or primary inputs, such that the labour input coefficients become 0.7087 for food, 3.1889 for clothing and 0.89 for fuel, then *per capita* labour input requirements are restored to 2.6 units. The deterioration in economic welfare accompanying the adaptation to the rupture of the initial ecological equilibrium is conceivably reversible if the adaptation results in the achievement of a new, sustainable ecological equilibrium. In such a situation the society can give its attention to the realisation of labour saving technological change" (Common, 1988). Further developments, assuming a maximum requirement of 3 units of labour, and assuming that non-renewable resource, R2, is declining down a quality gradient, prompts the development of new technology requiring a new non-renewable resource, R3, to be used. The numerical illustration is shown in Table 32 where entries above the dashed line are intermediate input requirements per unit of output of food and clothing; entries below the dashed line are primary input coefficients; numbers I, II and III are stages of economic development by which

Table 32   Input/output table of economic development (Adapted from Common, 1988)

Period I	Food	Clothing			
Food	0.25	0.40			
Clothing	0.14	0.12			
Labour	0.8	3.6			
R1	0.5	1			
Period II	*Food*	*Clothing*	*Fuels*		
Food	0.25	0.4	0.1		
Clothing	0.14	0.12	0.05		
Fuel	0.1	0.2	0.1		
Labour	0.8	3.6	1		
R1	0.4	0.8	0		
R2	0	0	1		
Period III	*Food*	*Clothing*	*Fuels 1*	*Fuels 2*	
Period n	*Food*	*Clothing*	*Fuels 1*	*Fuels 2*	*Fuels n*
Food	"	"	"	"	"
Clothing	"	"	"	"	"
Fuel	"	"	"	"	"
Labour	"	"	"	"	"
R1	"	"	"	"	"
R2	"	"	"	"	"

this hypothetical society exploits its environment. Economic development is, therefore, seen as a process of shifting through a succession of ecological niches, the shifts being necessitated by the fact that the means by which a new niche is created are such that eventually it will no longer serve its original purpose.

Common's essay is important in that it illustrates the way in which a hypothetical society develops economically by exploiting its environment. It could be argued that the contemporary global economic system is now attempting to exploit several ecological niches which cover the earth – with no new niche to be found then any development must perforce look at socio-economic restructuring or perish. If this is the case, and this lies at the heart of both the early *Limits to Growth* models (Meadows *et al.*, 1972), the *Report to the President* (Barney, 1980) and the *Brundtland Report* (WCED, 1987), then there is clearly an urgent need to make development sustainable. It should be noted that the hypothetical illustration is based on the requirement of meeting fixed *per capita* subsistence needs; hence economic welfare is measured unequivocally by *per capita* labour inputs. Common is aware that he ignores problems associated with social inequalities, whatever their basis. It should also be noted that economic development does not necessarily imply any long-term improvement in the quality of human welfare or the welfare of other species. This latter assumption can be challenged by adopting an ecocentric position. Adopting such a position does imply that ethical concerns are fundamental to the creation of sustainable societies.

Several implications for sustainable development flow from the unconventional idea of economic development being some form of adaptation to a changing environment and *vice versa*. First, the role of population change is vitally important in the debate over sustainable development. Next, even with a constant population, changes in the ecological equilibrium result in the quest to use new non-renewable resources in order "to run to keep up". Third, the use of energy as a way of measuring the human impact on the environment and the economy shows, in general terms, that economic development has been about increasing environmental exploitation. It would be interesting to see the use of new environmentally-friendly technologies based on renewable resources to solve this problem. Fourth, it is acknowledged that subsistence levels change with economic development. For many people in developed countries the use of a fridge is a basic necessity in the 1990s, yet in the UK it was a luxury item in the 1950s. Whether all the "basic" items used today are essential rather than the result of heavy advertising is debatable. The question of what defines and determines basic needs – which underlies sustainable development – needs further consideration. Fifth, and more controversial, is the view that "while the economy is still delivering subsistence, a combination of a change in the way subsistence requirements are met has resulted in an increase in the cost of meeting subsistence, a welfare loss and an increase in *per capita* national income" (Common, 1988). Whilst Common is clear that economic development might work out otherwise and that different trends could be expected as particular circumstances differ, he notes that it is possible on philosophical and aesthetic or religious criteria to prefer earlier stages of development to later stages. He adds that those adopting such criteria are generally regarded as 'odd' (Common, 1988). It should be noted that there is no need to return to earlier patterns of development. This is particularly the case in attempting to pursue sustainable development where the expectation is that it is possible to transform past historical patterns of economic development and associated exploitation of other people and the environment to enter a new relationship in ecological equilibrium with the environment. The daunting task before us is to improve human welfare in a just manner; alter economic development so that the output/input ratios fall and re-establish ecological equilibrium with the rest of nature whilst maintaining biodiversity. This is a major task and one way in which we can move towards such a goal is by use of dynamic simulation modelling.

Currently, humankind's use of the earth's resources through either market mechanisms or state-planned economies has plundered the earth of its materials and polluted the planet, all in the name of economic growth and development. As many of the planned economies have now become part of the global market system, the problem of environmental abuses has not receded – in fact many of them have worsened. As Marx (1867) noted, "Capitalist production . . . disturbs the metabolism of the man (*sic*) and the Earth, i.e. the return of the soil to its elements consumed by man in the form of food and clothing, and therefore violates the eternal condition for lasting fertility of the soil . . . capitalist production, therefore, develops technology, and the combining together of various processes into a social whole, only by sapping the original sources of wealth: soil and the labourer" (Marx, 1867 in Daly, 1977).

The idea that capitalist productive processes are ecologically unsustainable re-appears in Boulding's (1980) characterisation of the market economy as a "cowboy" rather than "spaceship" economy. The image of a cowboy economy is "symbolic" of the illimitable plains and also associated with reckless, exploitive, romantic and violent behaviour, which is characterised by open societies. The closed economy of the future might similarly be called the 'spaceman' economy, in which the earth has become a single spaceship, without unlimited reservoirs of anything, either for extraction or for pollution, and where, therefore, man must find his place in a cyclical ecological system which is capable of continuous reproduction of material form even though it cannot escape having inputs of energy.

Whilst Boulding noted the need to develop an economic system as a subset of ecological activities, it was Daly who provided the main twentieth century impetus to developing a steady-state economy. The starting point of his analysis was an appreciation of both the materialistic basis of economic activity and a moral imperative that we need to embrace a form of stewardship for the planet rather than adopting an uncaring exploitation. Daly's (1973, 1977) ideas of a steady-state economy placed emphasis on the flows of energy and materials through the system rather than the attempts to live on borrowed natural capital stock.

There are, of course, a variety of ways of contemplating possible future ecological–economic interactions. At a conceptual level the neo-classical conventional economic optimistic view is one of ever increasing continuing growth of the human made components of capital (K_m) at the expense of natural capital (K_n). Within this camp environmentally-minded individuals would be keen to see some percentage of growth used to fund environmental protection. The logic of this approach suggests that natural capital could be driven down to zero without causing the collapse of the economy (Figure 19A). Alternatively, Figure 19B illustrates a more realistic, but pessimistic view, that shows over-expansion of the human economy causing collapse of the ecological life-support system and ultimately either a collapse of the economy which depends upon it or a massively reduced economy eking out a living in an environmentally impoverished world. The third alternative makes the distinction between growth

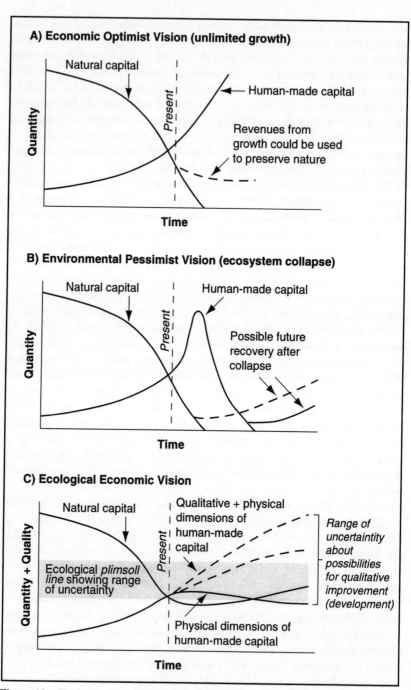

Figure 19 Economic–ecological interactions and alternative futures. (After Folke *et al.*, 1994)

and development. The former implies a material increase in size, while development implies an improvement in organisation without size change. In Figure 19C ecological natural capital (K_n) has declined but may increase by replanting and careful harvesting of renewable resources and pollution control measures. The human-made capital (K_m) reaches a certain physical limit – although qualitatively there may be changes in the quality of life which are not necessarily based upon the acquisition of more material goods beyond a threshold (Zolotas, 1981). There are ranges of uncertainty about both the possibilities for qualitative improvement in life as well as uncertainties associated with the "plimsoll line" of ecological sustainability. This third economic–ecological vision may allow various socially-just patterns of sustainable development to evolve within the constraints of a steady-state economy.

It is possible to extend the ideas of a steady-state economy into a model of sustainable development by using energy accounting and dynamic simulation modelling. In Figure 20 a simplified flow chart of a macro-model of sustainable development is shown. This model consists of several positive and negative feedback loops which interconnect the major state-variables in the model. These major state-variables include: a demographic sector, crude industrial and resource-base sectors, energy sector, and agricultural and natural vegetation sectors. The major exogenous sectors are climate change and world trade. As far as possible the material flows are expressed in energy terms rather than in monetary units. Several policy switches can be applied to some of the negative loops so that the trajectory of the system can be guided onto a sustainable form of development.

The major state-variables in the model were initialised for Australia for 1980 and a 'business as usual' base run was simulated. As can be observed from Table 33 the base run is not sustainable. By the time the simulation has reached 2020, the endogenous energy required by the system is exhausted and, to compensate for this shortfall, large imports of oil have to be imported resulting in a massive trade deficit. The standard of living has an index of 19 compared with the 1980 index of 100. The population growth is over twice the sustainable population. Obviously, this would be an unsatisfactory state of affairs for Australians. The federal, state/territory governments and others would need to take decisive action to prevent this critical simulated event from actually occurring.

Several simulation experiments were performed to try and steer the unsustainable trajectory onto a path of sustainable development. This is achieved by introducing a series of policies in the model *via* activating several negative feedback loops. By stabilising population growth and conserving energy requirements, as well as altering the national goal to self-sufficiency in energy, using renewable resources and some fossil fuels, it is possible, in theory, to achieve a condition of dynamic equilibrium in the macro-model of Australia. Under this scenario the simulation shows a reduced population with an index of 111 and a sustainable population potential of 113, i.e. a population still within

151

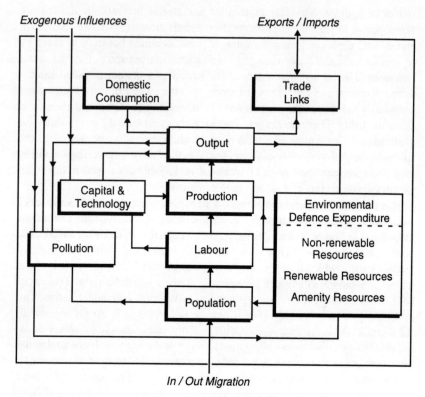

Figure 20   A generic model of sustainable development

Table 33   Unsustainable and sustainable simulations for Australia, 1980–2020

Major state variables	Unsustainable trajectory (U)			Sustainable trajectory (S)		
	Parameter	*1980*	*2020*	*Parameter*	*1980*	*2020*
Population growth	0.02	100	221	0.00	100	111
Sustainable population	–	100	93	–	100	113
Investment	0.24	100	–	0.50	100	–
Energy self-sufficency	0.21	100	0	1.00	100	464
Food self-sufficiency	1.00	100	42	1.00	100	102
Interest rate	0.50	100	100	0.50	100	100
Imports	–	100	315 000	–	100	58
Standard of living	–	100	19	–	100	89

Table 34 Unsustainable and sustainable simulations for Scotland, 1980–2020

Major state variables	Unsustainable trajectory (U)			Sustainable trajectory (S)		
	Parameter	1980	2020	Parameter	1980	2020
Population growth	0.02	100	200	0.00	100	111
Sustainable population	–	100	110	–	100	113
Investment	0.24	100	–	0.50	100	–
Energy self-sufficency	0.21	100	380	1.00	100	474
Food self-sufficiency	1.00	100	99	1.00	100	102
Interest rate	0.05	100	100	0.05	100	100
Imports	–	100	128	–	100	58
Standard of living	–	100	19	–	100	54

the bounds of sustainability. The nation appears to be self-sufficient in food and energy, although the standard of living is slightly reduced when compared with the 1980 index base. This simulated condition can be interpreted as a steady-state or a state of ecologically sustainable development.

In the case of Scotland the model was re-initialised and the business as usual scenario was run. Again an unsustainable trajectory was noted. By simulated year 2020 the population had risen to over twice the 1980 total and the standard of living fallen to below 20, when compared with the 1980 base data. Capital formation had substantially declined and cereal imports had risen. As in the Australian case study, it is possible to mitigate the worst impacts of the business as usual scenario by introducing several policies simultaneously. First, by reducing vital rates to zero and maintaining stable and low interest rates a more sustainable pattern of development can be simulated. Under these policy options the populaton only rises by 11% of the 1980 figure – although the standard of living falls by 46% of the 1980 base year level. Capital formation is positive but net imports are still lower than the 1980 figure (see Table 34).

Obviously, the model used in these two case studies in Australia and Scotland is very simple. Similarly, the policy prescriptions need further attention. Nevertheless, the research reported here is indicative of the possibility of developing a detailed macroeconomic–ecological model of sustainable development. Many more detailed investigations need to be made including the collection of better data, further sensitivity analysis, and the detailed testing of the model with some or all of the sustainable development indicators described in Part Two. This latter task can be achieved by disaggregating the model by sectors as well as spatially. At present the model merely indicates the potential of this approach to resolving some of the issues which surround the term sustainable development. At the national level this simple model can illustrate some ways in which sustainable trajectories can be realised in theory; translating the model's recommendations into practice requires some careful ethical consideration and brave political judgements.

EXTENDING THE MODELLING APPROACHES

The energy-based systems approach is, as shown in the previous section, a novel and useful way of simulating sustainable development. It is, however, only one way in which we can attempt to move the concept of sustainable development into an operational form. The systems approach can be extended by integrating it with other methods to provide more useful information for those interested in promoting sustainable development. In particular, it will be argued that the use of geographical information systems (GIS) and expert systems can help to provide decision-makers with tools appropriate to the development of management strategies which could promote sustainable development.

In the UK the *Chorley Report* (1987) has had a major impact on the development and implementation of GIS in several academic institutions as well as in Government departments. Essentially, a GIS allows various layers of data to be held in a large relational data base. Each item of the data is given a geographical co-ordinate so that after manipulation, the location of that specific item can be represented as a map or as part of a table or statistical diagram. If, for example, the locations of all deciduous forests in the UK were stored in a GIS then it is possible to indicate the locations of all these forests as mapped output.

The major strength of GIS resides in its ability to handle several layers of data, where each layer represents a specific set of data, such as the deciduous forest cover of the UK. If relationships between this forest cover and altitude, soil type and precipitation were required then a GIS could effectively show all these layers in a composite map. More importantly, the areal association between altitude and forest cover can be ascertained by combining sets of the spatial data. Several economic–ecological studies have benefitted by using GIS.

A growing trend in the use of GIS is to move beyond relatively simple analysis of map overlays and descriptive digital terrain models to explore the various processes underlying complex spatial patterns. In 1988 Wadge and Isaacs evaluated environmental hazards associated with volcanic eruptions for the Soufriere Hills Volcano on Montserrat in the West Indies which is only 5 km from Plymouth, the island's capital. The model consisted of a computer simulation of volcanic eruptions linked with a digital elevation model to simulate likely impacts of a volcanic event on the island. This type of research has obvious benefits for short-term planning of evacuation priorities and routes in the event of a real volcanic eruption (Wadge and Isaacs, 1988).

It is not too difficult to envisage that the application of process models of sustainable development could be interconnected with a GIS so that alternative scenarios of the future could be examined. Such integration would allow the exploration of sustainable futures in both the temporal and spatial domain. It could also act as a guide to interested parties, such as NGOs and Government Departments as well as other citizens to examine alternative paths of sustainable development, both locally and globally. In complex cases the use of expert systems to give some advice on the alternative scenarios can also be envisaged. Indeed, in some limited environmental studies, such as farming in the Australian outback, expert systems are helping farmers to tackle land degradation problems locally and thereby assist in the fight to move food production onto a sustainable path.

Some ways in which a systems model of sustainable development can be extended have been described. It is not suggested that movement towards sustainable development needs to await further developments in information technology but rather to suggest that political moves towards sustainable development can be aided by using the currently available technology. Clearly, system modelling can be used to highlight the dynamic processes which drive an ecological–economic system but, by itself, it is of limited use to describe the spatial manifestation and regional differences in patterns of sustainability. The spatial patterns of sustainable development can be portrayed by the use of GIS. In fact it could be argued that such applications readily assist environmental managers and other decision-makers with a tool suitable for spatial planning. For real-time monitoring of the ways in which specific pollutants are altering ecosystems, remote sensing by aeroplane and satellite is an important adjunct to GIS. In sustainable development the issues we are dealing with pose very difficult problems and in these cases the use of expert systems may be helpful as a guide to the use of complex modelling. More importantly, for the decision-makers the use of expert systems represents one way of providing useful advice and the underlying reasons for choosing one path of sustainable development rather than another. But these tools of information technology are just that – and as any craftsperson knows sharp tools handled carelessly are more likely to injure than help with the job in hand.

Clearly, the dynamic model of sustainable development outlined in this chapter has its usefulness. The full potential of its application will not however be realised until it is integrated with other tools of information technology. As discussed in this Chapter, by using energy as the basis of the modelling endeavour, it is possible to indicate clearly what is physically possible without pre-determining what is socially, economically or politically desirable. It is obvious that if a path of sustainable development is not physically possible then it cannot work. Nevertheless, to remain on an unsustainable trajectory or to explore possible scenarios so that society can choose to move onto a path of sustainable development, is one of ethical choice and political judgement.

CONCLUDING COMMENT

This Chapter has examined the role of dynamic simulation modelling in exploring sustainable development trajectories. After discussing some of the methodological problems associated with modelling, it was suggested that simulation models can help us in our quest to develop sustainable scenarios of development for different spatial and temporal scales. If current forebodings concerning the likelihood of unsustainable development – with all the horrors and misery that it implies – then there is a degree of urgency in attempting to ensure that we make changes to policy decisions sooner rather than later, if we are to leave this planet in good condition for our children, future generations, and other species.

Throughout this chapter emphasis has been placed upon dynamic simulation models to show the type of trajectories that, if put into practice, can lead to sustainable development options rather than to remain on an unsustainable path of development by maintaining the status quo. Obviously, the need to incorporate a spatial aspect of this work is essential and links to GIS and other forms of information technology can be used to help in this endeavour.

This chapter has argued that energetic considerations and a systems approach can be used as one way of modelling sustainable development. It has been demonstrated that this approach is useful in that it indicates what is physically possible from an energetic perspective. From the case studies described above it is clear that this approach has some usefulness for those people who wish to examine sustainable development from a personal, organisational or governmental perspective. Furthermore, it has been noted that this systems approach can be integrated with other approaches to aid the transition towards sustainable forms of development. It should, of course, be noted that the development of any type of model of sustainable development is not a panacea for the continuation of life on this planet. As usual, the laws of thermodynamics will inexorably result in the demise of all life-support systems. This rather pessimistic conclusion should, however, be tempered with cautious optimism in that we can, if we are willing to struggle for a sustainable world, develop this goal which can last as long as the sun shines.

To some environmentalists this technocentric approach may appear unwarranted – but surely exploring alternative life-styles for nations or the entire world cannot be left to mere chance processes or to the normal political practice, often called the "muddling through" approach. We have both a moral and practical responsibility to ourselves and others to use our brains and hands to resolve the problems that we, and earlier generations, have created. To believe in purely spiritual regeneration and small-scale communal life (for all the advantages they do offer) is both utopian and irresponsible. The ecological and economic problems are already present and attention must be directed now towards implementing policies which are sustainable.

CHAPTER 9

MAKING DEVELOPMENT SUSTAINABLE

INTRODUCTION

The previous chapters have examined sustainable development from a variety of perspectives. The development and historical evolution of the concept was described in Chapter Two, followed by the ethical basis of sustainable development in Chapter Three, and Chapters Four to Seven discussed environmental, economic and socio-political indicators of the concept. This then led to a description of a generic dynamic model of sustainable development and the ways in which it could be developed to help in the progress towards sustainable development globally, nationally, or locally. Obviously, the decision to promote sustainable development represents a new way of interconnecting or re-connecting human activities with the rest of the environment so that development can be sustainable. This new view depends, in part, on the political ideology of the different players in the system. Throughout this book an ecocentric perspective, as distinct from a technocentric position, has been implicitly adopted. There are however a vast number of "Green" positions adopted under the ecocentric banner. In this chapter we adopt the ecoliberalist ideology as one way of describing a vision of a sustainable world. This vision may not appeal to all, but without a vision it is clear that the goal of making development sustainable may be lost sight of as we become embroiled in detailed work on smaller facets of sustainable development.

In the following section we describe briefly various political ideologies which can be classified as "Green". This is then followed by describing a vision of a sustainable society. It will be suggested that many of the contours of this Green society can be discerned as vague outlines from some of the literature. In particular, the German Green Party programme of 1983, the Common Statement of the European Greens for the 1989 elections to the European Parliament, the ideas on the Common Good (Daly and Cobb, 1989), and the *Brundtland Report* (WCED, 1987), as well as several political texts have been used to sketch this outline (Eckersley, 1992; Dobson, 1991; Goodin, 1992; O'Neill, 1993). This is followed by some ways in which policies can be used to translate this vision of a sustainable society into reality and by a description of the role of strategic environmental assessment to aid sustainable development policies. Finally, some of the major unresolved problems underpinning this work will be noted.

COMPETING IDEOLOGIES AND SUSTAINABLE DEVELOPMENT

There have been many attempts to classify the alternative and often conflicting attitudes and values to environmental problems in general and to sustainable development in particular. These classifications range from the technocentric to the environmentalist through to the deep ecologists' views (O'Riordan, 1981). The technocratic ideology is almost arrogant in its assumption that man is supremely able to understand and control events to suit his purposes. The technocentrics believe in environmental management and are reactive, as distinct from pro-active, to pollution control strategies. In particular the technocentrics believe that technology and scientific progress can ensure humankind's continued existence on the planet. In contrast, ecocentricism preaches the virtues of reverence, humility, responsibility, and care; it argues for low impact technology (but is not anti-technological); it decries bigness and impersonality in all forms (but especially in the city); and demands a code of behaviour that seeks permanence and stability based upon ecological principles of diversity and homeostasis (O'Riordan, 1981). The ecocentrists focus on nature's rights and on the limits to growth. It is possible to subdivide these two broad classes further with the ecocentric group being sub-divided to form the trans-personal ecology or deep ecology and moderate ecology. The technocentric group can also be sub-divided into accommodating and cornucopian environmentalists (Table 35).

While there are other possible ways of classifying "green thought", such as dark green through to light green and on to grey (Dobson, 1992), the classification in Table 35 does provide some guide to the diverse ideologies and beliefs underpinning environmental debates. To unravel these differences is important as such understanding provides an insight into the views expressed by people writing, talking and actively participating in environmental affairs. The cornucopian environmentalists have a firm belief in the ability of the market and scientific technology to resolve any current environmental problem. For some of the Green groups these cornucopian ideas are anthropocentric and do not attempt to link human societies into an ecological relationship with the rest of the biosphere. The ecocentrists, however, suggest that a change in the ways in which we interact with the rest of nature (as we are part of nature and not apart from it) depends ultimately upon adopting a specific ideological position. In some cases the ecocentric perspective views science as a necessary but not sufficient condition for human and nature's emancipation; other subgroups of ecocentricism are more concerned with mysticism rather than science as an alternative way of interacting with the rest of nature.

Most environmentalists are concerned with environmental issues in which the physical or ecological basis of real world problems are examined, together

Table 35   Green political ideologies

		Green political ideology	
Outside politics		Eco-anarchism	
Part of conventional political groups	Eco-socialism	Eco-liberals	Eco-fascism
New groups	Eco-feminism		
		Deep ecologists	

with the social, economic, political and ethical dimensions. Within the ecocentric perspectives of environmentalism there are many different ideological positions. Despite these differences all ecocentric ideologies have the following five features in common. First, they recognise the full range of human interests in the non-human world; next, they recognise the interests of non-human communities; they also recognise the interests of future generations of humans and non-humans; they are in favour of science and technology but against scientism (i.e. the conviction that empirical – analytical science is the only valid way of knowing) and technocentricism (i.e. anthropocentric technological optimism); they adopt a holistic rather than an atomistic methodology which incorporates organisms as well as populations, species and ecosystems including the ecosphere (Eckersley, 1992).

Within the ecocentric perspective, however, there are numerous ideologies including eco-anarchism through to eco-socialism. These different groupings are shown in Table 35. Most of these ideologies are left of centre in political orientation, and seek to transcend the current global market-based system so that ecologically sustainable economic development for current and future generations can be achieved. Many of the ecocentric ideologies also stress themes of equity as well as economic efficiency; concern for non-human communities and their habitats; and concern for the growing disparities between the rich and poor, both within various nations and between the developing and developed world. These ecocentric ideals of sustainable development have been termed the three Es: environmental integrity, economic efficiency, and equity (Young, 1992); all three depend on adopting different ethical positions.

It will be noted that the Deep Ecology and Eco-feminist movements are classified as part of conventional political positions although they are, in their different ways, an influential part of contemporary ecological thought. Both of these views have had some impact on ecocentric thought, but to date, have failed to attract large numbers of people to their cause. The Deep Ecology movement (Naess, 1973), or as it is sometimes called the transpersonal ecological movement (after Fox, 1990), is critical of scientism and a purely instrumental orientation towards the non-human world; similarly ecofeminism stresses caring relationships between people and nature. Both groups support small-scale decentralised communities, cultural and biological diversity, as well as appropriate or alternative (soft) technology. In this sense Deep Ecology or transpersonal ecology is part of the ecocentric movement.

Unfortunately, Deep Ecologists have difficulty in deciding how to solve specific environmental problems; in particular they appear incapable of developing any approaches which would move the current unsustainable patterns of development onto a sustainable path. They rely heavily on individual spiritual awakening and awareness of the environment in order to change individual attitudes. Whilst this may be admirable, the singing of hymns or other chants is neither a necessary or sufficient condition to change the current practices of unsustainable activity.

Similarly, the eco-feminist world view seeks to establish mutalistic, social and ecological relationships based upon caring or nuturing characteristics often wrongly attributed solely to women. Whilst this aspect of ecocentricism has some merits the primary causal process underpinning their perspective is that male domination of women and nature is the major factor preventing a more caring attitude to our relationships with nature. Obviously, there is some empirical support for this perspective; the unpaid domestic labour often carrried out by women, as noted in the ISEW measures (see Chapter 6), being a case in point. More generally, many households in the developed and developing world undervalue the role played by women in society. Nevertheless, the eco-feminists' view is flawed in that the domination of nature or other people can take many forms such as racism or imperialism and there is no need to suggest that a person's gender is essential for this process of domination. What a truly ecocentic ideology is concerned with is cultivating the best qualities of human beings, regardless of the traditional association of aggressiveness and domination with the male and nuturing and caring with the female gender (Plumwood, 1986; Plumwood, 1988).

According to Woodcock (1983) the anarchist's world view depends on an acceptance of natural laws manifested through evolution, and this means that the anarchist sees himself *(sic)* as the representative of the true evolution of human society and regards authoritian political organisations as a perversion of that evolution. Eco-anarchists would generally embrace this perspective. A key feature of eco-anarchist thought is to abolish or bypass the modern nation state and confer social, economic and political autonomy on decentralised local communities. A second feature is that it is argued that eco-anarchism is compatible with an ecological perspective (Bookchin, 1980). Third, eco-anarchists view local initiatives and extra-parliamentary activity as ways of promoting ecocentric aims.

These characterisitics of eco-anarchism give rise to different types of communalism. Communalism may be described as small-scale localised communities living peacefully with each other and their environment. At least two different types of communities have been identified: ecomonasticism

(Eckersley, 1992) and bioregionalism (Sale, 1984). In Ecomonasticism a group or commune of people live largely self-sufficient lives often under the influence or guidance of a spiritual or charismatic leader in charge of the commune. Such communes are similar to medieval monastic settlements but often have a different spiritual base. In this sense they are similar to the deep ecologists.

Bioregionalism is a North American phenomenon often associated with Sale's writings (1984). The basic idea underpinning bioregionalism is that local communities live in harmony with each other and their immediate surroundings. It is of course very debatable to assume that bioregional communities linked to a geographical area such as a drainage basin can be insulated from changes in the larger world outside the region. Changes to the climate, for example, may alter the bioregion's net primary productivity so that the human community would have to adapt, move on, or perish. Similarly, there is no guarantee that different bioregional groups will live peacefully with each other. As one writer, notes "stateless, moneyless, small-scale communes, or other informal alternatives are not viable without complex administrative and social structures necessary to guarantee democratic participation, civil rights and egalitarian co-ordination of economic resources" (Frankel in Pepper, 1994). Finally, if outside groups decide to threaten such biocommunities, who would offer protection when the state with its police and judiciary are no longer present in this eco-anarchist society?

Within democratic pluralist societies there has been a growing recognition that environmental problems are to some extent the result of unbridled economic activity. Several economists have argued that these environmental problems can be resolved by the application of market-based mechanisms, in addition to the usual pattern of government regulation. As noted in earlier chapters the dominant paradigm to tackle these environmental problems is neo-classical economics. However, within the economic profession a growing number of economists are attempting to develop ecological economics to tackle environmental problems from a broader economic basis which does not rely on neo-classical economics. To date co-evolutionary economists (Norgaard, 1988) and other sub-groups are attempting to develop a new economic paradigm to challenge the dominant neo-classical view (Costanza, 1991).

At a theoretical level, eco-liberals are attempting to reformulate the dominant neo-classical theory to incorporate ecological and environmental problems. As noted in Part Two, the development of ecological economics has attempted to address these complex questions. At present, however, the development of an articulate eco-liberal theoretical position has not been achieved.

From a pragmatic perspective, eco-liberals still believe in the market system, with the price mechanism acting as the method of resource allocation. The price mechanism has many problems associated with it, such as the unquestioned belief in the *status quo* in terms of the distribution of money and wealth in a society; or the vexed problems associated with the accounting for ecological "goods and services" which are not part of a market system. In the growing discipline of ecological economics there is an assumption of the necessity to use a single measure (money) which is used to compare ecological questions of interest including ecological–economic interactions. There is, however, the problem of confusing commensurability with comparability.

Both the neo-classical economists and those of the Austrian school assume that price is simply a neutral measuring rod of the marginal utility a person expects to receive from some goods or service from an ecosystem. This approach ignores the fact that economic transactions incorporate social as well as economic aspects of the real world. More importantly, it ignores the self-evident fact that the use of a single measure, such as money, confuses comparability with commensurability. The latter can be used when all things are measured in the same units; comparability is required only when preferences are given by a person when comparing, for example, a tundra and tropical forest ecosystem.

The key feature of the eco-liberals is their belief in the modification of market mechanisms through active government involvement to try and reduce, and resolve, many environmental problems. Unfortunately, at present, no new theoretical framework has been developed which seriously challenges the neo-classical perspective. Ideas such as co-evolutionary and alternative Green economics are proposed but, as yet, they have not provided the cogent theoretical or empirical work which is required to successfully challenge the neo-classical perspective (Jacobs, 1991). Whether this heterogenous group will be able to overthrow the dogma of the neo-classical paradigm is part of an important on-going debate in economics. More importantly the resolution of this debate has ramifications on the way individuals within the market economy interact with each other and the rest of nature.

According to Pepper (1994) eco-socialism is anthropocentric. In this text, however, it will be argued that eco-socialism is actually part of the eco-centric approach. Pepper sees eco-socialism as an extension of the basic socialist principles of egalitarianism, eliminating poverty, and incorporating resource distribution according to need rather than the ability to pay and includes the democratic control of our lives and communities. These traditional socialist principles are embraced in eco-socialism but attempt to address environmental problems by mobilising the labour movement to exert their power as producers of goods rather than mere (green) consumers. He does note that, "An ecologically-sound socialist society will not come about until most people want it enough to be prepared to create and maintain it. Probably, and regrettably, the bigger catalyst will be the failure of capitalism (a) to produce the goods which it promises, even for a small minority (b) to create a physical and non-material environment for the rest which is tolerable enough to contain discontent". Clearly, a move towards eco-socialism will require a fundamental restructuring of society and an overthrow of the capitalist class. Whilst this is a fundamental part of the socialist vision it should be noted that the various struggles to create a socialist world have not, as yet, been successful.

There are, of course numerous criticisms that can be aimed at the eco-socialist vision of a democratically-run planned economy interacting in an environmentally benign way with the ecological systems. Eckersley (1992) suggests that a theoretical case may be made for eco-socialism if it is superior to the market system in several ways. These include provision of goods and services on the basis of needs rather than the ability to pay; the minimisation or avoidance of negative externalities of a market system causing pollution; ironing out excessive social and regional inequalities; ensuring that scale of the macro-economy respects the carrying capacity of ecosystems (unlike a market economy, a planned economy has no inbuilt imperative to grow, but it can develop); generally to take a longer term view of collective needs of current and future generations of human and non-human populations.

Unfortunately, this eco-socialist future requires both access to full information and complete trust in the elected officials' ways of running the complex system. One of the key problems in any eco-socialist new world order is to co-ordinate a range of public agencies which will be arrived at by consensus rather than through the "impersonal" workings of a market, and that each agency charged with some duties will interpret these duties in a uniform way and follow them through correctly. There are obvious problems with such a system. Dryzek (1987), for example, suggests that goal-directed socio-economic and ecological systems require a continuing consensus on values if they are to produce, distribute and ensure a desired common good. The problem with this approach is that "the administered structure cannot waiver in its commitment, for it is only that commitment which can keep the system on course" (Dryzek, 1987). This tells against the feasibility of a well functioning AND democratic planned economy. Clearly, the promise of creating an eco-socialist world has as many structural problems as the capitalist system which it is attempting to overthrow.

Whilst most ecocentric views tend to be to the left of centre of the conventional political spectrum in contemporary democracies, one group is distinctly to the extreme right of centre, namely eco-fascism. Eco-fascist ideas are found throughout the 20th century (Bramwell, 1989) and, like conventional fascism, stress the importance of a dominant group of people. Often eco-fascist groups have a charismatic leader who appeals to violent instincts in some humans.

Eco-fascists accept that there are major environmental problems, such as over-population and resource scarcity and, at this level, they are similar to many other ecocentric groups. Their responses to these environmental problems are, however, fundamentally different. They believe that problems such as over-population should be resolved by allowing starvation – no aid is suggested. This approach is often based on the metaphor of the "lifeboat ethic" (Hardin, 1974), where those in the lifeboat offer no help to drowning people. This analogy is powerful but false (Luper-Foy, 1995). Such policies would actively NOT help the poor or starving – in extreme cases eco-fascists would assist by practising genocide or ethnic cleansing. Similarly, in a world of scarce resources, they would take a disproportionate amount of any given resource by force if necessary. Such extreme right-wing behaviour is not compatible with either civilised co-operative behaviour or with respect to other life forms. As Russell (1969) notes in his discussion on Nietzsche and fascism, "to formulate any satisfactory modern ethic of human relationships, it will be essential to recognise the necessary limitations of men's power over the non-human environment and the desirable limitation of their power over each other". Fascism ignores both and encourages barbarism to the detriment of all – eco-fascism is not excepted from this indictment.

This brief account of major political ideologies currently being developed within the ecocentric movement is not exhaustive. It does however indicate that there are differences within the "Green" movement as there are within conventional political parties. The eco-fascist ideal can be summarily dismissed as the road to barbarism; the eco-anarchists assume a benign character not often encountered within the human species and still needs to consider competition between different communes. Leaving aside these two ecocentric extremes we are then left with ways of promoting sustainable development which are eco-liberal or eco-socialist or a mixture. In the following section we examine a vision of sustainable development from an eco-liberal perspective. Such a vision accepts the current realities of unsustainable development and then suggests ways in which a sustainable society can be developed from within the corpus of society.

A VISION OF A SUSTAINABLE SOCIETY

The competing ideologies briefly discussed in the previous section contain within them alternative visions of a sustainable society. It is, of course, clear that if sustainable development is to be translated from a concept into an operational form then culturally-specific and environmentally-sensitive economic development must be of paramount importance. No monolithic one dimensional view of the world shall dominate (Marcuse, 1964). The seeds of sustainable development will undoubtedly bloom according to local custom, environmental needs, and political practice. Nevertheless, it is important to provide a description of a sustainable society so that the key differences between possible sustainable futures and the current position can be appreciated.

There have, of course, been several attempts to define the outlines of a sustainable society (More, 1910; Pirages, 1977). These attempts are, to some degree, utopian. Dobson (1992) defends such utopian thinking as an essential aspect of moving towards a sustainable society. He wrote that "The Utopian vision provides the indispensible fundamental well of inspiration from which the green activists, even the most reformist and respectable, need continually to draw. Green reformers need a radically alternative picture of post-industrial society, they need deep ecological visionaries, they need the phantom studies of the sustainable society and they need, paradoxically, occasionally to be brought down to earth and be reminded about the limits to growth". Perhaps the main reason for portraying utopian visions of a sustainable society, was noted by Oscar Wilde who wrote that "A map of the world that does not include Utopia is not worth even glancing at" (Quoted in Jacobs 1991). But knowing where utopia is located is one thing, actually achieving this destination is a problem of quite another order of magnitude.

Several writers have described their vision of a sustainable society (Dobson, 1992). Several characteristics of a sustainable society can be gleaned from such descriptions. In particular, it is noted that the general direction in which humanity should be moving to establish a "sustainable" society is known. Generally, the world should move towards population decline rather than growth and toward efficiency rather than wasteful use of energy and other resources. It should be moving towards economic equity rather than increasing the gap between rich and poor. Humanity should be struggling to empower rather than to marginalize women and to pursue religious, ethnic, and racial tolerance rather than strife. All nations should be working hard to preserve and restore biodiversity rather than to destroy it. The following sketch represents one view of a sustainable society which may act as a guide to reach this destination.

(A) Energy

From the previous chapter it is clear that any ecological and economic system depends ultimately upon energy for it to function. The extraction of energy from renewable or non-renewable resources is not free. In energetic terms there is no merit in mining, for example, 1 tonne of coal if it requires the energy equivalent of 1 tonne of coal to extract. In the case of non-renewable resources it is obvious that various sources of energy are used. These resources include coal, natural gas, oil and uranium. The latter is used for nuclear power which is not only non-renewable but has major problems with long-term safety of both the immediate populations and the life-support systems of the planet, as witnessed in the Chernobyl disaster. Civil use of nuclear power has yet to be resolved. Similarly, British Energy and the government are locked in a power struggle over an estimated £7.6 billion bill for decommissioning (Sunday Times, 1996). Furthermore, the problems of safely disposing of the waste products from military and civil use of nuclear power have yet to be resolved. If we are to apply the precautionary principle it would appear sensible to stop further production of nuclear power rather than hope that one day these problems will be resolved. Green policies would stop all nuclear power operations and move towards safe and renewable forms of energy.

A sustainable society under current proven technology would rely upon the use of renewable resources for its energy supplies. These renewable resources include wind, wave, hydro-power, biomass, wet and dry rock technology, trapping methane gases from landfill sites, as well as the use of photovoltaic cells and other forms of capture of solar power. It must be remembered that, under the laws of thermodynamics, it is not possible to have 100% energy-efficient machines. Even if we moved towards an energy supply wholly based upon renewable energy supplies there would still be a need for careful energy conservation. The Ecology House experiment in Toronto, Canada, for example, provides some physical demonstration of the ways in which sustainable living can be achieved without recourse to poorer living standards. The recent EUROPA study indicated that 95% of Europe's energy needs can be met by use of potentially renewable resources. It is clear that relying solely upon renewable energy may not meet the current lifestyles of the rich in industrialised countries. This would imply that, in a sustainable society, a small reduction in current energy use would have to follow in addition to reduced demand brought about by increased prices and conservation. For a sustainable society there is a real need to make the transition to energy derived from renewable resources sooner rather than later. Such an action would satisfy our culturally reduced energy needs without robbing future generations of their energy supply.

(B) Population

Obviously, in a world of finite assimilative capacities for the various ecosystems, and one which has finite resources of land and sea for food production, there is a limit to population and other forms of growth. This statement reinforces the earlier conclusions reached by the limits to growth model builders of the 1970s (Meadows *et al.*, 1974). In their study they wrote that "If present trends continue unchanged, then the limits to growth on this planet will be reached sometime in the next one hundred years. The most probable result will be a collapse (sudden and uncontrollable) in both population and industrial capital". Whilst the conclusions they reached have been subject to much criticism, it could be argued that you do not need a computer to prove that in a finite world it is impossible to continue to have population and economic growth. As Porritt (1969) notes, "in terms of reducing overall consumption, there's nothing more effective than reducing the number of people doing the consuming".

The reduction in the number of people doing the consuming so that the environment can be protected raises ethical, political and social problems. The recent Population Summit held in Cairo in 1994 was unable to reach any consensus on population control for two major reasons. First, the Roman Catholic church continues to argue that most forms of birth control are morally wrong. Similarly, many cultures do not like the idea or practice of euthanasia. Clearly, if all of these options are excluded, the world's population will continue to grow and with it, further damage to ecosystems, the resource base and other living forms will inevitably ensue.

Several demographers have argued persuasively that if there were two children per family then, after a period of population growth, the world's population would stabilise as the number of births equalled the death rate. On the basis of current population trends and projections (Brown and Kane, 1994) this pattern of growth has not yet been achieved, nor is it likely by the year 2050. There are, of course, major political problems associated with the stabilising of a nation's population. First, a numerically small nation may have less voting rights in large international organisations. Obviously, these institutional patterns can be changed but there is no certainty that larger nations would welcome or endorse such changes. If the alternative to institutional reform is procreation then further population problems are bound to arise. Secondly, in warfare larger populations have a better probability of leaving some survivors. Again, such political realities should not be thought of as an endorsement for larger populations but do indicate some of the political problems of moving towards a stable and smaller population.

Given the actual growth rate of population in various countries, one political practice has been to limit the number of children to one child per family, as in China. By the 1980s there was a major change in thinking when it was announced that one child per family would be the norm unless a couple were blessed with double happiness (twins). Unfortunately, this sound demographic policy has failed to take into account the social preferences for boys in a Chinese family.

Clearly, the moral, social and political problems which surround population policies are immense. Nevertheless, it is clear to those in the Green movement that population policies have to be addressed and put into operation if we are to develop a sustainable pattern of development.

(C) Employment

With the recent collapse of the many socialist nations (the exceptions being China, North Korea and Cuba) there has been a spread of the capitalist world market system. One of the consequences of this has been the need for wage labour. In many nations of the world economic employment is the main way of gaining a livelihood. In the rich nations of the world, especially the United States of America, a forty-hour week with holidays brings a balance between work and leisure; back-breaking work and degrading conditions have been greatly reduced (Cobb, 1993). Nevertheless, for many ethnic minorities and for women the search for gainful employment is demoralising.

In many nations, however, the development of economic growth is a mixed blessing. On one hand it is claimed by orthodox economists that it creates wealth and employment, but others state that such changes destroy the earlier forms of labour, and marginalise traditional forms of authority. Furthermore, the development of the world economy has resulted in conditions of wage labour closer akin to slavery than to gainful employment in some countries. All the hardships to children and the environment are part of the 'success' of the unbridled growth of the world market, with its promise of increased material wealth at the expense of both the labourer and nature.

There is of course no need for patterns of exploitation to be perpetuated. During the 1930s Keynes (1936) was able to present a general theory of employment, money and interest, as a basis for a civilised way of ensuring that the worst excesses of the global economy were managed to ensure that essential social needs could be met, such as hospitals, care for the young, infirm and elderly, public transport, and publicly owned utilities.

(D) Agriculture

Whatever population size a future sustainable society would have is a moot point. It is clear that, even with a small population, it is essential that food and fibre production would need to be of a *minimium*, sufficient to meet current protein, vitamin, calorie and fibre requirements. The industrial-based agricultural practices in the OECD countries, whilst responsible for producing surpluses, may have a major impact on ecosystems. Apart from the remaining natural ecosystems which they inevitably alter, modern agriculture is intensively chemically-based. The negative side of the application of agro-chemicals has been witnessed in high levels of nitrogen in watersheds in the UK; in the algal blooms of the Murray–Darling and other freshwater systems; salinization of the land in Southern Europe and Australia through irrigation; and in dust bowl conditions due to ecologically unsound farming practices in the USA, Australia and parts of the UK. More damaging changes have also been reported in the reduction in male fertility due, perhaps, to chemicals used for food packaging (pthalenes) and chlorine.

One aspect of a Green economy would be to substitute labour for fossil fuel-fired machinery in the agricultural sector. Goldsmith, for example, has suggested that a four- or five-fold increase in the agricultural labour force in the UK would enable the country to forego much of the input of machinery and chemicals which have been used in the past thirty years (Goldsmith in Dobson, 1992). Other writers suggest that the search for agricultural self-sufficiency is as much spiritual and ideological as it is one of trying to reap the basic necessities of life out of the bare minimum of our surroundings (Bunyard and Morgan-Grenville, 1987). We need not go for this minimalist approach to agriculture but there is a need to re-examine the economic basis of agricultural production, with its grants and subsidies, as well as the pattern of land ownership through which the ecological resources are brought into service for human well-being. Economics and land ownership play an important part in changing the ecology of the landscape for all other species.

(E) Water

Water is indispensable for human life and for the growth and reproduction of plants and animals. In many parts of the world the problem of water supply is not one of absolute shortages but of a poor distribution of the resource. Even in Britain the distribution of water is uneven, with East Anglia suffering drought-like conditions while the Scottish Highlands have excess water all year round. Furthermore, the pollution of coastal waters continues with more investment required in an attempt to clean up beaches and waterways. In some cases there have been improvements in the condition of some rivers. A sustainable society requires a plentiful supply of good quality water.

(F) Manufacturing and service industries

One of the major strengths of the ecocentric perspectives is the need to develop employment opportunities for all people who wish to work. Obviously, ecocentrics stress the importance of jobs which rely on the use of potentially renewable resources. The immediate impact of such an approach would be to open up more jobs in existing primary sectors such as forestry, fishing and agriculture as well as to provide new opportunities for collective development of small scale industries for local consumption. Another benefit of such co-operatives would be to reduce the amount of transport between places and hence further reduce pollution.

Obviously, some movement of goods between centres would be required but much of the communication could be undertaken by electronic devices, with the energy for the units coming from renewable energy sources. Often the new employment will be in cybernetic services with the use of computing to interconnect different groups. These services are already available, but from an ecocentric viewpoint they would be used for supporting life rather than purely generating economic growth for a wealthy minority.

From an ecological perspective the idea of producing goods and services in an environmentally benign manner is appealing. Socially, the idea of returning to labour which is not alienating and demeaning would be a welcome change for many people either in currently low paid jobs or unemployed. The idea of wages and salaries, which are historically-conditioned modes of payment peculiar to capitalism, will be replaced with new forms of currency. The idea of using local currencies in a local employment and trade system (LETS) to support local economies has some merit but needs to be examined in more detail to see how these localised economies would interact with a system of exchange across the global community.

(G) Shelter

For most societies shelter, either permanent or temporary, is essential for survival. Throughout this century there has been a global trend towards urbanisation. The metabolism of cities has been examined since the UNESCO *Man and the Biosphere* programme began in the 1970s. At present cities have a major ecological footprint on the earth. Jefferson, as early as 1917, realised that the then largest city, London, used the whole world for its "sustenance space". In the last sixty years, however, the burgeoning of urban areas has resulted in a greater number of ecological footprints stamping across the world in seven-league boots in a futile search for sustainable sustenance space (Jefferson, 1917).

Yet, the ecological impact of cities is not an essential aspect of urban life. Paris in the nineteenth century was almost 80% self-sufficient in food and water. The recycling of manure from horse transport as a fertiliser for small gardens resulted in a healthy diet for many Parisians. This self-sufficiency was broken with the introduction of new modes of transport, and from urban building activity. Nevertheless, the example does show that cities are not always ecologically bad environments. Furthermore, the cultural life and anonymity, which is part of urban living, does appeal to many residents.

These examples of city living do not mean that we need to return to the nineteenth century city. Indeed, such a step would be retrograde; the evils of urban squalor and homelessness were noted by Engels (1969) in his study of Salford and Manchester. One wonders if he would have noticed any basic changes in the conditions of working and unemployed people in the same city at the end of the twentieth century.

It may be possible to make cities sustainable. The use of permaculture in urban gardens, the reorganisation of urban space and the possibility of using new transport systems could contribute to these developments but the way in which they can be achieved is still being investigated. Similarly, experimental work in Toronto and the UK in developing ecologically-sound housing demonstrates the creative possibilities that can be achieved by combining ecological sense with artisitic sensibilities in architecture. To realise good quality housing which is energy efficient, ecologically harmonious, socially acceptable and affordable for all, is not a utopian vision. Some planners have suggested that taxes on energy inefficient homes could be raised to ensure that such shelter became the norm in the 21st century whilst people in energy-efficient homes would be helped. Obviously, such energy taxes would need to consider the problems of social equity (i.e. by not making life harder for the less well-off) as well as the natural variation in climatic conditions. Such taxes could also help towards reducing the enhanced greenhouse effect.

(H) Diversity and wilderness

Many ecocentrics stress the need for biodiversity (as well as cultural diversity) and areas of wilderness to be left untouched for other species. With the spread of human population it has been shown that 40% of the net primary productivity of the planet is already being appropriated by human kind. (Vitousek *et al.*, 1986). It is therefore essential that any further development of the human species be restricted in both numbers and in its impacts on the rest of nature. Earlier it was argued that setting aside land for other species is not just an ethical point but it also makes excellent sense from an ecological perspective. When planners talk about Ecumenopolis – a world city open 24 hours a day and spanning the globe – one wonders at the lack of ecological sense and sensibility underpinning such grandiose notions (Doxiadis, 1968).

(I) Religious tolerance

For many people Green ideas have a quasi-religious significance. Under eco-centricism religious beliefs would all be tolerated with the exception of any one religion which attempted to coerce people to accept it as the only truth or light. For some of the world religions this may be problematic – although there are signs of a rapprochement between many of the world religious faiths and the celebration of differences is currently being developed (Smart, 1989).

There are, however, problems with the acceptance of some specific aspects of some religions such as the use of contraceptives to prevent unwanted births. Yet from an ecocentric perspective the need to reduce total population (and for some their excessive consumption patterns) is opposed to some religious orthodoxy. Even more difficult are the theological conflicts between some of the world religious groups. These disputes appear inevitable even when they threaten life and make it difficult to reconcile some aspects of religion with sustainable development.

(J) Science, arts, technology and education

The development of green awareness and practice is not taking place in a socio-economic vacuum. Since the publication of *Agenda 21* much emphasis has been placed on greening the curriculum in all forms of education. Raising the awareness of current ecological and environmental problems is part of the ongoing process to achieve sustainable development. Education has a pivotal role in this process but it cannot be left to education alone to provide the where-with-all for sustainable development to become a reality; science, the arts and technology can also play their role. Science is very important as it provides one independent way of critically evaluating someone else's conclusions from experiments; the arts because they provide both pleasure and recreation as well a critique of contemporary affairs; and technology as it can help to provide environmentally benign ways of producing goods and assimilating wastes. These social activities can all play a part in developing a sustainable world.

(K) Trade and travel

Ecocentrics stress the need for local production, distribution and consumption. Some people perceive this type of development as a move towards self-sufficiency with no trade or travel between places and groups. In a sense the idea of making local communities more self-sufficient is part of the ecocentric world view. It must, however, be noted that in order to maintain or improve current living standards then trade between different groups is essential. The terms of trade must, however, be changed so that enormous debts do not arise between the rich and developing nations. Similarly, movement of people for social intercourse is part of a useful, and for many an enjoyable, multi-cultural lifestyle.

(L) Communications

As we move towards the twenty-first century there is a growing awareness of the power of electronic communications to form and mould opinion on sustainable futures. The much-vaunted super-highway of information technology is being made available. This communications technology is like a doubled-edged sword in that it can be both liberating and dominating. The domination of cyberspace is due to the increasing ownership of communication channels (printed word, television, the radio, as well perhaps as the internet) by a few large corporations. The liberation of communication channels gives individuals the opportunity to openly engage in discussions around the world but also permits the transmission of ethically unsound activities.

(M) Political systems and international relations

The attempt to promote sustainable development has been seized by many political groups. In Western democracies, which only account for 20% of the world's population and absorbed over 80% of the world's resources in 1989, most major political parties have a green strand to their manifestos. Few of these formal parties have, however, actually scrutinised the full implications of implementing green policies. Usually, some 'greenwash' is applied to environmental issues to try and reassure the electorate that they are doing a good job and are able to cope with the ideas of sustainable development as another item on the political agenda.

Real political activity for sustainable development is more concerned with active public participation rather than political posturing. One of the main aspects of *Agenda 21* is to involve people at the local level to ensure that their views are actually being taken on-board when any decisions directly affecting them are made. It remains an open question whether or not politics will give way to a broad-based democratic movement with open access to information and safeguards for individual citizens rights.

Many environmental problems are international or global in extent. The protection of the atmosphere or the oceans, for example, requires international rather than just local efforts. Green international policy must be developed to preserve human life (and the life of other species) by protecting the ecosystems and physical basis of life on earth. Next, the decommissioning and safe disposal of all weapons of mass destruction (nuclear, chemical and biological) would have to be agreed and implemented globally. These positive developments coupled with a pursuit of peace are cherished aims of many ecocentric groups. It should, however, be noted that the role of conventional military defence has not been adequately addressed by the Green parties.

This brief description of the outline of sustainable society is applicable to most contemporary societies. Obviously, the ways in which individuals, groups and nations respond to the challenges posed by altering current unsustainable practices lies in the realm of human endeavour and political practice. In the contemporary world there is much political posturing about the attempts to (somehow) move the current unsustainable practices onto a sustainable trajectory without much understanding of how the latter can be achieved.

In some small communities it could be argued that the living of essentially sustainable life styles have been practiced for many years. In the case of some aboriginal or first peoples there is a case that their traditional ways of life have been sustainable for many hundreds and in some cases thousands of years. In contemporary industrial nations some small groups are attempting to evolve lifestyles which, over a limited domain, are sustainable. For the vast majority of people and especially for the political representatives the move towards a communitarian way of life is quantitatively insufficient and qualitatively unacceptable to current generations. This need not be the case, in fact it is possible to learn from these "living social experiments" to find out actual practices which allow the move towards more sustainable forms of living in the face of apparently massive inertia.

One of the major log-jams in implementing sustainable development policies and practices is the difficulty of reconciling current bureaucratic practices, as witnessed in governmental behaviour, with the need to develop a more accountable and responsive action by elected representatives of the people. This may require a sea-change in attitudes and behaviour to implement sustainable development. It is likely that there will be much resistance to change on behalf of many political parties and the bureaucracies including the planning authorities. Nevertheless, there are signs that making local authorities more accountable to the electorate is happening, but this should not be achieved by economic incentives alone. The complex processes of making development sustainable can be helped by strategic environmental assessment.

POLICIES FOR SUSTAINABLE DEVELOPMENT

The vision of a sustainable society sketched in the previous section can give rise to numerous policies to promote sustainable development. These policies, together with the use of different instruments, could assist the government, organisations and individuals in their pursuit of making development sustainable. However, several important pre-conditions need to be satisfied, including the need for a stable political system and effective participation in decision-making at the appropriate level. The latter aspect is important if we are to galvanise all sectors of the community into purposeful action. Next, an administrative system which is just, flexible and willing to resolve any tensions arising from disharmonious development is also required. It could be argued that liberal democratic societies are the closest to satisfying these pre-conditions and are, therefore, likely to be the main agents of change toward sustainable development.

Many of the pre-conditions for sustainable development were identified in the *Brundtland Report* (WCED, 1987) – but the ways in which such broad ideas can be translated into specific policies were not discussed in detail. The rest of this section provides some details of the policies which, if taken together, are likely to move society towards a path of sustainable development. Naturally, the portfolio of policies are based on the eco-liberal perspective described above and also use the rule that there must be a separate policy instrument for each policy objective.

The primary consideration of sustainable development policy is to maintain and enhance the ecological and environmental systems of the planet so that other objectives such as the maintenance of biodiversity, the eradication of poverty and the improvement to the quality of all life can be accomplished early in the twenty-first century. Policies which are directed towards energy, water, agriculture and biodiversity could achieve some of these goals.

Many environmentalists wish to see biodiversity maintained rather than diminished. There are several ways in which this aspect of natural capital can be maintained. First, large areas of wilderness or less altered landscapes can be set aside so preserving the natural capital of a nation. Actually determining the amount and specific sites is, of course, a major problem. One way of achieving this goal is to introduce economic incentives for both private and public landowners NOT to use some areas of their land with the proviso that only environmentally-sound developments would be permitted through the usual planning processes. Next, the nutrient and material cycles of ecosystems must be allowed to function naturally. This would imply that efforts to overload the natural systems must be restricted by pollution-control measures. Furthermore, the assimilative capacity of the natural systems must be maintained. At low levels of biodegradable pollutants the natural environmental systems can operate normally. When critical thresholds are exceeded for specific pollutants then there are dangers to the rest of life in the ecosystem.

At a global scale the persistent pollution of the atmosphere with CFCs and several other greenhouse gases must be substantially reduced. The CFC problem has been brought under control by international action under the Montreal Protocol and the London agreement. By reducing to zero the emissions of CFCs then, in time, it is hoped that the hole in the ozone layer will repair or, at least, not become any larger. When other aspects of pollution are considered then the use of carbon taxes to reduce carbon dioxide content in the atmosphere has been proposed but still needs to be ratified internationally before being implemented. At sub-global scales the use of polluter pays principles and best available technology for pollution control should be implemented. These two principles together with the use of emission standards and economic incentives could make substantial reductions in our contribution to the pollution of the ecosystems.

The primary policy in the energy sector is to move towards complete reliance upon renewable energy sources with the relatively quick transition from nuclear and other non-renewable resource use such as coal, gas and oil. The use of biomass, water, wave, wind, solar, thermal and tidal power are all less environmentally damaging than the use of non-renewables. It should be noted that phasing out of the major energy industries should not cause large-scale unemployment as the move towards environmentally-friendly energy production, using renewable energy sources, would call upon the initiative, capital and skills already available in the current energy industries. Some moves in this direction have already been made with the use of wind and other renewable energy resource use.

Most environmentalists would wish to see the complete phasing out of nuclear energy and the abandonment of any further proposed buildings of nuclear reactors. Sweden has moved towards this goal and it is not inconceivable that this pattern could be developed in the UK. Currently, insurance companies are not willing to underwrite the insurance relating to accidents at nuclear plants and the UK Government's policy to privatise this sector of energy has led to the peculiar view that the taxpayer should subsidise any insurance claims and underwrite the costs of decommissioning any nuclear plant. This assumes that the latter can be dismantled safely and that high-level waste can also be safely disposed of. On both these counts there are major problems which many environmental scientists would consider insoluble. Hence, the precautionary principle should be invoked to ensure the safety of current and future generations and their environment. Obviously, the use of nuclear weapons should also be eliminated.

One way of making the transition from the use of non-renewable energy resources to a sustained use of renewable energy resources is through taxation. By introducing progressively higher taxes for failing to produce a growing percentage of energy from renewable resources, energy companies would be encouraged to make this rather difficult transition in an organised and planned manner. If, for example, the nation wished to move to a complete renewable energy future by 2050 then companies achieving the target would be rewarded by the use of economic incentives: those failing to reach the target would be penalised through heavier taxation.

Water is essential for most life forms and indispensable for human beings. Obviously, there are great geographical variations in the patterns of precipitation and the demands for water, both spatially and temporally. It is essential that demand should fall well short of water supply. This implies that a national grid of water supply be built and maintained so that areas of deficit can still have water from other wetter areas. Obviously, the volume of water located in natural aquifers cannot be increased, so reservoirs will need to be built – based upon the assumptions of changing rainfall patterns predicted in climate change scenarios, and the differential patterns of demand. Furthermore, pipelines connecting water supply to consumers must be maintained so that vast quantities of water "lost" through leaking pipes is substantially reduced. In the UK the current attempts to meter consumers' water use, whilst admirable from a conservation perspective, actually pales into insignificance when compared to water losses through badly maintained pipes. An eco-liberal perspective would ensure that the basic needs of water are actually maintained through accountable and efficient public ownership rather than relying on private companies. Under a publicly-owned system the re-allocation of water to areas of need would be met as a public duty rather than as a business. Obviously, the water supply in any country has a finite limit for a given period and measures to control other aspects of the economy are required to conserve this precious resource.

Food is also essential to life and one of the major changes in environmental history has been the agricultural revolution (Ponting, 1992). Obviously, the use of any renewable resource, such as fish farming or forestery, should only be harvested at no more than the generation rate. Furthermore, incentives could be made to ensure that the reduction in non-renewable resources could be substituted by a planned replanting of the land to increase biomass for fuel, fibre and food production.

Recently, the agri-business has, under various forms of economic incentives such as the EU Common Agricultural Policy, produced massive food surpluses. Obviously, this policy has been good insofar as no one wishes to return to the food rationing of the Second World War – but the impact on the landscape and on other farming regions has been very high. In many areas of Europe the loss of hedgerows to expand the size of fields has resulted in the loss of biodiversity and, in some areas, soil erosion. Outwith the European Union several areas, such as Australia, have found competition with subsidised food production difficult (Young, 1992). Clearly, there is a need to ensure that a plentiful and good quality supply of food is available. This can be achieved by use of incentives and, if need be, by subsidies to farmers to diversify their agricultural production. Such diversity would include coppicing, for contributing to renewable energy supply, as well as moving to less intensive use of fertilisers. This latter strategy would help to minimise the pollution damage to aquifers by pollutants such as nitrate. Furthermore, there could be an incentive for farmers to move towards organic production of foodstuffs and a humane treatment of animals and poultry. Some writers have suggested that less reliance upon mechanised farming methods and a return to the land of employment would be a desirable feature of a less intensive and mechanised lifestyle. Again, a mix of land-use controls, economic incentives and disincentives together with some guidelines including the banning of some fertilisers would be required.

Central to any sustainable development strategy must be the reduction in population numbers. In some nations, such as the UK, the population is reaching replacement levels but in other countries, with a younger population pyramid, birth rates are outstripping death rates. Obviously, the introduction of contraception and financial incentives to move to family sizes which are self-replicating need to be encouraged. In the UK education for all sectors of the population is desirable and the opening up of nursery and higher education is important for an educated citizenship. Similarly, the provision of good quality public health care is essential for all people from before the cradle and to the grave. In a sustainable society these aspects of civilised living need to be funded in a caring and accountable manner. As many Western Governments are concerned over the rising costs of public services such as health and education, serious consideration needs to be given to finding ways of funding these services. One radical way of enhancing human welfare would be to provide income from a land tax so that a re-distribution of wealth can be channelled into service provision.

Much economic activity takes place in secondary, tertiary and quaternary activities. Primary activities such as farming, forestry, fishing and mining account for a small proportion of the work-force in many advanced industrial nations – although, as noted above, the move to repopulate the countryside by moving to less intensive use of machinery has been proposed by some writers (Morgan-Grenville, 1987). Currently, however, the other sectors of the economy are also responsible for economic growth and employment. In a quest to move towards a sustainable form of development it is essential that these other sectors of the economy pursue technical efficiency so as to reduce the production of waste. Daly (1977) suggests that a sustainable economy would be one in which emphasis is placed on reducing the throughput of energy and materials. Similarly, an emphasis on re-use, repair and recycling of materials is given a higher profile and is actively encouraged. Some ways in which these important aspects of a sustainable society can be achieved are by use of polluter pays mechanisms, emission standards, and economic incentives, such as tradeable discharge permits for some forms of pollution control and tradeable resource extraction permits. A tax on resource extraction and use could also be introduced to ensure that wanton misuse of non-renewable resources is prevented. Furthermore, the use of non-renewables should be offset by investments that enhance the value of renewable resources by the equivalent amount.

Most of the prescription described above refers to economic activity within a nation. Obviously, the international dimensions of sustainable development need to be mentioned. One of the primary aims of the *Brundtland Report* was to reduce poverty between nations. This can be achieved by facilitating the transfer

177

of wealth to *per capita* poor countries – to promote freer trade by encouraging trading partners to export goods which are produced in a sustainable manner and to tax severely those areas of trade, such as non-renewable resources, which are clearly unsustainable. To prevent the relocation of polluting activities it is essential that equivalent trading standards be met. Such standards would go back to the Rio Principles of preventing the "export" of polluting practices (see Chapter 3). Obviously, international lending agencies would have to re-examine their practices to ensure that investment is both ethically and environmentally sound.

These recommendations to assist in the transition to a sustainable future need to be pursued by both formal political processes as well as by involving local communities to assist in the implementation of such actions. Ethical and political judgements will need to be made as to the best way of implementing sustainable policies. Some of the ways in which these recommendations can be translated into policy prescriptions are given in Table 36. The table represents a summary of the policy portfolio for assisting in implementing the sustainable development strategy. The ways in which these ideas can be translated into practice are now briefly examined.

THE ROLE OF STRATEGIC ENVIRONMENTAL ASSESSMENT IN SUSTAINABLE DEVELOPMENT

For many decades governments of different political colours have promoted the idea of implementing policies, plans and projects to achieve some political goal. The political goal could be to encourage secure employment in, say, Northern England or to attract inward investment into the silicon valley in Scotland. This idea of developing policies, plans and projects to achieve a democratically chosen goal is not confined to Keynesian economic policies of the pre-Thatcher UK Government but is also practised in many other industrialised nations such as USA, Japan as well as by our European partners. The move towards market-based economics and the collapse of centralised planning in Eastern Europe has not delivered a death blow to the policies, plans and projects approach – although it has severely damaged their political credibility. Nevertheless, there is a feeling that some form of planning is essential if we are to protect ourselves and the rest of nature from the ravages of unbridled market forces. This section briefly examines the ways in which sustainable development could be promoted within the context of the current economic system by developing new policies, plans and projects.

Since the publication of the US National Environmental Protection Act (NEPA, 1970) in 1969 there has been considerable interest in developing both national environmental impact analysis guidelines and techniques associated with Environmental Impact Analysis (EIA) (Wathern, 1990). Numerous countries have official EIA systems established through regulations and others

Table 36 Sustainable development: policies and instruments

Sector	Policy	Instruments
Energy	1) Phase out nuclear power	Give full costs to producers/ shareholders
	2) Invest in renewables	Phase in more capital from nuclear to renewable
	3) Pollution control	Polluter pays / Best Available Technology (BAT)
	4) Energy conservation	Grants and Taxes
Population	5) Stabilise population	Education & healthcare
	6) Reduce population	Financial incentives; licenses
Employment	7) 'Full' employment	Keynesian incentives
	8) Minimum wage	Social charter in EU
	9) Good conditions for work	Health & safety checks
Agriculture	10) Increase labour on farms	Tax incentives
	11) Reduce fossil fuel	Carbon tax
	12) Reduce fertiliser	Fertiliser tax / land use control
Water	13) Social ownership	Compensation
	14) Reservoir construction	Tradeable extraction permits
	15) National pipe-line	Tradeable extraction permits
	16) Conservation	Meters: Pipe maintenance tax
Industry	17) Minimise throughput	Tax resource extraction
	18) Durability	Increase VAT on short-life manufactured goods
	19) Pollution control	Polluter pays / BAT / tradeable discharge permits
	20) Encourage small firms	Tax incentives for small/ medium firms
Shelter	21) Energy efficient homes	Tax energy inefficient homes
	22) Passive heating	Encourage possible energy use; package to help poor
	23) Green the environment	Land use planning
Biodiversity	24) Conserve nutrients & natural ecological cycle	Land use zonation
	25) Harvest renewables	Use maximimum sustainable yield
	26) Limit waste emissions	Encourage recycling & re use/ pollution control via regulation and fines
Religions	27) Protect religious freedom	Education
Education	28) Encourage arts, sciences	Core funding by the government & technology
Trade & travel	29) Provide bicycle ways	Land use planning
	30) Encourage rail transport	Real investment in social ownership
	31) Reduce fossil fuel use	Carbon tax
	32) Promote trade in sustainable resources	Tax unsustainable resource use

Continued

Table 36 Continued

Sector	Policy	Instruments
Communications	33) Increase access	Support for public use
International relations	34) Reduce armaments	Encourage 'arms' for peace / tax weapon production
	35) Reduce armed forces	
	36) Abolish nuclear, chemical / biological weapons	
	37) Debt reduction	Encourage sustainable resource projects in less developed countries / debts for nature swaps

have non-mandatory EIA guidelines. EIA regulations are found in several countries including Canada (1973), Australia (1974), West Germany (1975) and France (1976) and in forty nations worldwide. In 1985, EC directive 85/337 made EIA mandatory in certain circumstances, and more uniform throughout the European Community than previously. EIA is now used in some form or other in many nations of the world.

These legislative changes have been accompanied by the development of methods to put into operation actual EIA. Generally, EIA methods have been applied to specific projects such as the Australian Federal Government's decision to undertake uranium mining adjacent to Kakadu National Park (Moffatt and Webb,1992). Often Leopold matrices or similar methods are used to weigh up the negative, neutral and positive aspects of a proposed project. Economists have also contributed to this *a priori* appraisal by examining the cost-benefits associated with the use of say a national park when compared to mining in the same region (Press *et al.*, 1995). The lessons learnt from the development of EIA have, to date, been useful but much more research and application needs to be underaken if the EIA are to live up to the expectations associated with the NEPA and similar acts to protect the environment from unbridled development projects in OECD countries and other areas of the world.

Despite the growing interest and application of EIA some writers have suggested that a broader more comprehensive analysis of environmental assessment is required if we are to promote sustainable development. This broader approach has been called Strategic Environmental Assessment (SEA). Two alternative approaches to the development of SEA have been suggested. The first is to use SEA as a broader framework for individual EIAs but the second, and potentially more powerful way of using SEA, is as a means of influencing the ways in which sustainable development could be put into practice. In this latter context SEA is viewed as a way of overcoming some of the problems associated with the existing system project of EIA, but would also become a practical and pro-active step towards attaining sustainable development. It is this latter aspect which is considered below.

Several international organisations have recognised the need for SEA and are actively discussing the ways in which SEA could be implemented. In the UK, for example, the government is committed to the integration of environmental concerns into policy appraisal and decision making; this is reflected in the recent UK Sustainable Development Strategy (Anon., 1994) which stresses the need for the UK to pursue sustainable development. Similarly, in New Zealand sections outlining the content of SEA are given in Part V of the Resource and Management Act, which came into force in October, 1991. The World Bank's *Environmental Assessment Sourcebook* of 1991 also discusses the need for SEA, claiming that such a system could reduce the time and effort required for project specific EIAs, by identifying issues, initiating the collection of baseline data and assembling data. Clearly, there are several government and international organisations considering the possibility of SEA. At least two questions are raised by these discussions. First, what type of environmental problems should be covered by SEA? Secondly, what types of methods could be employed to ensure that SEA aids sustainable development?

It would appear obvious that many of the local scale environmental problems concerned with the setting up of a new industrial plant or other project can be estimated by use of EIA procedures. It could be argued the EIA should be extended to include both pro-active and re-active action to cope with specific environmental problems. Many environmental problems, although located locally, contribute to national, international and even global problems. It would, therefore, be sensible to introduce SEA to examine these multi-regional and often multi-sectoral environmental problems. In the case of energy use, for example, it is clear that some pollutants which are derived from e.g. car exhausts have a local, regional and indeed a global impact. Given the global nature of these problems it is quite clear that global problems cannot be analysed simply in terms of individual planning applications in e.g. the UK. In this sense there is a need for the use of EIA types of methodologies to be applied at local, regional, national, international and global levels as the acknowledged way of dealing with distributed and global effects of power plant emissions. The implementation of SEAs for sustainable development must come from a Keynesian type of approach to environmental and economic problems. If eco-socialism is unable to displace capitalism then a Keynesian type of approach to transform the system from within will allow the excesses of the market to be controlled so that both the environmental resources, the rest of nature and public participation in a democratic and accountable global community can thrive. Such a Keynesian paradigm offers the opportunity to make development sustainable – rather than continuing with the Monetarist policy. The advantage of a return to a Keynesian approach allows micro-economic matters to be conducted through market mechanisms whilst the broader macro-economic and ecological problems can be managed by political intervention. This Keynesian type of approach will not of course be welcomed by eco-anarchists or eco-facists; eco-liberals may like the idea and eco-socialists may see this as a step towards a better world. We have, of course, a choice either to return to scarcity or relearn the ways of managing the global system through Keynesian-like policy instruments.

CONCLUSION

This chapter has outlined some of the ways in which development can be made sustainable. Obviously, there are a whole host of competing and sometimes conflicting ideologies underpinning the discussion over sustainable development, some of these positions have been described. This was followed by a description of a green view of a sustainable society. Whilst such ideas may seem utopian, in that real societies may differ radically from that described, these radical departures will hopefully illustrate the rich diversity of social solutions to the present unsustainable paths of current business as usual development.

In order to try and promote more sustainable paths of development for different regions a portfolio of policies have been suggested. It has also been suggested that SEA could be introduced from within a broadly Keynesian framework to implement these policies. From the experience gained in the use of EIA it is possible that further developments on sectoral and regional lines could be implemented in an attempt to move the essential and ongoing discussion of sustainable development into practical application. It has also been suggested that models, similar to that described in the previous chapter, would have a role to play in these developments. Obviously, the future is not ours to determine but if we use the environmental systems wisely then we offer a planet fit for our children and their descendants. There is nothing predetermined about these possible futures but there is the strong possibility that current uncaring, uncontrolled, chaotic market-based economics is driving the earth's life-support systems beyond the edge of recovery. Do we wish to organise our lifestyles in a sustainable way? As Coombs (1990) so eloquently states there are lifestyles which are "more modest in their material demands, less destructive of the physical environment – lifestyles which are simpler, whose excitements are found primarily in the human relationships they provide scope for. The search for those lifestyles is the essential task of the rising generation. Upon their success in that search will depend the future of humankind".

CHAPTER 10

AFTERWORD: TOWARDS SUSTAINABLE SOCIETIES

EVOLUTION OR REVOLUTION?

The previous chapters have explored the concept of sustainable development from a variety of perspectives. The evolution of the concept was examined in Chapter two where it was argued that whilst it is possible to trace an evolutionary path, the ideas and practices of sustainable development are potentially revolutionary. The early ideas of attempting to integrate environmental concerns with economic development were traced back to the Stockholm conference and no doubt earlier precursors for sustainable development could be cited. Clearly, the work of Aldo Leopold's *Land Ethic* (Leopold, 1949), and the idea of Carsons' *Silent Spring* (Carsons, 1965) and Commoner's *Closing Circle* (Commoner, 1972) and Fraser Darling's study of the Western Isles (Darling, 1955) all contributed to make sustainable development an idea whose time had come. But, as we have seen, the idea of sustainable development did not follow a simple linear path but moved from ecodevelopment to *Limits to Growth* and *World Conservation Strategies* as well as national responses to these international political activities. These activities were given new breath by the WCED Brundtland Commission and the report *"Our Common Future"* which placed the concept of sustainable development on the political agenda. These international environmental actions culminated in the internationally agreed *Agenda 21* with its avowed aim of making development sustainable in the 21st century.

Whilst the second chapter stressed the evolution of the idea of sustainable development it could be argued that *Agenda 21*, with its emphasis upon local action is potentially more revolutionary in concept than simply a further development along the evolutionary path. The reason for this potentially revolutionary development in the operation of sustainable development is due to the ways in which local participation and the freedom of information are urged as essential conditions for sustainable development to become a reality in everyday practice. As Mikesell (1995) notes, "sustainable development is a revolutionary political and social concept. It will not succeed without the conviction and participation of the masses of people who must bring it about. Gaining that conviction and participation is a more important challenge for

183

external assistance agencies than providing capital and technical assistance". If this participation is to happen then the twin needs of social and natural justice must be given careful scrutiny and support.

SOCIAL AND NATURE'S JUSTICE?

In the third chapter it was argued that one of the important aspects of the Rio meeting was the statement of the various principles of sustainable development. Obviously, sustainable development is an anthropocentric view in the sense that development is for human survival and improving human welfare. It has, however, been argued that an ecocentric approach to sustainable development is desirable. In particular, several philosophers have suggested that abiotic and other biotic forms as well as *Homo sapiens* need to be given careful consideration when assessing the impact of human interactions with the rest of nature. It is at this juncture that Taylor's (1986) priority principles for considering the rights of nature come into play. It has been argued that these principles, while very difficult to put into practice, can guide us onto a path of sustainable development.

It was argued that these priority principles need to be examined from the perspective of equality rather than giving the top priority to economic efficiency. In particular it was suggested that a reworking of the ideas of Rawls' (1971) *Theory of Social Justice* could form a framework for establishing a just basis for sustainable development. As he suggests that both inter- and intra-generational equity need to be considered in any serious discussion of sustainable development, then ideas of justice, justly arrived at, must take precedence over lesser tasks of improving economic efficiency. Some conventional measures of equity as witnessed in the work of Smith (1975; 1994) can be used to arrive at a just distribution of the global cake.

The ideas of Taylor and Rawls were suggested as one way of drawing together an ethical framework for discussing sustainable development by re-connecting the worlds of humanity and nature. Many of the substantive issues involved in this approach need to be addressed in this area of work, but it does give an ethically sound basis for making decisions concerning our relations with each other and the rest of the planet in a just manner.

MEASURING SUSTAINABLE DEVELOPMENT

Chapters four to seven examined the various ways in which sustainable development can be measured. Underlying this emphasis upon measurement is the need to demonstrate: (a) that the current paths of economic growth and development are not sustainable, and (b) that if we are to change these unsustainable patterns onto sustainable paths then we need to be able to monitor the planet's ecosystems (including humanity's impacts) to ensure that these new patterns of development are sustainable.

Several different types of measures of sustainable development have been suggested in the literature. In some cases the detailed data are not easily ascertained and in other cases the temporal and/or spatial quality of the data coverage is not very good. Using several measures of sustainable development it was shown that Scotland was only, at best, marginally sustainable. Only one measure (which has major limitations) demonstrated that Scotland was sustainable. These empirical studies illustrate some of the difficulties involved in determining whether or not a nation is on a sustainable trajectory. More empirical research is continuing on the development of these measures.

To some environmentalists and other groups the fact that current patterns of resource exploitation and human degradation need to be shown to be unsustainable may cause surprise. Surely, they would argue that the *Report to the President* (Barney, 1980); the *Limits to Growth* (Meadows *et al.*,1972) and the Stockholm conference (Ward and Dubois, 1972) all demonstrated this many years ago. Whilst many would agree with this some, others such as Simon and Khan (1984), suggest that there are no limits to growth; although, as Erhlich and Erlich (1994) note Simon's arguments are indeed simple. Other economists suggest that the apparent problems we face represent the final aspect of working within one niche prior to a move towards the exploitation of a new set of resources. While this latter argument has some merit, it applied only when new lands were to be "discovered". We now know, in broad terms, both the limits to the earth and to its assimilative capacities. Hence, it would be sensible to acknowledge these limits and try to live within them rather than try to exceed these natural constraints. This implies that we need to examine ways of changing our practices as the world is unable to change its ecological niches and natural primary productivity as fast as some economists and other people would like to assume.

SUSTAINABLE DEVELOPMENT: MODELS AND POLICIES

Assuming that we are indeed confronted by the current global market system which is attempting to live beyond the ecological limits of the earth and also that current market-driven business appears incapable of self-regulation, then what guidance can we give to move the current paths of unsustainble development onto sustainable trajectories? In Chapter 8 an attempt was made to highlight the ways in which a sustainable simulation model could be used, along with other methods, in an attempt to search for alternative forms of living which would develop into sustainable, peaceful and creative forms of development within the ecologically possible constraints. By making some reasonable value judgements concerning the basic needs for humanity and respect for the abiotic and biotic communities on the earth, some simulations of possible paths of sustainable development were given. These paths resulted from work at different spatio-temporal scales undertaken in Australia and Scotland in different environmental and socio-economic settings. Obviously, the choice of a specific simulated pattern of development may be preferred by the model-builder but this is not necessarily the one which may be selected by a government or other decision-makers. Even if we make the basic assumption, which underpins all human endeavour, that life on earth is worth living or ought to be worth living then it is clear that some ethical framework is required to guide our choice over which path of sustainable development we move toward. It is at this point in the text that we returned to the ordering principles, outlined in Chapter 3, whereby socially-just and environmentally-sound principles could be utilised in a just way to encourage paths of development which are sustainable.

In an attempt to illustrate the ways in which these principles can be brought into the arena of public policy and private practice some of the ill-defined contours of a possible sustainable society were described. This society was based upon an eco-liberal political ideology operating within a democratic system. These policies, described in the previous chapter, are based upon the need to develop a sustainable society. Many of the policies are unexceptional, but they need to be implemented as a portfolio of green policies rather than an *ad hoc* mixture of policies. In some cases the policies need to be agreed and implemented at the global level. The changes in trade, for example, cannot be tackled unilaterally. Many other policies can be introduced simultaneously by countries within a particular bloc. Some policies, such as pollution regulation can also be implemented at the local level. It has been suggested that, by using these various policies in combination with various economic instruments, it is possible to move unsustainable societies onto a path of sustainable development. More detailed work on the ways that this portfolio of policies can be implemented needs to be undertaken.

Whilst this attempt to outline the policies for one possible realisation of a sustainable society may be perjoratively described as 'utopian' it has two major advantages over continuing to talk about a better sustainable future without attempting to describe it. First, it shows how the principles, practices and measures of sustainable development can be integrated, albeit crudely, to act as a guide to sustainable living. Second, it also demonstrates starkly the distance we still have to travel to move from the current unsustainable position to realising a just, participatory and sustainable society. A vision of such a possibility, and the means by which sustainable development can be achieved, have been described in this book.

REFERENCES

Ahmed Y. S., El Serafy E. and Lutz E. (eds.) (1989) *Environmental Accounting for sustainable development.* (Proceedings of a UNEP/World Bank Symposium)

Allen R. (1980) *How to Save the World.* (London: Kogan Page)

Anderson V. (1991) *Alternative Economic Instruments.* (London: Routledge)

Anon. (1994) *Sustainable Development: The UK Strategy.* (London: HMSO)

Anon. (1994) Britain's very own Brundtland Strategy. *Nature* 367: 395

Asheim G. B. (1991) Defining sustainability when resource management does not have deterministic consequences. Mimeo, Department of Economics, University of Oslo

Atkinson A. B. and Micklewright J. (1992) *Economic transformations in Europe and the Distribution of Income.* (Cambridge: Cambridge University Press)

Atkinson G. and Pearce D. (1993) Capital theory and the measure of sustainable development: an indicator of weak sustainability. *Ecological Economics* 8: 103–8

Barbier E. (1989) *Economics, Natural Resources, Scarcity and Development.* (London: Earthscan)

Barbier E. B. (ed.) (1993) *Economics and Ecology: New Frontiers in Sustainable Development.* (London: Chapman Hall)

Barney G. O.(ed.) (1980) *The Global 2000 Report to the President of the U.S.* (New York: Pergamon)

Bennett K. D. (1989) A Provisional map of forest types for the British Isles 5000 years ago. *Journal of Quaternary Science* 42:141–4

Binns W. O. (1979) The hydrological impact of afforestation in Great Britain. In Hollis G.E. (ed.) *Mans' Impact on the Hydrological Cycle in the UK,* pp. 55–70. (Norwich: Geobooks)

Bookchin M.(1980) *Toward an Ecological Society.* (Montreal: BlackRose)

Boulding K. E. (1980) The economics of the coming space-ship Earth. In Daly H.E. (eds.) *Economics, Ecology, Ethics: Essays Towards a Steady-State Economy,* pp. 253–63. (San Francisco: W H Freeman)

Boyden S. V. (1981) *The Ecology of a city and its people: the case of Hong Kong.* (Canberra: ANU Press)

Bramwell A. (1989) *Ecology in the 20th Century: A History.* (Cambridge: Cambridge University Press)

Brandt Commission (1980) *North-South: A Programme for Survival*. (London: Pan)

Brennan A. (1988) *Thinking about Nature: An Investigation of Nature, Value and Ecology*. (London: Routledge)

BRF, British Road Federation (1993) Basic Road Statistics. (London: British Road Federation)

Brookfield H. (1989) Boldness and caution in the face of global change. *Australian Geographical Studies* 27 (2): 199–207

Brown B. J., Hanson M. E., Liverman D. M. and Merideth R. W. (1987) Global sustainability: toward a definition. *Environmental Management* 11,(6): 713–19

Brown L. R. and Kane H. (1994) *Full House: reassessing the Earth's population Carrying Capacity*. (New York and London: W W Norton)

Buitenkamp M., Venner H. and Wams T. (eds.) (1992) *Action Plan Netherlands*. (Netherlands: Friends of the Earth)

Bunyard P. and Morgan-Grenville F. (eds.) (1987) *The Green Alternative to Good Living*. (London: Methuen)

Calow P. and Berry R. J. (eds.) (1989) *Evolution, Ecology and Environmental Stress*. (London: Academic Press)

Carsons R. (1965) *Silent Spring*. (Harmondsworth: Penguin)

CDP Commonwealth Discussion Paper (1990) Ecologically Sustainable Development. (Canberra: Australian Government Publication)

Chorley, Lord (1987) *Handling Geographic Information*. Report to the Committee of Enquiry. (London: HMSO)

Clark W. C. and Munn R. F. (eds.) (1986) *Sustainable Development of the Biosphere*. (Cambridge: Cambridge University Press)

Cobb C. and Cobb J. (eds.) (1993) *The Green National Product*. (Washington: University of America Press)

Cobb J. B. (1993) *Sustainability: Economics, Ecology and Justice*. (New York: Orbis)

Coates B. E., Johnston R. J. and Knox P. (1977) *Geography and Inequality*. (Oxford: Oxford University Press)

Cole H. S. D., Freeman C., Jahoda M. and Pavitt, K. L. R. (1973) *Thinking About the Future: A Critique of the Limits to Growth*. (London: Chatto and Windus)

Common M. (1988) 'Poverty and Progress' Revisited. In Collard D., Pearce D. and Ulph D. (eds.) *Economic Growth and Sustainable Environments*, pp. 15–39. (London: McMillan Press)

Common M. and Perrings C. (1991) Toward an ecological economics of sustainability. *Ecological Economics* 61: 7–34

Commoner B. (1972) *The Closing Circle*. (London: Cape)

Coombs H. C. (1990) *The Return to Scarcity: Strategies for an Economic Future*. (Cambridge: Cambridge University Press)

Conway G. R. (1985) Agroecosystems analysis. *Agricultural Administration* 20: 31–5

Costanza R. (ed.) (1991) *Ecological Economics: The Science of Management of Sustainability.* (New York: Columbia University Press)

Cotgrove S. (1982) *Catastrophe and Cornucopia: the Environment, Politics and the Future.* (Chichester: John Wiley and Sons)

Daily G. C. and Ehrlich P. R. (1992) Population, sustainability, and earth's carrying capacity. *Bioscience* 42: 761–71

Daly H. E. (1973) *Toward a Steady-State Economy.* (San Francisco: W H Freeman)

Daly H. E. (1977) *Steady-State Economics: The Economics of Biophysical and Moral growth.* (San Francisco: W H Freeman)

Daly H. E. (1987) The economic growth debate: What some economists have learned but many have not. *Journal of Environmental Economics and Management,* 14 (4), 323–36

Daly H. E. and Cobb J. B. (1989) *For the Common Good: Redirecting the Economy toward the Community, the Environment and a Sustainable Future.* (Boston: Beacon Press)

Darling F. F. (1955) *The West Highland Survey: An essay in human ecology.* (Oxford: Oxford University Press)

Dasgupta P. (1982) *The Control of Resources.* (Oxford: Basil Blackwell)

Desai M. (1994) The measurement problem in economics. *The Scottish Journal of Political Economy* 41: 34–42

Dempsey R. and Power R. (1972) The politics of the environment. In: Rapoport A. (ed.) *Australia as Human Setting.* (Sydney: Angus and Robertson)

Dobson A. (1991). *The Green Reader.* (London: Andre Deutsch)

Dobson A. (1992) *Green Political Thought.* (London: Unwin)

DoEn, Department of Energy (1993) *Digest of Energy Statistics 1992* (London: HMSO)

DoE, Department of Environment (1990) *Countryside Survey.* (London: HMSO)

DoE, Department of Environment (1989) *Sustaining our Common Future: A Progress Report by the United Kingdom on implementing Sustainable Development.* (London: DoE)

DoE, Department of Environment (1992) Digest of Environmental Protection and Water Statistics (London: DoE)

DHAE, Department of Home Affairs and the Environment (1983) *A National Conservation Strategy for Australia.* (Canberra: Australian Government Publication Service)

DASETT, Department of the Arts, Sport, the Environment, Tourism and Territories (1991) *Australian National Report to the United Nations Conference on Environment and Development.* (Canberra: Public Discussion Paper)

Doxiadis C. A. (1968) *Ekistics.* (London: Hutchinson)

Drenowski J. and Scott W. (1968) The level of living index. *Ekistics* 25: 226–75

Drenowski J. (1974) *On Measuring and Planning the Quality of Life.* (The Hague: Mouton Press)

Dryzek J. (1987) *Rational Ecology: Environment and Political Economy.* (Oxford: Blackwell)

Eckersley R. (1992) *Enviromentalism and Political Theory: Toward an Ecocentric Approach.* (London: UCL Press)

ESD, Ecologically Sustainable Development Working Group (1991) *Draft report* (10 Volumes). (Canberra: Australian Government Publishing Service)

Edel M.(1973) *Economics and the Environment.* (Englewood Cliffs: Prentice Hall)

Ehrlich A. H. and Ehrlich P. R. (1994) Simple Simon Environmental Analysis. In Miller G. T. *Living in the Environment.* (Belmont: Wadsworth)

Ekins P. (1990) *Wealth beyond measure: An atlas of new economics.* (London: Gaia Books)

Ekins P. and Max-Neef M.(1992) *Real-life economics. Understanding wealth creation.* (London: Routledge)

Elliot J. A. (1994) *An Introduction to Sustainable Development: The Developing World.* (London: Routledge)

Engel J. R. and Engel J. G.(eds.) (1990) *Ethics of Environmental Development: Global Challenge and International Response.* (London: Belhaven)

Engels F. (1969) *The Condition of the Working Class in England.* (London: Panther)

ET, Economic Trends (1992 *et seq*). Economic Trends in the UK Regional Accounts 1992, Part 1 (London: HMSO)

European Commission (1992) *Towards Sustainability – European Community Programmes of Policy and Action in Relation to Environmental and Sustainable Development.* COM (92) 23 final, vol II. (Brussels: Commission of European Communities)

Farman J. C., Gardiner B. G. and Shanklin J. D. (1985) Large losses of total ozone in Antarctica reveal seasonal Cl_{ox}/NO_x interaction. *Nature* 315: 207

Farvar M. T. and Glaeser B. (1979). *The Politics of Ecodevelopment.* (Berlin: International Institute for Environment and Society)

FES, Family Expenditure Survey (various years) *Family Spending.* (London: HMSO)

Folke C., Hammer M., Costanza R. and Jansson M. (1994) Investing in Natural Capital – Why? What and How? In: Jansson A. M., Hammer M., Folke C. and Costanza R. (eds.) *Investing in Natural Capital* pp. 1–20. (Washington DC: Island Press)

Forrester, J. W. (1971) *World Dynamics.* (Massachusetts: Wright-Allen)

Fox W. (1990) *Towards a Transpersonal Ecology: Developing New Foundations for Environmentalism.* (Boston: Shambhala)

Georgescu-Roegen N. (1971) *The Entropy Law and the Economic Process.* (Massachusetts: Harvard University Press)

Goodin R. E. (1992) *Green Political Theory.* (Cambridge: Polity Press)

GSS, Government Statistical Service (various years) The Scottish Environmental Statistics. (Edinburgh: HMSO)

Hardin G. (1968) The Tragedy of the Commons. *Science* 162: 1243–8

Hardin G. (1974) Living on a Lifeboat. In Hardin G. and Baden J. *Managing the Commons*, pp. 261–79. (San Francisco: W. H. Freeman and Co.)

Hare W. L. (ed.) (1990) *Ecologically Sustainable Development.* (Canberra: Australian Conservation Foundation)

Hartwick J. M. (1977) Intergenerational equity and the investing of rents from exhaustible resources. *American Economic Review* 67,5: 972–4

Hartwick J. M. (1978) Investing returns from depleting renewable resource stocks and intergenerational equity. *Economic Letters* 85–8

Hartwick J. M. (1978) Substitution among exhaustible resources and intergenerational equity. *Review of Economic Studies* 45, 347–54

Hartwick J. M. (1990) Natural resources, national accounting and economic depreciation. *Journal of Public Economics* 43: 291–304

Harvey D. (1973) *Social Justice and the City.* (London: Edward Arnold)

Harvey D. (1974) Population, resources and the ideology of science. *Economic Geography* 50: 265–77

Harvey D. (1982) *The Limits to Capital.* (Oxford: Blackwell)

Hawke R. J. L. (1989) *Our Country Our Future.* (Canberra: Australian Government Publishing Service)

Henderson-Sellers A. and Blong R. (1989) *The Greenhouse Effect: Living in a Warmer Australia.* (Kensington: New South Wales University Press)

Hicks J. R. (1948) *Value and Capital.* (Oxford: Clarendon)

HMSO (1994) *Sustainable Development: The UK Strategy.* (London: HMSO)

United Kingdom National Accounts (various years) (London: HMSO)

RT, Regional Trends (various years) Central Statistical Office, (London: HMSO)

Hollings C. S. (1973) Resilience and stability of ecological systems. *Annual Review of Ecology and Systematics* 4: 1–23

Hollings C. S. (1994) *Adaptive Environmental Assessment and Management.* (London: Wiley)

Hope C., Parker J. and Peake S. (1992) A pilot environmental index for the UK in the 1980s. *Energy Policy* 20, 4: 335–8

Howarth R. and Norgaard R.(1992) Environmental valuation under sustainable development. *American Economic Review* 82, 2: 473–77

IPCC, Intergovernmental Panel on Climate Change (1990) Climate Change – The IPCC Scientific Assessment (WMO–UNEP). (Cambridge: Cambridge University Press)

IUCN (1980) *World Conservation Strategy.* (Gland: IUCN)

IUCN/UNEP/WWF (1991) *Caring for the Earth: A Strategy for sustainable Development.* (Gland: IUCN)

Jacobs M. (1991). *The Green Economy: Sustainable Development, the Environment and the Future of Politics.* (London: Pluto)

Jackson T. and Marks N. (1994) *Measuring Sustainable Economic Welfare: a Pilot Index, 1950–1990.* (Stockholm: Stockholm Environmental Institute/ New Economics Foundation)

Jefferson M. (1917) The distribution of British cities and the Empire. *Geographical Review* 4: 387–94

Jones G. (1979) *Vegetation Productivity.* (New York: Longman)

Keating M. (1989) *Toward a Common Future: A Report on Sustainable development and its implications for Canada.* (Ottawa: Environment Canada)

Keynes J. M. (1936). *The General Theory of Employment, Interest and Money.* (London: MacMillan)

Kuik O. and Verbruiggen H. (eds.) (1991) *In Search of Indicators of Sustainable Development.* (Dordrecht: Kluwer)

Kukathas C. and Petit P. (1992) *Rawls: A Theory of Justice and its Critics.* (London: Polity Press)

Leach G. (1976) *Energy and Food Production.* (London: IPC Science and Technology Press)

Leipert C. and Simonis U. E. (1989) Environmental Damage – Environmental Expenditures: Statistical Evidence of the Federal Republic of Germany. *International Journal of Social Economics* 15,7: 37–52

Leopold A. (1949) A Sand County Almanac and Sketches Here and There. (New York: OUP)

Luper-Foy S. (1995) International justice and the environment. In Cooper D. E. and Cooper J. A. (eds.) *Just Environments.* (London: Routledge)

Lowe P. and Goyder J. (1983). *Environmental Groups in Politics.* (London: George, Allen and Unwin)

Marcuse H. (1964) *One Dimensional Man: The Ideology of Industrial Society.* (London: Sphere)

Marx K. (1867) *Capital.* (3 Volumes) (London: Wishart)

Maslow A. (1968) *Towards a Psychology of Being.* (New Jersey: Princetown University Press)

May R. M. (1976) Simple mathematical models with very complicated dynamics. *Nature* 261: 459–67

McCormick J. (1989) *The Global Environmental Movement: Reclaiming Paradise.* (London: Belhaven Press)

McNeeley J. A. (1990) How conservation strategies contribute to sustainable development. *Environmental Conservation* 17 (1): 9–13

Meadows D. H., Meadows D. L., Randers J. and Behrens W. W. (1972) *The Limits to Growth.* (New York: New American Library)

Meadows D. L., Behrens W. W., Meadows D. H., Naill R.F., Randers J. and Zahn E. K. O. (1974) *The Dynamics of Growth in a Finite World.* (Massachusetts: Wright-Allen)

Meadows D. H. (1990) A reaction to the multitude. In Woodwell G. M. (ed.) *The Earth in Transition.* (Cambridge: Cambridge University Press)

Mikesell R. F. (1995) *Economic Development and the Environment: A Comparison of Sustainable Development with Conventional Development Economics.* (London: Mansell)

Miles H. and Jackson B. (1991) *The Great Wood of Caledon.* (Lanark: Colin Baxter)

Mill J. S. (1867) *The Principles of Political Economy.* (London: Parker and Sons)

Moffat A. J. (1988) Forestry and soil erosion in Britain, a review. *Soil Use and Management* 4: 41–4

Moffatt I. (1984a) Environmental Management, Models and Policies. In: Murray-Smith D.J. (ed.) *Proceedings of the 1984 UKSC Conference on Computer Simulation.* pp182–90 (London: Butterworths)

Moffatt I. (1984b) Environmental Quality in Stirling. In Pacione M. and Gordon G. (eds.) *Quality of Life and Human Welfare.* (Norwich: Geobooks)

Moffatt I. (1990) The potentialities and problems associated with applying information technology to environmental problems. *Journal of Environmental Management* 30: 209–20

Moffatt I. (1992a) *The Greenhouse Effect: Science and Policy in the Northern Territory, Australia.* (Darwin: North Australia Research Unit, ANU Press)

Moffatt I. (1992b) The evolution of the sustainable development concept: a perspective from Australia. *Australian Geographical Studies* 30: 1, 27–42

Moffatt I. and Webb A. (eds.) (1992) *Conservation and Development Issues in North Australia.* (Darwin: North Australia Research Unit, ANU Press)

Moffatt I. (1994) On measuring sustainable development indicators. *International Journal of Sustainable Development and World Ecology* 1: 97–109

Moffatt I., Hanley N. and Gill J. P. S. (1994) Measuring and Assessing Indicators of Sustainable Development for Scotland. (Stirling: SOAFD/SNH)

Moffatt I. and Wilson M. (1994) An Index of Sustainable Economic Welfare for Scotland, 1980–1991. *International Journal of Sustainable Development and World Ecology* 1: 264–91

More T. (1910) *Utopia.* (London: Blackie)

Naess A.(1973) The Shallow and the Deep, Long-Range Ecology Movement: A Summary. *Inquiry* 16, 95–100

NEPA (1970) National Environmental Policy Act. (Washington: US Government)

Nordhaus W. D. and Tobin J. (1973) Is growth obsolete? In: Moss M. (ed.) *The Measurement of Economic and Social Performance, Studies in Income and Wealth,* pp. 509–64. (New York: National Bureau of Economic Research)

Norgaard R.B. (1988) Sustainable Development: A Co-evolutionary View. *Futures* December: 606–20

Norton G. (1987) Book Review: Respect for Nature. *Environmental Ethics* 9, 3: 261–67

NTS National Travel Survey (various years) *National Travel Survey*. (London: HMSO)

OECD, Overseas Economic Development Council (1991) *Environmental Indicators: A Preliminary Set*. (Paris: OECD)

Openshaw S. (1995). Neuroclassification of spatial data. In Hewitson B. C. and Crane R. G. (eds.) Neural Nets: Applications in Geography, pp. 53–70 (Dordrecht: Kluwer)

Opschoor J. B. (1991) Economic modelling and Sustainable Development. In Gilbert A. J. and Braat L. C. (eds.) *Modelling for Population and Sustainable Development*, pp. 191–210. (London and New York: Routledge)

O'Riordan T. (1981) *Environmentalism*. (London: Pion)

O'Riordan T. (1988) The politics of sustainability. In Turner, R. K. (ed.) *Sustainable Environmental Management: Principles and Practice*. (London: Belhaven Press)

O'Riordan T. (ed.) (1995) *Environmental Science for Environmental Management*. (Harlow: Longman)

Park C. C. (1994) *Sacred Worlds: An Introduction to Geography and Religion*. (London: Routledge)

Passmore J. A. (1974) *Man's Responsibility for Nature: Ecological problems and Western tradition*. (London: Duckworth)

Patterson K. (1992) The service flow from consumption goods with an application to Friedman's Permanent Income Hypothesis. *Oxford Economic Papers* 44: 289–305

Pearce D. W. and Atkinson G. D. (1993) Capital Theory and the measurement of sustainable development: an indicator of weak sustainability. *Ecological Economics* 8: 103–8

Pearce D., Markandya A. and Barbier E. B. (1989) *Blueprint for a Green Economy*. (London: Earthscan)

Pearce D. (1993) *Blueprint 3: Measuring Sustainable Development*. (London: Earthscan)

Pearman G. I. (ed.) (1988) *Greenhouse Planning for Climate Change*. (Melbourne: CSIRO Division of Atmospheric Research)

Peet J. (1992) *Energy and the Ecological Economics of Sustainability*. (Washington: Island Press)

Pepper D. (1994) *Ecosocialism: From Deep Ecology to Social Justice*. (London: Routledge)

Perrings C. (1987) *Economy and Environment*. (Cambridge: Cambridge University Press)

Pezzey J. (1989) *Economic Analysis of Sustainable Growth and Sustainable Development*. (Washington: World Bank)

Pirages D. (ed.) (1977) *The Sustainable Society: Implications for Limited Growth*. (London and New York: Prager)

Pittock A. B. (1988) Actual and anticipated changes in Australia's climate In: Pearman G.I. (ed.) *Greenhouse: Planning for Climate Change.* (Melbourne: CSIRO Division of Atmospheric Research)

Ponting C. (1992) *A Green History of the World: The Environment and the collapse of Great Civilisations.* (Harmondsworth: Penguin).

Porritt J. (1969) *Seeing Green.* (Oxford: Blackwell)

Plumwood V. (1986) Ecofeminism: An Overview and discussion of positions and arguments. *Australasian Journal of Philosophy* Spring: 16–24

Plumwood V. (1988) Women, Humanity and Nature. *Radical Philosophy* Spring: 16–24

Press T., Lea D., Webb A. and Graham A. (eds.), (1995) *Kakadu: Natural and Cultural Heritage and Management.* (Darwin: ANCA and NARU)

PT, Population Trends (various years) *Population Trends.* (London: HMSO)

Rapoport A. (ed.) (1972) *Australia as Human Setting.* (Sydney: Angus and Robertson)

RAS, Road Accidents Scotland (1992). (London: HMSO)

Rawls J. R. (1971) *A Theory of Justice.* (Oxford: Blackwell)

Redclift M. (1987) *Sustainable Development: Exploring the Contradictions.* (London: Methuen)

Rees W. E. and Wackernagel M. (1994) Ecological footprints and appropriated carrying capacity: measuring the natural capital requirements of the human economy. In: *Investing in Natural capital: the Ecological Economics approach to sustainability.* (Island Press: Washington)

Repetto R., McGrath W.,Wells M., Beer C. and Roisini F. (1987) *Wasting Assets: Natural Resources in the National Income Acccounts.* (Washington: World Resources Institute)

Riddell R. (1981) *Ecodevelopment: Economics, Ecology and Development; an alternative to growth imperative models.* (Farnborough: Gower)

Roberts N. (ed.) (1994) *The Changing Global Climate.* (Oxford: Blackwell)

Russell B. (1969) *History of Western Philosophy.* (London: George, Allen and Unwin)

Sachs I. (1984) The Strategies of Ecodevelopment. *Ceres* 17, 4: 20–35

Sale K. (1984) Bioregionalism – A New Way to Treat the Land. *The Ecologist* 14: 167–73

Sandbrook R. (1983) The UK's overseas environmental policy. In WWF, The Conservation and Development Programme for the UK: A Response to the World Conservation Strategy. (London: Kogan Page)

SAS, Scottish Abstracts of Statistics (various years). (Edinburgh: Scottish Office)

SOAFD, Scottish Office, Agriculture and Fisheries Department (1992) *Economic Report on Scottish Agriculture.* (Edinburgh: SOAFD)

SEB, Scottish Economics Bulletin (1993). (Edinburgh: HMSO)

Selman P. (1985) Responding to the World Conservation Strategy. *The Environmentalist* 4(2): 20–35

Selman P. (1987) *Implementation of the national conservation strategy for Australia.* (Canberra: CRES ANU Press)

SES, Scottish Environmental Statistics (1992). (Edinburgh: Scottish Office)

Simon J. L. and Kahn H. (eds.) (1984) *The resourceful Earth: a response to Global 2000.* (Oxford: Blackwell)

Smart N. (1989) *The World's Religions: Old Traditions and Modern Transformations.* (Cambridge: Cambridge University Press).

Smith A. (1976) *The Wealth of Nations.* (Harmondsworth: Penguin)

Smith D. (1994) *Geography and Social Justice.* (London: Edward Arnold)

Smith D. H. (1975) *Patterns in Human Geography.* (Hammondsworth: Penguin)

SNH, Scottish National Heritage (1992) *First Operational Plan.* (Edinburgh: Scottish National Heritage)

Sohn L.B. (1974) The Stockholm declaration on the human environment. *The Harvard International Law Journal* 14(3): 423–515

Solow R. (1974) The economics of resources or the resources of economics. *American Economic Review* 64: 1–14

Solow R. (1993) An almost practical step toward sustainability. *Resources Policy* 19: 162–72

Standing Committee on the Environment, Recreation and the Arts (1991) *The Injured Coastline: protection of the coastal environment.* (Canberra: Australian Government Publishing Service)

Stigliani W. and Salomons W. (1993) Our Father's Toxic Sins. *New Scientist*, Dec. 11, pp. 38–42

Strong M. F. (1977) The International Community and the Environment. *Environmental Conservation* 4(3): 165–72

Struik G. J. (1967) Growth habits of Dandelion, Daisy, Catsear and Hawkbit in some New Zealand grasslands. *Journals of Agricultural Research* 10: 331–44

Sunday Times (1996) *Nuclear Friction* (Sunday Times Business Focus) p. 3

Taylor P. W. (1986) *Respect for Nature: A Theory of Environmental Ethics.* (New Jersey: Princetown University Press)

The Ecologist (1972) Blueprint for Survival. *The Ecologist* 2(10): 1–43

Turner R. K. (ed.) (1988) *Sustainable Environmental Management: Principles and Practice.* (London: Belhaven Press)

Turner R. K. (ed) (1995) *Sustainable Environmental Economics and Management: Principles and Practice.* (Chichester: John Wiley)

UN, United Nations (1968) *A Series of national Accounts. Statistical Methods* Series F, No.4. (New York: United Nations)

UN, United Nations (1990) SNA Handbook of Integrated Environmental and Economic Accounting Draft. (New York: United Nations Statistics Office)

UNCED, United Nations Council for Economic Development (1992) *Earth Summit '92.* (London: The Regency Press)

UNDP, United Nations Development Programme (1990) *Human Development Report.* (Oxford: Oxford University Press)

UNEP, United Nations Environment Programme (1995) *The proposed Programme Nairobi.* (New York: United Nations)

Uno K. (1988) *Economic Growth and Environmental Change in Japan – Net National Welfare and Beyond.* (mimeo, University of Tsukuba: Institute of Socio-Economic Planning)

Van Pelt M. J. F. (1993) *Ecological Sustainability and Project Appraisal: case Studies in Developing Countries.* (Aldershot: Avebury)

Victoria (1984) *Ensuring our Future – Draft Conservation Strategy overview for public comment.* (Melbourne: Ministry for Planning and Environment)

Vitousek P. M., Ehrlich P. R., Ehrlich A. H. and Matson P. A. (1986) Human appropriation of the products of photosynthesis. *Bioscience* 36, 6: 368–73

Wadge G. and Isaacs M. C. (1988) Mapping the volcanic hazards from Soufriere Hills Volcano, Montserrat, West Indies using an image processor. *Journal of the Geological Society* 145: 541–51

Walker G. J. and Kirby K. J. (1989) *Inventories of ancient, long-established and semi-natural woodland for Scotland.* (Edinburgh: Research and Survey in Nature Conservation)

Wall G. (1974) Public responses to air pollution in Sheffield, England. *International Journal of Environmental Studies* 5, 4: 259–70

Ward B. and Dubois R. (1972) *Only One Earth.* (Harmondsworth: Penguin)

Wathern P. (ed.) (1990) *Environmental Impact Assessment: Theory and Practice* (London: Routledge)

Western Australia (1987) *A state conservation strategy for Western Australia: a sense of place.* (Perth: Department of Conservation and the Environment)

Wilkinson R. G. (1973) *Poverty and Progress: An Ecological Model of Economic Development.* (London: Methuen)

Wilson D. (1988) *Biodiversity.* (Washington: National Academy of Sciences)

Wilson M. D. (1994) *Measuring Sustainable Development in Scotland.* MSc Environmental Management Thesis, University of Stirling

World Bank (1991) *Environmental Assessment Sourcebook.* (Washington: World Bank)

WCED, World Commission on Environment and Development (1987) *Our Common Future.* (Oxford: Oxford University Press)

Woodcock G. (1983) *The Anarchist Reader.* (London: Fontana)

WWF, World Wide Fund for Nature (1983) *The Conservation and Development Programme for the UK: A response to the World Conservation Strategy.* (London: Kogan Page)

Young M. D. (1990) Natural resource accounting. In: Common M. and Dovers S. (eds.) *Moving Towards Global Sustainability: Policies and Implications for Australia.* (Canberra: ANU Press)

Young M. D. (1992) *Sustainable Investment and Resource Use: Equity, Environmental Integrity and Economic Efficiency.* (Paris: UNESCO)

Zolatos X. (1981) *Economic Growth and Declining Social Welfare.* (New York: University Press)

INDEX